COMPUTER SCIENCE, TECHNOLOGY AND APPLICATIONS

VEHICULAR NETWORKS

APPLICATIONS, PERFORMANCE ANALYSIS AND CHALLENGES

COMPUTER SCIENCE, TECHNOLOGY AND APPLICATIONS

COMPUTER SCIENCE, TECHNOLOGY AND APPLICATIONS

VEHICULAR NETWORKS

APPLICATIONS, PERFORMANCE ANALYSIS AND CHALLENGES

PETER HAN JOO CHONG

AND

IVAN WANG-HEI HO

EDITORS

nova science publishers
New York

NOTICE TO THE READER

Library of Congress Cataloging-in-Publication Data

ISBN: 978-1-53615-978-3
Library of Congress Control Number: 2019946604

Published by Nova Science Publishers, Inc. † *New York*

CONTENTS

PREFACE

With the forthcoming enforcement of installing wireless units for Dedicated Short Range Communications (DSRC) on newly manufactured light-duty vehicles in the US, and the development of the Cellular V2X (C-V2X) standard in 3GPP, vehicle-to-everything (V2X) communications and vehicular networking for improving road safety, enhancing traffic efficiency, and supporting heterogeneous vehicular applications is foreseeable in the near future.

V2X communications for enhancing road safety has been a hot research topic in Intelligent Transportation Systems (ITS), and a number of communication protocols and networking functions (e.g., routing protocols and warning message broadcast strategies) have been proposed in this context. However, a major drawback is that most of them are developed based on heuristic approaches or predominated models in mobile ad-hoc network (MANET) research(e.g., random mobility models), which are obviously insufficient to capture the major characteristics of real-world vehicle motions, and may result in low performance and limited capabilities for vehicular networks. In view of this inadequacy, we first introduce in this book a novel modeling framework for characterizing the space and time dynamics of vehicular communication protocol performance, such as 802.11p (which forms the PHY and MAC layers of DSRC), in signalized urban road systems. Such modeling framework is expected to generate fundamental understanding of the connection between vehicular mobility and communication connectivity, and establish a brand-new methodology that provides practical directions and guidelines for the design and optimization of vehicular networks in the long term.

On the other hand, the fast development of self-driving systems and autonomous vehicles in recent years has attracted a lot of interest from the industry and research community. Although autonomous vehicles are usually installed with a number of advanced sensors (e.g., LIDAR for light detection and ranging of surrounding obstacles), most of the existing self-driving systems are standalone. To achieve level 5 of autonomous driving that is applicable to every driving scenario, communications and networking among autonomous vehicles as well as the road infrastructure for extending the sights of vehicles and better coordination among them is a prerequisite. However, positioning of vehicles in dense urban canyons has long been a challenging issue, as non-line-of-sight and multipath GPS signals greatly degrade the positioning accuracy, which is crucial in vehicular safety applications. Therefore, we have a chapter on vehicular positioning in urban areas via integrating multiple sensors on autonomous vehicles. Other than safety applications, the collected vehicular mobility traces also have tremendous value in various kinds of traffic flow prediction and data mining tasks to optimize the efficiency of the transportation network.

It has long been expected that future vehicular networks will be cloud-based, so that various data collected by pervasive vehicular sensor nodes can be readily available on the cloud for big data analysis. However, with the recent growing interest of mobile edge computing (MEC), it is believed that near-edge computing can lead to lower latency and better resource management, which is especially suitable for time-critical applications that are common in highly-dynamic vehicular networks. In addition, MEC is usually implemented through the software-defined networking (SDN) technology, which will also be introduced and discussed in this book.

Finally, security and privacy is always a major issue in communication networks. This is of paramount importance in vehicular networks since the data traversed contain a lot of location information of end users, and intruded self-driving system would be a catastrophe. How to preserve privacy and system security, while not disrupting the normal operation of the network is a pivotal challenge to overcome.

This book consists of seven chapters, and here is a brief synopsis of each chapter:

Chapter 1. Performance Evaluation of the 802.11p VANET protocol based on Realistic Vehicular Traffic Flow: We illustrate in this chapter how empirical velocity profiles of vehicles can be exploited to evaluate the communication performance of generic vehicular network protocols such as 802.11p.

Chapter 2. Vehicular Positioning System: This chapter focuses on the multi-sensor integrated positioning method for robust and sub-meter level positioning for vehicular navigation.

Chapter 3. Vehicle Trajectory Processing and Big Data Mining: This chapter talks about advanced methods and machine learning techniques for vehicle location awareness, traffic flow prediction, and private car trajectory data mining.

Chapter 4. Software-Defined Vehicular Ad-hoc Networks: We introduce in this chapter how software-defined networking (SDN) technology can be applied to vehicular ad-hoc networks to improve its overall efficiency.

Chapter 5. Mobile Edge Computing: Architecture, Technology and Direction: This chapter enlightens different aspects of Mobile Edge Computing (MEC) such as architecture, security and privacy, economic traits, potential challenges, applications, mobility management, computation offloading, and future directions.

Chapter 6. Location Privacy for the Next Generation Networks: Achieving location privacy in highly connected and autonomous vehicles: This chapter proposes an Infrastructure-Assisted Pseudonym Changing Scheme (IPCS). IPCS aims to provide location privacy against trajectory attacks thereby reducing the likability of the pseudonyms.

Chapter 7. Secure and Tamper-Resilient Data Aggregation for Autonomous Vehicles and Smart Mobility: In this chapter, we focus on the security and tamper-resilience of data aggregation in autonomous vehicles as a part of the smart mobility infrastructure, based on the backbone of a distributed ledger.

Overall, Chapters 1 to 3 are regarded as fundamental problems in vehicular networking including protocol performance modeling, positioning, traffic flow prediction, and trajectory data mining. Chapters 4 and 5 are related to MEC powered by SDN and related technologies and its applications in vehicular networks. Chapters 6 and 7 are related to security and privacy in vehicular networks, including the location privacy and secure data aggregation for smart mobility. This book covers relatively advanced and cutting-edge topics in vehicular networks, including its applications, performance analysis, and major challenges. It is suitable for a survey course for college engineering postgraduate students who aspire for an in-depth study and understanding of the upcoming trend in vehicular networking and related technologies.

Peter Han Joo Chong
Ivan Wang-Hei Ho

In: Vehicular Networks
Editors: P. H. J. Chong and I. W-H. Ho

ISBN: 978-1-53615-978-3
© 2019 Nova Science Publishers, Inc.

Chapter 1

PERFORMANCE EVALUATION OF THE 802.11P VANET PROTOCOL BASED ON REALISTIC VEHICULAR TRAFFIC FLOW

Ivan Wang-Hei Ho[1]*and Elmer R. Magsino[12]

[1]Department of Electronic and Information Engineering, The Hong Kong Polytechnic University, Kowloon, Hong Kong
[2]Department of Electronics and Communications Engineering, De La Salle University, Manila, Philippines

ABSTRACT

Vehicular networks play a vital role in an Intelligent Transportation System (ITS). They enable connectivity and communications among infrastructure and vehicles everywhere to deliver safety and application-specific messages for travel comfort, driving convenience and coordinated traffic flow. In this regard, the performance of the broadcast and unicast communication protocols needs to be evaluated under the influence of a realistic vehicular distribution and traffic rules and regulations. In this work, empirical traffic models are employed to generate real-world urban

*Corresponding Author's E-mail: ivanwh.ho@polyu.edu.hk

traffic density profiles for investigating the developed IEEE 802.11p performance models. Based on the location-dependent vehicular density, the developed performance models can predict the vehicular network's delay, throughput and efficiency. We also validate the 802.11p broadcasting and unicast performance based on a realistic vehicular road distribution through extensive simulation. Our results indicate that both the spatial and temporal changes in an urban road setup have been adequately captured. The proposed novel framework can provide researchers and network designers various insights into the future design of communication protocols to be implemented in vehicular networks.

INTRODUCTION

Intelligent Transportation System (ITS) supports information exchange among vehicles (V2V) and vehicles and infrastructure (V2I). It enables efficient routing of environmental data, the delivery of up-to-date services for both information and entertainment, and real-time traffic control and safety (Baskar et al. 2011). An integral part of ITS is the Vehicular Ad-Hoc Network (VANET) that provides short-range wireless connection between infrastructure and vehicles without any wireless access points. Through VANETs, vehicles can easily connect/disconnect to/from a network by utilizing the IEEE 802.11p standard (Standards Committee 1997). Such protocol defines the medium access control (MAC) and physical (PHY) layers in the Dedicated Short Range Communications (DSRC) stack. The DSRC band has seven 10 MHz channels, where one of the channels is used as the control channel (CCH) for broadcasting safety messages (Omar, Zhuang, and Li 2013). The other six channels are denoted as service channels (SCH) for different applications, e.g., disseminating 3D road map data to intelligent vehicles (Chu et al. 2017)).

Assisting road drivers by informing them of road danger and emergency situations is best achieved by broadcast transmission. Broadcasting quickly provides drivers and passengers safety-related information by covering multiple vehicles and infrastructure within the transmission range (Mchergui et al. 2017). On the other hand, unicast transmission is suitable when the messages being transmitted requires an automatic repeat request (ARQ). This is accomplished because unicast involves a mechanism for message retransmission and a confirmation technique from the recipient to the origin after there is a successful reception. Unicast transmission can also avoid the broadcasting storm problem (Chakroun, Cherkaoui, and Rezgui 2012).

As the number of vehicles increases across the globe (Statista 2018), incorporating empirical vehicular traffic in the analysis and performance of the 802.11p protocol becomes an important issue, since vehicles automatically become the 802.11p transceivers. Their mobility and presence on the roads create a research paradigm that must be addressed by including realistic approaches in modeling traffic and vehicular distribution. Existing literatures focused on assuming homogeneous vehicular distribution, and neglecting the influence of traffic signals and vehicular interactions (Han et al. 2012; Ma et al. 2012; Wu et al. 2015). This work investigates the IEEE 802.11p performance for vehicular information dissemination/exchange via broadcast and unicast by providing an original framework involving a realistic traffic distribution. The block diagram of our novel methodology is illustrated in Figure 1. A stochastic traffic model, modified from (Ho, Leung, and Polak 2011), is derived by considering a practical traffic scenario that includes traffic lights and realistic vehicular traffic flow. The 802.11p models are then developed on top of this modified traffic model. For broadcast, we demonstrate our analytical framework by studying the control channel used in broadcasting beacon messages. For unicast, the contention process for both the idle and busy states are modeled by a 2D Markov chain. On the other hand, the interference model, based on packet collisions, is evaluated by considering four various scenarios involving vehicles that are either transmitting, receiving or being interfered. At time t and at any location along the road, the delay and throughput metrics are computed to characterize the performance of IEEE 802.11p in both broadcast and unicast transmission modes. Additionally, the packet delivery success rate is used to evaluate the broadcasting efficiency.

The structure of the chapter is outlined as follows. A detailed literature review regarding the modeling of vehicular traffic and 802.11p network for broadcast and unicast is given in Section 2. The proposed methodology for VANET modeling and performance metrics are described in Section 3. The results and discussion of our simulation are then presented in Section 4. Lastly, the summary and conclusion of the work are found in Section 5.

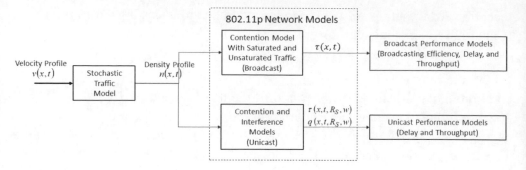

Figure 1. The proposed block diagram of the novel methodology for evaluating 802.11p VANET employing realistic vehicular traffic flow.

REVIEW OF RELATED LITERATURE

IEEE 802.11p Protocol for Vehicular Networks

The IEEE 802.11p (Jiang and Delgrossi 2008) was devised to enable wireless access and communication among vehicles and roadside infrastructure. The 802.11p PHY layer follows the OFDM technology to accommodate the highly dynamic channel conditions and multipath fading present in a vehicular network. The MAC layer of the 802.11p standard employs the Carrier-Sense Multiple Access with Collision Avoidance (CSMA/CA) having the capability to repeat retransmissions. The 802.11p protocol improves the quality of service (QoS) by adopting the Enhanced Distributed Channel Access (EDCA) from the 802.11e standard (Standards Committee 2005).

Research studies have employed the use of Markov chains to analyze the 802.11p protocol. In (Ma and Chen 2007b) and (Ma, Chen, and Refai 2007), saturated and unsaturated conditions were studied by analyzing the broadcast throughput, delay, and packet reception ratio using a 1D Markov chain. In another paper, (Wang and Hassan 2009) considered both reliability and broadcast throughput by identifying a function that will provide the appropriate contention window sizes. In (Vinel, Staehle, and Turlikov 2009), a 3D Markov model, which has many states, was used to evaluate the performance of beacon broadcasting.

(Bianci 2000) employed a 2D Markov chain in deriving the transmission and collision probability relationship due to simultaneous transmissions and the presence of hidden nodes. In (Han et al. 2012), a 2D Markov chain is also applied for analyzing the EDCA mechanism while also adding a retransmission limit. In (Wang et al. 2010), the busy or idle channel status was incorporated by considering the multi-channel MAC protocol presented in the IEEE 1609.4 standard.

Vehicular Traffic Flow Modeling

Previous analytical studies have focused more on evaluating the 802.11p protocol under simple traffic flow conditions to simplify the analysis, e.g., homogeneous vehicular distribution, disregard of traffic lights and rules, constant vehicular speed, etc. The works in (Ma and Chen 2007a; Ma et al. 2012) randomly generated moving vehicles on a one-dimensional (1D) highway and assumed that the vehicular arrival follows a Poisson distribution. On the other hand, Wu, et. al, (Wu et al. 2015) used the freeway mobility model for generating vehicular traffic on a highway. The synthetic vehicular traffic flow constrained the vehicles to have constant speeds and the following vehicles' speeds are always less than that of the vehicles in front of them. Low- and high-density highway and urban traffic flows are studied in (Booysen, Zeadally, and Van Rooyen 2012).

Realistic approaches were considered in the works published in (Khabazian and Ali 2008) and (Umer et al. 2010). In (Khabazian and Ali 2008), the highway entry and exit points were considered to integrate the heterogeneity of vehicular traffic flow in their study. The work seen in (Umer et al. 2010) characterized the heterogeneous vehicular traffic and density by incorporating the deterministic fluid dynamic model into the traffic flow, with the assumption that it follows the conservation law. To become more realistic, the study also included road junctions and vehicular density, emphasizing locations where congestions occurs.

To characterize realistic vehicular flow, the randomness of each vehicle and the corresponding effect as well as the influence of traffic lights must be included in the analysis. Such considerations are addressed by the work in (Ho, Leung, and Polak 2011). The vehicular traffic model presented in (Ho, Leung, and Polak 2011) utilizes a stochastic fluid dynamic for obtaining the mean vehicular density profile with distribution knowledge while at the same time, using a density-dependent velocity profile to approximate the vehicular interactions.

TRAFFIC AND NETWORK MODELING

This section discusses the realistic urban traffic setup that captures both the temporal and spatial dynamics of the vehicular traffic flow. Based on a practical traffic model, our methodology for estimating the 802.11p VANETs broadcast and unicast performance is investigated. In simple words, given the traffic velocity profile, various metrics for estimating the network performance can be computed.

Stochastic and Empirical Vehicular Traffic Model

The urban vehicular traffic modeling studied in this work combines the macroscopic flow with a stochastic approach. Consider the vehicular flow of a signalized and semi-infinite urban road setup shown in Figure 2, and limiting the discussion to a single-lane and one-directional traffic flow model. Multi-lane and bi-directional scenarios can be built by superimposing numerous basic blocks of this derived model.

At location $x = 0$, vehicle arrival follows a non-homogeneous Poisson distribution $\{A(t)| - \infty < t < +\infty\}$, having an expected rate of arrival equal to $\alpha(t)$ that is non-negative and integrable for $t > 0$. Vehicular flow is in the direction of the arrow and is controlled by a traffic light as it approaches the junction. Vehicles can only enter or leave the road segment at the junction.

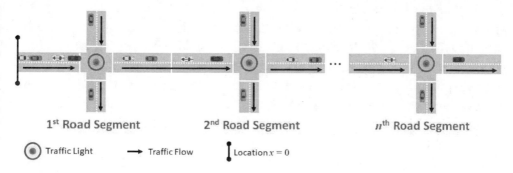

Figure 2. An urban single-lane road setup that has a one-directional flow of vehicular traffic.

Consider the vehicular traffic found in the first road segment of Figure 2, we can model this as an incompressible fluid depicted in Figure 3, where $C^+(x, t)$

and $C^-(x,t)$ represent the amount of entering and exiting vehicles at $(0,x]$ during the time interval $(-\infty, t)$, respectively. $Q(x,t)$ denotes the amount of passing vehicles at location x within $(-\infty, t)$ while $N(x,t)$ corresponds to the amount of remaining vehicles on the first road segment $(0,x]$ during time t.

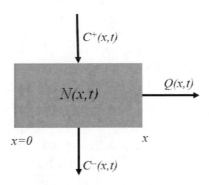

Figure 3. Traffic flow modeled as an incompressible fluid.

By applying the conservation principle and the relationships between flow rate, flow speed and fluid density, we have:

$$c^+(x,t) - c^-(x,t) - \frac{\partial q(x,t)}{\partial x} = \frac{\partial n(x,t)}{\partial t} \tag{1}$$

where $c^+(x,t)$ defines the rate of change of entering vehicular density $C^+(x,t)$ with respect to x and t. On the other hand, $c^-(x,t)$ defines the rate of change of exiting vehicular density $C^-(x,t)$ with respect to x and t. $q(x,t)$ and $n(x,t)$ are the rate of vehicles passing through and the density of vehicles at location x and at time t, respectively.

We assume that the velocity, $v(x,t)$, and vehicular density, $n(x,t)$, are independent of each other, thus (1) can be written as (2).

$$c^+(x,t) - c^-(x,t) - \frac{\partial v(x,t)}{\partial x} n(x,t) = \frac{dn(x,t)}{dt} \tag{2}$$

To include randomness of traffic into the model, the following deterministic variables in (1) and (2) become:

$$c^+(x,t) = \frac{\partial^2 E[C^+(x,t)]}{\partial x \partial t}, \quad c^-(x,t) = \frac{\partial^2 E[C^-(x,t)]}{\partial x \partial t}$$

$$q(x,t) = \frac{\partial E[Q(x,t)]}{\partial t}, \text{ and } \quad n(x,t) = \frac{\partial E[N(x,t)]}{\partial x} \tag{3}$$

where $E[\bullet]$ denotes the expectation of $[\bullet]$.

For a given road segment, if the vehicle arrival follows a Poisson distribution, then, the vehicle density also follows the Poisson distribution. This has been empirically validated in (Ho, Leung, and Polak 2011). Given this finding, the average density of vehicles and its distribution in terms of space, x, and time, t, can be obtained. In addition, if we let the arrival process, $A(t)$, follow the non-homogeneous Poisson process with a mean arrival rate of $\alpha(t)$, then, at time t, the average vehicular density for two regions, e.g., $(x_1, x_2]$ and $(x_3, x_4]$, that are non-overlapping, are independent and can be represented by:

$$\bar{N}(x_1, x_2, t) = E[N(x_1, x_2, t)] = \int_{x_1}^{x_2} n(s,t)ds$$

$$\bar{N}(x_3, x_4, t) = E[N(x_3, x_4, t)] = \int_{x_3}^{x_4} n(s,t)ds \tag{4}$$

Note that from (1) to (2), we assume that $v(x,t)$ and $n(x,t)$ are independent of each other and possibly not be true empirically. Nonetheless, if there is not much traffic load, e.g., < 30 vehicles/min in the network, the proposed stochastic traffic model will still be a suitable approximation. To incorporate interactions among vehicles, the revised Greenshield's model (5) is employed.

$$v(x,t) = v_f \left(1 - \frac{n(x + \Delta x, t)}{k_j} \right) \tag{5}$$

where k_j indicates the congestion/jamming density and v_f defines the vehicular mean free speed.

Network Models for the IEEE 802.11p Broadcast and Unicast Transmission Modes

We derive network models focusing on beacon broadcasting that considers packet contention and collision for investigating the 802.11p broadcast performance. On the other hand, the contention and interference models are obtained when employing the 802.11p unicast transmission. In our analysis, the IEEE 802.11p PHY and MAC layer assumptions for broadcast and unicast transmissions are tabulated in Table 1.

IEEE 802.11p Broadcast Contention Models

Broadcasting of vehicle status (e.g., location, speed and bearing) and safety-related messages (e.g., road conditions, accidents) operates in the control channel (CCH). A vehicle generates a beacon message every 100 ms and broadcast them when the vehicle is in the CCH. Vehicles compete for channel access following the CSMA/CA mechanism. If by the end of the CCH interval the beacon has not been sent, it will automatically be dropped. However, according to (Campolo et al. 2011), the dropping of beacons rarely occurs. Additionally, there will be no retransmission of collided beacons.

Saturated Traffic Condition   During saturated traffic condition, our assumptions follow that of (Wang and Hassan 2009) where the channel sensed by a vehicle at location a is busy with a probability equal to p and the vehicle's transmission probability equal to τ. Figure 4 characterizes the contention model of any vehicle, where the contention window size is represented by W_{ss}. Each state corresponds to the counter value during contention. The counter value remains the same during busy time slots and decrements during idle time slots. If the counter reaches zero, then, the broadcasting of messages will happen at the next idle state, and a non-zero random value is loaded to the counter.

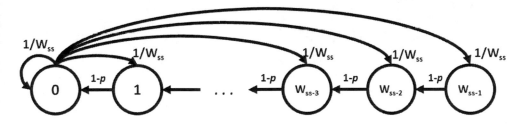

Figure 4. Markov chain model during saturated traffic condition.

From Figure 4, the transmission probability τ can be expressed as (6), while

Table 1. 802.11p Network Model Assumptions

	Broadcast Assumptions	Unicast Assumptions
PHY Layer	1. The one dimensional road has an isotropic and homogeneous channel.	
	2. Vehicles have identical transmission range, R_S, and sensing/interference range, R_I, where $R_S < R_I$.	
	3. Collision happens when vehicles within R_I of the receiver transmit at the same time as the sender. There is a successful reception if there is no packet collision.	
	4. The only cause of transmission failure is due to collision, including the hidden nodes.	
MAC Layer	1. There is only beaconing message in the system queue.	1. The saturated condition, i.e., there are continuous packets available for transmissions during the SCH interval, is considered to make a perpetual non-empty queue.
	2. There is a beacon message ready to be transported at the beginning of each CCH.	
	3. Beacons are generated every 100 ms (10 Hz).	
	4. Since we are modeling a single queue scenario, the arbitrary inter-frame space (AIFS) interval is neglected. If this is needed, then it can be incorporated by adding extra states to the Markov chain.	2. All nodes share the same EDCA settings.
	5. Every vehicle in the road segment is assumed to share the same MAC settings (e.g., contention window size, slot time, etc.).	
	The channel time is characterized as infinitely long (Vinel, Staehle, and Turlikov 2009; Stanica, Chaput, and Beylot 2011).	

the busy channel probability is denoted by (7). $\bar{N}(R_I)$ represents the mean number of vehicles located in the sensing region.

$$\tau = b_0 = \frac{2(1-p)}{1-2p+W_{ss}} \tag{6}$$

$$p = 1 - \Sigma_{k=0}^{\infty} \frac{(1-\tau)^k \, \bar{N}(R_I)^k \, e^{-\bar{N}(R_I)}}{k!} = 1 - e^{-\bar{N}(R_I)\tau}. \tag{7}$$

Unsaturated Traffic Condition   Most traffic comes from beacon messages used for positioning instead of emergency messages. Thus, in the control channel, the queue is not saturated (Daneshgaran et al. 2008). This unsaturated condition is illustrated in Figure 5.

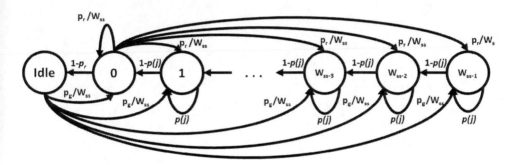

Figure 5. Markov chain model during unsaturated traffic condition.

In Figure 5, four additions were made. First, there is an 'Idle' state to accommodate vehicles with empty message queues, indicating that these vehicles are not in contention mode. Second, at the beginning of the CCH duration, the number of vehicles in contention is at maximum and decreases when vehicles send their beacons, then going to the 'Idle' state. Therefore, the channel busy probability is a function of time, i.e., $p(j)$. Third, time j is measured in terms of "virtual time slots". Lastly, the probability of generating other safety-related messages are p_g or p_r. p_g refers to the probability of generating an emergency packet in the next virtual time slot while the vehicle is 'Idle'. On the other hand, p_r pertains to the probability that a newly generated packet happens before the message queue becomes empty.

At each state, the number of vehicles is calculated recursively as

$$\pi_{idle}(1) = 0 \tag{8}$$

$$\pi_i(1) = \frac{1}{W_{ss}} \tag{9}$$

$$\text{for } i = 0, 1 \dots, W_{ss} - 1$$

$$\pi_{idle}(j) = \pi_{idle}(j-1) + \pi_0(j-1) * (1 - p(j-1)) \tag{10}$$

$$\text{for } j = 2, 3, \dots$$

$$\pi_k(j) = \pi_{k+1}(j-1) * [1 - p(j-1)] + p(j-1) * \pi_k(j-1) \tag{11}$$

$$\text{for } k = 0, 1 \dots, W_{ss} - 2, j = 2, 3, \dots$$

$$\pi_{W_{ss}-1}(j) = \pi_{W_{ss}-1}(j-1) * p(j-1) \tag{12}$$

$$\text{for } j = 2, 3, \dots$$

$$p(j) = 1 - e^{-\bar{N}(R_I)\pi_0(j)} \tag{13}$$

$$\text{for } j = 1, 2 \dots$$

(8) and (9) are the initial conditions. (10) – (12) are the state transition conditions. (13) computes if there is at least one vehicle that is transmitting, thus, $p(j)$ is calculated.

IEEE 802.11p Unicast Models

Contention Models   In this work, modeling of V2V unicast transmissions will focus on the single access queue. The contention process, for a vehicle a found at location a, is modeled by the 2D Markov chain shown in Figure 6, where state i is the back-off stage and k is the counter value of i. Lastly, w_i counts at each stage i the total values for the contention window (W_{ss}) size. It is equal to $w_i = W_{ssi} + 1$. We derive the probability τ of a vehicle a when transmitting a packet at the start of a time slot.

Vehicle a senses a busy channel if other vehicles are inside its sensing range R_I and are also transmitting. In this case, the busy channel probability p is given in (14), provided that the vehicles are Poisson-distributed.

$$p = 1 - e^{-\bar{N}(R_I)\tau R_I} \tag{14}$$

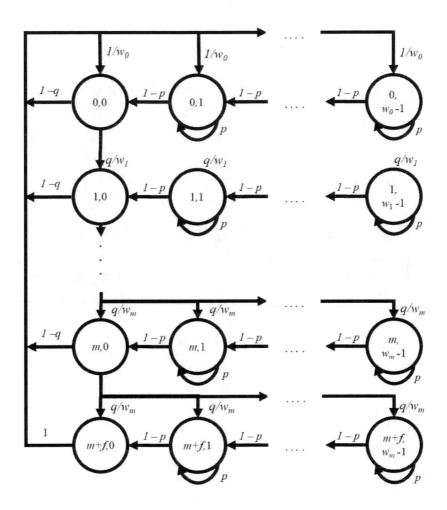

Figure 6. The 2D Markov chain for a single access class in 802.11p unicast.

τ_{R_I} denotes the average transmission probability of all vehicles within the sensing range of vehicle a. $\bar{N}(R_I) = \int_{a-R_I}^{a} n(x)dx + \int_{a}^{a+R_I} n(x)dx$ because the vehicular distribution is considered static due to an extremely small SCH interval.

Based from Figure 6, the expression for the transmission probability, as a function of the collision probability, q, is given by (15).

$$\tau = \frac{1 - q^{m+f+1}}{\gamma \left[\frac{1-q^{m+f+1}}{1-q} + \frac{1}{2(1-p)} \left(w_o \frac{1-(2q)^{m+1}}{1-2q} - \frac{1-q^{m+1}}{1-q} \right) + \frac{w_m-1}{2(1-p)} \left(\frac{q^{m+1}(1-q^f)}{1-q} \right) \right]}$$

$$(15)$$

where $\gamma = (1 - q)$.

Finally, setting the conditions $m = 1$ and $f = \infty$, vehicle a's transmission probability τ is depicted in (16). m and f are defined as the maximum limit on how much the initial contention window size will be doubled and the maximum number of retransmissions before discarding the packet, right after m stages, respectively. In these conditions, the maximum contention window size is twice the original contention window size even if there are future retransmissions. w_0 is a constant EDCA setting value.

$$\tau = \frac{2(1 - p)}{1 - 2p + w_0(1 + q)} \tag{16}$$

Interference Models   Vehicles performing unicast transmission suffer from packet collision if there are sources of interference. We consider a case where vehicle a is transmitting data to a vehicle behind it, e.g., vehicle x. If at least one other vehicle is in the vicinity of vehicle x's sensing range, R_I, then packet collision can occur. In such scenario, four models of interference need to be derived, as shown in Figure 7.

(17) gives the probability of having i vehicles within the transmission range of vehicle a, assuming that the vehicular arrival follows a Poisson process.

$$P\{i \text{ vehicles in } [a - R_S, a)\} = \frac{(\bar{N}_{R_S})^i e^{-\bar{N}_{R_S}}}{i!} \tag{17}$$

where $\bar{N}_{R_S} = \int_{a-R_S}^{a} n(x)dx$ is the average number of vehicles within vehicle a's transmission range R_S for $0 \le i < +\infty$. A vehicle k, where $1 \le k \le i$, within vehicle a's transmission range R_S is randomly chosen with a probability $P(k) = 1/i$.

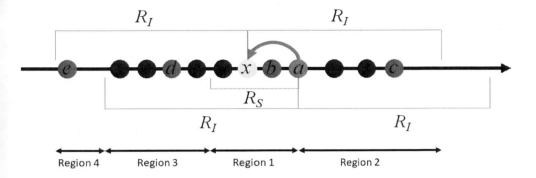

Figure 7. Various interference regions.

Region 1 (R1) $[a - R_S, a)$ In R1, at least one vehicle is transmitting with a probability equal to (18), where τ_{R_S} denotes the mean transmission probability of vehicles situated in R1.

$$B = 1 - (1 - \tau_{R_S})^i \tag{18}$$

The k-th vehicle receiver is interfered among i vehicles with a probability equal to (19).

$$P_{Intf1}(k) = P(k)B \tag{19}$$

For R1, the interference probability, P_1, is given by (20).

$$P_1 = \sum_{i=1}^{\infty} P\{i \text{ vehicles in R1}\} \sum_{k=1}^{i} P_{Intf1}(k) = 1 - e^{-\tau_{R_S}\bar{N}_{R_S}} \tag{20}$$

Region 2 (R2) $(a, x + R_I]$ For R2, the probability that there is at least one vehicle transmitting is given by (21), where τ_C is the vehicles' average transmission probability.

$$C(x) = 1 - \sum_{n=0}^{\infty} P\{n \text{ vehicles in R2}\} P(n \text{ vehicles not transmitting})$$

$$= 1 - e^{-\tau_C \left(\int_a^{x+R_I} n(s)ds \right)} \tag{21}$$

The k-th vehicle receiver is interfered among i vehicles with a probability equal to (22).

$$P_{Intf2}(k) = P(k) \int_{a-R_S}^{a} f(x)C(x)dx \tag{22}$$

where from (Ho, Leung, and Polak 2011), $f(x)$ is:

$$f(x) = \begin{cases} \frac{n(x)}{\bar{N}_{R_S}} & a - R_S \leq x < a \\ 0 & \text{otherwise} \end{cases} \tag{23}$$

For R2, the interference probability, P_2, is shown in (24).

$$P_2 = \sum_{i=1}^{\infty} P\{i \text{ vehicles in R1}\} \sum_{k=1}^{i} P_{Intf2}(k)$$

$$= \frac{1 - e^{-\bar{N}_{R_S}}}{\bar{N}_{R_S}} \int_{a-R_S}^{a} n(x) \left[1 - e^{-\tau_C \bar{N}_C(x)} \right] dx \tag{24}$$

Region 3 (R3) $[a - R_I, a - R_S)$ For R3, the probability, D, that there is at least one vehicle transmitting is given by (25), where τ_D is the vehicles' mean transmission probability and $\bar{N}_D = \int_{a-R_I}^{a-R_S} n(s)ds$ defines the mean number of vehicles in the region.

$$D = 1 - \sum_{n=0}^{\infty} P\{n \text{ vehicles in R3}\} P(n \text{ vehicles not transmitting})$$

$$= 1 - e^{-\tau_D \bar{N}_D} \tag{25}$$

For R3, the interference probability, P_3, is shown in (26).

$$P_3 = \sum_{i=1}^{\infty} P\{i \text{ vehicles in R1}\} \sum_{k=1}^{i} P(k)D \int_{a-R_S}^{a} f(x)dx$$

$$= \frac{(1 - e^{-\bar{N}_{RS}})(1 - e^{-\tau_D \bar{N}_D})}{\bar{N}_{RS}} \int_{a-R_S}^{a} n(x)dx \qquad (26)$$

Region 4 (R4) $[x - R_I, a - R_I)$ For R4, the probability that there is at least one vehicle transmitting is given by (27), where τ_E is the vehicles' mean transmission probability and $\bar{N}_E = \int_{a-R_I}^{x-R_I} n(s)ds$ defines the mean number of vehicles in the region.

$$E(x) = 1 - \sum_{n=0}^{\infty} P\{n \text{ vehicles in R4}\}P(n \text{ vehicles not transmitting})$$

$$- 1 - e^{-\tau_E \bar{N}_E(x)} \qquad (27)$$

In Fig. 7, the interferers are situated outside vehicle a's sensing range which classifies them as hidden nodes. In R4, there are three scenarios that involve hidden node transmissions. These are: (1) simultaneous transmissions between the hidden nodes and vehicle a, (2) transmission by the hidden nodes first before transmission of vehicle a, and (3) transmission of vehicle a first before the transmissions of hidden nodes.

For scenarios 1 and 2, and starting from the time slot at which vehicle a starts to transmit, the probability that the k-th vehicle receiver found at x is interfered by vehicles transmitting in R4 is given by (28).

$$P_{Intf4\_1}(k) = P(k) \int_{a-R_S}^{a} f(x)E(x)dx \qquad (28)$$

For scenario 3, the time slot when vehicle a started to transmit and its state, whether in contention or transmission, in the expected time slot $pT + (1-p)$ are considered. Assume that there are J expected slots needed for completing one practical transmission time of T physical slots. Transmissions by the hidden nodes will take place when $J \geq 2$. When this happens, then, no vehicle has transmitted during the first expected time slot with the probability $1 - E(x)$.

Thus, during the $(j + 1)$-th expected time slot, the probability that there is at least one hidden node that transmits is given by (29).

$$P_{exp}(j) = [1 - E(x)]^j E(x), 1 \leq j \leq J - 1 \qquad (29)$$

The conditional interference probability when considering scenario 3 is expressed by (30).

$$P_{Intf4\_2}(k) = P(k) \int_{a-R_S}^{a} f(x) \sum_{j=1}^{J-1} P_{exp}(j) dx \qquad (30)$$

Therefore, the overall interference probability in R4 is shown in (31).

$$P_4 = \sum_{i=1}^{\infty} P\{i \text{ vehicles in R1}\} \sum_{k=1}^{i} [P_{Intf4\_1}(k) + P_{Intf4\_2}(k)]$$

$$= C_4 \int_{a-R_S}^{a} \left[1 - e^{-\tau_E \bar{N}_E(x)}\right] \left[1 + \sum_{j=1}^{J-1} e^{-j\tau_E \bar{N}_E}(x)\right] dx \qquad (31)$$

where $C_4 = \frac{1-e^{-\bar{N}R_S}}{\bar{N}R_S} n(x)$ and $J = \lceil \frac{T}{pT+1-p} \rceil$. $\lceil \bullet \rceil$ denotes the ceiling operator.

Finally, the collision probability, q, from vehicle a to vehicle x while taking into consideration the presence of any interferers is (32).

$$q = 1 - (1 - P_1)(1 - P_2)(1 - P_3)(1 - P_4) \qquad (32)$$

802.11p Protocol Performance Metrics

We evaluate the joint transport and network models by determining the expected delay and throughput (both broadcast and unicast) and the broadcasting performance index (broadcast only) at location a.

Broadcasting Performance Index   We define the Broadcasting Performance Index (BPI) at location a as the ratio of the total number of interference-free

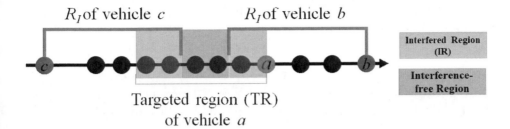

Figure 8. Determining the number of interference-free and targeted vehicles.

targeted vehicles (shaded by the red rectangular box in Figure 8) to the total number of targeted vehicles (TR in Figure 8) as defined in (33).

$$BPI = \frac{\text{\# of interference-free targeted vehicles}}{\text{\# number of targeted vehicles}} \qquad (33)$$

In the analysis of determining the number of intended receivers, we assume that vehicles at the back of a transmitter are the interested parties since drivers want to be informed of the preceding traffic instead of what has happened behind them. Among the targeted vehicles, some vehicles can be interfered by other simultaneous transmitters. Therefore, the overall BPI considering interference at locations b and c can be defined by (34).

$$BPI = \int_{-\infty}^{a-R_S} \int_{a}^{+\infty} \left(1 - \frac{\overline{N}_{IR}}{\overline{N}_{TR}} \right) * e^{-\tau_{TR}*\overline{N}_{TR}} * P(B = b) * P(C = c) db dc \qquad (34)$$

$\overline{N}_{IR}$ and $\overline{N}_{TR}$ are the average number of vehicles inside the interfered region (IR) and targeted region (TR), respectively. τ_{TR} can be obtained from (8) – (13) and is equivalent to the vehicles' estimated transmission rate. The probability $P(B = b)$ represents the effective interference source found at location b and is given by:

$$P(B = b) = \tau_{ab} n(b) e^{-\bar{N}_a^b \tau_{ab}} \qquad (35)$$

In (35), $\bar{N}_a^b$ and τ_{ab} denote the average number of vehicles and the average transmission rate in the interval $(a, b]$, respectively. The vehicular density at location b is represented by $n\,(b)$. We obtain $P(C = c)$ by following the same reasoning as $P(B = b)$.

Delay Metric   For broadcast transmission, the computation of delay is from packet contention until the actual transmission. The expected total broadcast delays for both the unsaturated and saturated traffic conditions are given by

$$E[D_B]_{Unsat} = E[T_x] + \sum_{k=0}^{+\infty} \sum_{j=1}^{k} \left(\left(E[T_x] * p(j) + [1 - p(j)] \right) * P(k+1) \right)$$

(36)

$$E[D_B]_{Sat} = E[T_x] + \sum_{k=0}^{+\infty} \left(k * \left(E[T_x] * p + (1 - p) \right) * P(k+1) \right)$$ (37)

$E[T_x]$ denotes the expected transmission time. p and $p(j)$ are the busy channel probabilities for the coming physical time slot and at the j-th virtual time slot, respectively. $P(k+1)$ is the probability that a vehicle starts to transmit in the $(k+1)^{th}$ virtual time slot.

For unicast transmission, the computation of delay commences at the start of contention until the reception of the ACK signal. Therefore, the total unicast delay D_U is equal to the number of failed transmission intervals and one successful transmission interval, as depicted in (38).

$$D_U = \eta \underbrace{\left(\overline{CT} + T \right)}_{T_F} + \underbrace{\left(\overline{CT} + T + SIFS + ACK \right)}_{T_S}$$ (38)

T_F and T_S are the failed and successful duration respectively. η denotes how many failed transmissions occurred. $\overline{CT}$ is the expected contention interval, while T, $SIFS$ and ACK are constants representing the transmission, Short Inter-Frame Space (SIFS) and ACK durations, respectively.

The expected delay for unicast transmission, $E[D_U]$, is given by (39).

$$E[D_U] = \frac{1}{1-q} \left[\left(\frac{p}{\tau} - p + 1 \right) T + \left(1 - \frac{1}{\tau} \right) p + \frac{1}{\tau} - 1 \right]$$ (39)

Throughput Metric For broadcast transmission, a successful transmission happens when all intended receivers get the message. The expected broadcast throughput, $E[\rho_B]$, is given by (40).

$$E[\rho_B] = \overline{N}_{TR} * \left(\frac{BPI}{E[D_B]} \right) \tag{40}$$

The expression for BPI is in (34), while the expressions for $E[D_B]$ are seen in equations (36) and (37) for the unsaturated and saturated conditions, respectively.

For unicast transmission, given L (packet size), the vehicle's expected unicast throughput, $E[\rho_U]$, is given by (41).

$$E[\rho_U] = \frac{L}{E[D_U]} \tag{41}$$

Interested readers are referred to (Qui et al. 2015) and (Xie, Ho, and Magsino 2018) for the complete derivation of the network models and performance metrics.

SIMULATION RESULTS AND DISCUSSION

Vehicular Traffic and Network Setups

We validate our analytical modeling of the IEEE 802.11p protocol by performing exhaustive simulations in C++ considering both the homogeneous and non-homogeneous vehicular traffic distributions. In the homogeneous scenario, we allowed the vehicle density, $n(x)$, to vary from 5 to 30 vehicles/km to observe the performance of the network under various traffic densities. When considering the non-homogeneous situation, we assume that the vehicle arrival follows the Poisson process with an arrival rate equal to 12 vehicles/min. When approaching the junction and at the same time, the traffic light turns RED, the vehicular mean free speed, $v_f(x, t)$, will follow (42) (Ho, Leung, and Polak 2011). For interactions among vehicle, k_j and Δx are set to 500 cars/km and 0.02 km in (5), respectively.

$$v_f(x,t) = \begin{cases} 1 & x < 1.98 \\ (100 - 50x) & 1.98 \leq x < 2 \\ 0 & 2 \leq x < 2.012 \\ (50x - 100.6) & 2.012 \leq x < 2.032 \\ 1 & x \geq 2.032 \end{cases} \qquad (42)$$

In simulating the network, all vehicles have the same transmission range, $R_S = 200$ m, and interference range, $R_I = 500$ m. The contention window sizes, W_{ss}, are set to 4, 8, 16, and 32. Each slot time is 16 μs while the channel period, i.e., CCH + SCH, equals 100 ms, where SCH = 50 ms. The (data rates, packet sizes) are (3 Mbps, 500 bytes) and (6 Mbps, 512 bytes) for the broadcast and unicast modes, respectively.

Broadcasting Performance Index Discussion

The simulated and analytical BPI's for both homogeneous and non-homogeneous traffic densities are shown in Figure 9. The mean BPI is obtained from averaging all vehicle instances on the road and in all simulation runs. Generally, there is a good match between the simulated and analytical BPI.

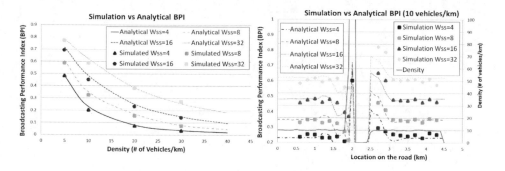

Figure 9. Analytical and simulated BPI given a homogeneous (left) and non-homogeneous (right) traffic densities.

For a homogeneous traffic density (left part of Figure 9), as the vehicular density increases, the channel becomes busier allowing more packet collisions to occur, effectively, decreasing the BPI. When the vehicular density is greater than 30 vehicles/km, we observe that two-thirds of the broadcasted packets can no longer be received by the intended receiving vehicles. To make sure that packets will be received even with an increasing vehicular density, a larger contention window size is recommended.

In (42), there is a vehicular mean speed equal to zero because a traffic light signal has turned RED, resulting to the bunching of vehicles at 2 km as indicated by an impulse. There is zero density at the region [2, 2.5] km (location of the traffic light). Elsewhere, we observe a constant traffic density. This setup illustrates the non-homogeneous scenario. As shown in the right part of Figure 9, as the vehicles approach the location of the traffic light (starting at 1.5 km), BPI decreases because of the presence of a high vehicular density. Also, once the vehicles have passed the junction (at 2.5 km), the BPI increases at a fast rate because there are no interferers. Overall, the maximum mean relative error between the simulated and analytical BPI's is 15%.

In any of the scenarios above, a high-valued BPI is desirable. To achieve this, communication parameters must be adaptive in the presence of any traffic density. For example, a larger contention window size is recommended when there is a high density of vehicles in the vicinity. In addition, the vehicle's transmission power can be decreased to reduce its transmission range, effectively minimizing interference and eliminating the effects of hidden nodes. Lastly, the transmission time for beacon can also be reduced to improve the BPI.

Delay Performance

For broadcasting, given a homogeneous vehicular density, as more vehicles are on the road at a specified location, the network delay increases due to the fact that more vehicles are competing to access the channel. There is also a large delay when the contention window is large because there is too much waiting time. This is illustrated in the left part of Figure 10.

In a non-homogeneous case (right part of Figure 10), there is a platoon of vehicles accumulating in front of the traffic light. Given this, naturally, there is a high rate of contention leading to a delay peak value found at location 1.5 km. However, the opposite can be found at location 2.5 km. Overall, the maximum mean relative error between the simulated and analytical delays is 8%.

The delay performance under the unicast transmission mode is shown in Figure 11. Like the broadcasting delay given a homogeneous density scenario,

Ivan Wang-Hei Ho and Elmer R. Magsino

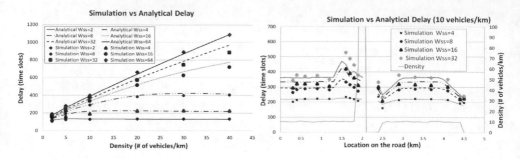

Figure 10. Analytical and simulated broadcast delay given homogeneous (left) and non-homogeneous (right) traffic densities.

the unicast delay also monotonically increases primarily because a vehicle experiences a longer contention time and there is a higher probability of packet collisions. For the non-homogeneous case, we can observe that the delay varies with the vehicular density. Before the location of 1.46 km, a constant transmission delay is observed for all contention window sizes. The delay escalates because of the presence of vehicles within the interference/sensing range up to location 1.6 km. Later on, the delay decreases because there are no vehicles found right after the traffic light. From the 2.53 km location, there is a gradual increase in delay since vehicles are now starting to form queues and well within the transmitting vehicle's interference range. Afterwards, another constant delay is observed. It is evident that a larger contention window size allows a smaller unicast delay.

Throughput Performance

The left part of Figure 12 demonstrates that the broadcasting throughput is at its highest when the homogeneous density approximately equals 5 vehicles/km, for any given contention window size, W_{ss}. When vehicular density is < 5 vehicles/km, the delay becomes the dominant factor. As the density increases, there is a decrease in throughput because the BPI is degraded, effectively, outweighing the increase in the number of target vehicular receivers. These findings bring us to a set of observations that 1) during low vehicle density, we can reduce the delay by adaptively reducing the contention window size and 2) we can improve

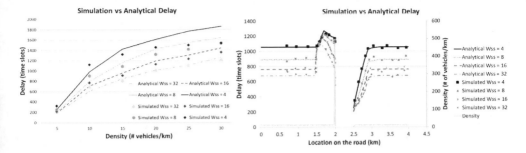

Figure 11. Analytical and simulated unicast delay given homogeneous (left) and non-homogeneous (right) traffic densities.

the *BPI* by increasing the contention window size when the density is not too low (> 5 vehicles/km).

On the other hand, for a non-homogeneous scenario (right part of Figure 12), the throughput performance is location-dependent and follows the *BPI* pattern in Fig. 9. At locations 1.5 and 2.5 km, throughput decreases and increases, respectively. At locations > 4.5 km, there are no vehicles in front, thereby, offering no interference. The mean relative error between the simulated and analytical throughput is less than 10%.

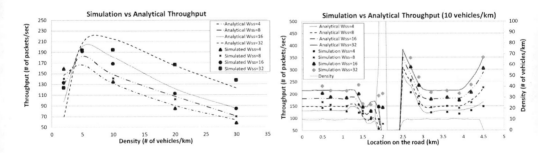

Figure 12. Analytical and simulated broadcast throughput given homogeneous (left) and non-homogeneous (right) traffic densities.

The unicast throughput results are shown in Figure 13. From (41), the throughput in the unicast transmission mode is simply the reciprocal of the unicast delay. For both the homogeneous and non-homogeneous cases, if there is an increase in the size of the contention window, there will also be an increase in the unicast throughput. This is due to the fact that in unicast, enough waiting time is guaranteed before the next transmission, resulting to less packet collisions.

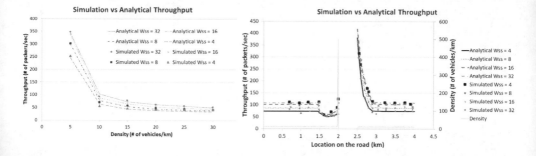

Figure 13. Analytical and simulated unicast throughput given homogeneous (left) and non-homogeneous (right) traffic densities.

CONCLUSION

This chapter investigated the IEEE 802.11p broadcast and unicast performance while considering empirical traffic distribution focusing on a signalized urban road setup. Our methodology proposed a joint transport and communications modeling framework that can capture real-world traffic dynamics and determine the network performance metrics that are necessary in the evaluation of the IEEE 802.11p standard. The stochastic traffic model incorporates the randomness, non-homogeneity, and traffic rules and regulations in an urbanized traffic flow, while the network models derive the contention and interference scenarios in both the broadcast and unicast setups.

Given a velocity profile, the traffic density as a function dependent on space and time is computed. From this, the network delay and throughput are obtained to evaluate the IEEE 802.11p broadcast and unicast performance. The developed models are validated by performing extensive simulation, and results have confirmed that the developed models can adequately predict the network performance in vehicular networks. These results can further be used in optimizing the network to achieve a higher efficiency.

Overall, we combined the traffic and network protocol models to investigate VANET performance in an urbanized road setup. The derived analytical models and its corresponding results provide insights into the future design and evaluation of VANET-related communication standards. This work can be easily extended by considering other road topologies, probabilistic connectivity, and fading and attenuation brought about by the roadside infrastructure.

REFERENCES

Baskar, Lakshmi Dhevi, Bart De Schutter, J. Hellendoorn, and Zoltan Papp. 2011. "Traffic control and intelligent vehicle highway systems: a survey." *IET Intelligent Transport Systems* 5, no. 1:38-52.

Bianchi, Giuseppe. 2000. "Performance analysis of the IEEE 802.11 distributed coordination function." *IEEE Journal on selected areas in communications* 18, no. 3:535-547.

Booysen, Marthinus J., Sherali Zeadally, and G-J. Van Rooyen. 2012. "Performance comparison of media access control protocols for vehicular ad hoc networks." *IET networks* 1, no. 1:10-19.

Campolo, Claudia, Alexey Vinel, Antonella Molinaro, and Yevgeni Koucheryavy. 2011. "Modeling broadcasting in IEEE 802.11 p/WAVE vehicular networks." *IEEE Communications letters* 15, no. 2:199-201.

Chakroun, Omar, Soumaya Cherkaoui, and Jihene Rezgui. 2012. "MUDDS: Multi-metric unicast data dissemination scheme for 802.11p VANETs." In *2012 8th International Wireless Communications and Mobile Computing Conference (IWCMC)*, pp. 1074-1079. IEEE.

Chu, Kai-Fung, Elmer R. Magsino, Ivan Wang-Hei Ho, and Chi-Kin Chau. 2017. "Index coding of point cloud-based road map data for autonomous driving." In *2017 IEEE 85th Vehicular Technology Conference (VTC Spring)*, pp. 1-7. IEEE.

Daneshgaran, Fred, Massimiliano Laddomada, Fabio Mesiti, and Marina Mondin. 2008. "Unsaturated throughput analysis of IEEE 802.11 in presence of non ideal transmission channel and capture effects." *IEEE Transactions on Wireless Communications* 7, no. 4:1276-1286.

Han, Chong, Mehrdad Dianati, Rahim Tafazolli, Ralf Kernchen, and Xuemin Shen. 2012 "Analytical study of the IEEE 802.11 p MAC sublayer in vehicular networks." *IEEE Transactions on Intelligent Transportation Systems* 13, no. 2:873-886.

Ho, Ivan Wang-Hei, Kin K. Leung, and John W. Polak. 2011. "Stochastic model and connectivity dynamics for VANETs in signalized road systems." *IEEE/ACM Transactions on Networking (TON)* 19, no. 1:195-208.

Jiang, Daniel, and Luca Delgrossi. 2008. "IEEE 802.11 p: Towards an international standard for wireless access in vehicular environments." In *VTC Spring 2008-IEEE Vehicular Technology Conference*, pp. 2036-2040. IEEE.

Khabazian, Mehdi, and Mustafa K. Mehmet Ali. 2008. "A performance modeling of connectivity in vehicular ad hoc networks." *IEEE Transactions on Vehicular Technology* 57, no. 4:2440-2450.

Ma, Xiaomin, and Xianbo Chen. 2007. "Delay and broadcast reception rates of highway safety applications in vehicular ad hoc networks." In *2007 Mobile networking for vehicular environments*, pp. 85-90. IEEE.

Ma, Xiaomin, and Xianbo Chen. 2007. "Saturation performance of IEEE 802.11 broadcast networks." *IEEE Communications Letters* 11, no. 8:686-688.

Ma, Xiaomin, Xianbo Chen, and Hazem H. Refai. 2007. "Unsaturated performance of IEEE 802.11 broadcast service in vehicle-to-vehicle networks." In *2007 IEEE 66th vehicular technology conference*, pp. 1957-1961. IEEE.

Ma, Xiaomin, Jinsong Zhang, Xiaoyan Yin, and Kishor S. Trivedi. 2012. "Design and analysis of a robust broadcast scheme for VANET safety-related services." *IEEE Transactions on Vehicular Technology* 61, no. 1:46-61.

Mchergui, Abir, Tarek Moulahi, Bechir Alaya, and Salem Nasri. 2017. "A survey and comparative study of QoS aware broadcasting techniques in VANET." *Telecommunication Systems* 66, no. 2: 253-281.

Omar, Hassan Aboubakr, Weihua Zhuang, and Li Li. 2013. "VeMAC: A TDMA-based MAC protocol for reliable broadcast in VANETs." *IEEE transactions on mobile computing* 12, no. 9:1724–1736.

Qiu, Harry JF, Ivan Wang-Hei Ho, K. Tse Chi, and Yu Xie. 2015. "A methodology for studying 802.11 p VANET broadcasting performance with practical vehicle distribution." *IEEE transactions on vehicular technology* 64, no. 10:4756-4769.

Standards Committee. 1997. Wireless lan medium access control (MAC) and physical layer (PHY) specifications. *IEEE Standard 802.11*.

Standards Committee. 2005. "Wireless LAN medium access control (MAC) and physical layer (PHY) specifications: Amendment 8: Medium Access Control (MAC) Quality of Service enhancements." *IEEE Computer Society*.

Stanica, Razvan, Emmanuel Chaput, and André-Luc Beylot. 2011. "Broadcast communication in vehicular ad-hoc network safety applications." In *2011 IEEE Consumer Communications and Networking Conference (CCNC)*, pp. 462-466. IEEE.

Statista. 2018. Number of vehicles in use worldwide 2006–2015.

Umer, Tariq, Zhiguo Ding, Bahram Honary, and Hasan Ahmad. 2010. "Implementation of microscopic parameters for density estimation of heterogeneous traffic flow for VANET." In *2010 7th International Symposium on Communication Systems, Networks & Digital Signal Processing (CSNDSP 2010)*, pp. 66-70. IEEE.

Vinel, Alexey, Dirk Staehle, and Andrey Turlikov. 2009. "Study of beaconing for car-to-car communication in vehicular ad-hoc networks." In *2009 IEEE International Conference on Communications Workshops*, pp. 1-5. IEEE.

Wang, Qing, Supeng Leng, Huirong Fu, Yan Zhang, and Hesiri Weerasinghe. 2010. "An enhanced multi-channel MAC for the IEEE 1609.4 based vehicular ad hoc networks." In *2010 INFOCOM IEEE Conference on Computer Communications Workshops*, pp. 1-2. IEEE.

Wang, Zhe, and Mahbub Hassan. 2009. "The throughput-reliability tradeoff in 802.11-based vehicular safety communications." In *2009 6th IEEE Consumer Communications and Networking Conference*, pp. 1-5. IEEE.

Wu, Celimuge, Xianfu Chen, Yusheng Ji, Satoshi Ohzahata, and Toshihiko Kato. 2015. "Efficient broadcasting in VANETs using dynamic backbone and network coding." *IEEE Transactions on Wireless Communications* 14, no. 11:6057-6071.

Xie, Yu, Ivan Wang-Hei Ho, and Elmer R. Magsino. 2018. "The modeling and cross-layer optimization of 802.11 p VANET unicast." *IEEE access* 6:171-186.

In: Vehicular Networks   ISBN: 978-1-53615-978-3
Editors: P. H. J. Chong and I. W-H. Ho © 2019 Nova Science Publishers, Inc.

Chapter 2

VEHICULAR POSITIONING SYSTEM

Li-Ta Hsu, Weisong Wen and Guohao Zhang*

Interdisciplinary Division of Aeronautical and Aviation Engineering,
The Hong Kong Polytechnic University, Hong Kong, China

ABSTRACT

This chapter focuses on the multi-sensor integrated positioning method for vehicular navigation. The most well-known and public-used positioning technology is global navigation satellite system (GNSS). The GNSS provides globally referenced positioning service under allweather conditions throughout the years. It easily obtains a positioning performance with less than 5 meters of horizontal positioning error in open-sky areas. With the aid of the differential correction provided by base stations or the sophisticated error models generated, GNSS precise positioning can be achieved with an error less than one meter. However, GNSS suffers severely from the multipath effect and non-line-of-sight (NLOS) receptions in urban areas. To increase the availability and reliability of the positioning service, the dead reckoning provided by on-board system is usually employed to assist the GNSS. The integrated positioning system is widely regarded as a solution in the applications of vehicle navigation. For autonomous driving, a robust centimeter-level positioning system is essential. GNSS/on-board sensors integrated positioning system cannot satisfy the requirement of autonomous vehicle. With the rapid development and implementation of light detection and ranging (LiDAR), localization

---

*Corresponding Author's E-mail: lt.hsu@polyu.edu.hk.

technologies are introduced to provide precise localization for autonomous vehicle in diverse scenarios. In a very sparse environment, however, the performance of the LiDAR localization is degraded due to the lack of sufficient features. To obtain the most preciseand robust localization solution, the GNSS/on-board sensors/LiDAR integrated system is developed. This multi-sensor integrated solution takes advantages of each sensor. Firstly, GNSS receiver provides globally referenced but low-frequency positioning. Secondly, on-board sensors provide the system dynamics at high update frequency. Thirdly, the matching between the consecutive LiDAR scanning provides high-frequency and precise positioning based on enough environment features. It is believed to be the ultimate solution for providing robust and sub-meter level positioning for autonomous vehicles in all environments.

GNSS POSITIONING

Vehicles generally adopt the GNSS to provide the positioning, velocity and timing (PVT) service to numerous applications globally. Currently, GNSS includes American GPS, European Galileo, Russian GLONASS, and Chinese Beidou. Among the GNSSs, GPS is the most popular system developed and operated by the U.S. Department of Defense. The working principles of different GNSSs are similar. In this section, GPS is used as an example to introduce the system and methodology of GNSS.

Today, GPS's horizontal Standard Positioning Service (SPS) and Precise Positioning Service (PPS) reach 3.8 meters (1σ) and 1.2 meters (1σ), respectively (ICD 2013). GPS is consisted of ground control, space, and user segments, as shown in the Figure 1. The ground segment controls and transmits the satellite orbit and clock data to satellites. The satellite receives the data and then broadcasts the signal to all users globally (Kaplan and Hegarty 2005, Misra and Enge 2011). This section will focus on the receiver (user segment) of the GNSS.

A GPS receiver architecture is shown in Figure 2. The front-end firstly down-coverts the GPS signal to the intermediate-frequency band, then it digitalizes the GPS signal. Signal acquisition is to determine visible satellites, coarse values of carrier frequency and code delay of received satellite signals. Signal tracking is followed to refine these values and keep tracking the signal and demodulate navigation data from satellites. The navigation data is then used to obtain pseudorange measurements, ephemeris, almanac, and Klobuchar information.

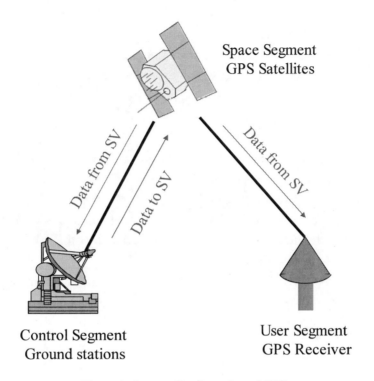

Figure 1. System Configuration of GPS.

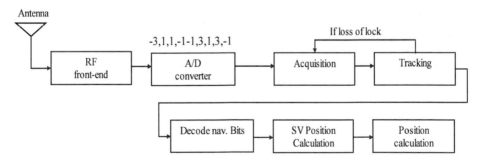

Figure 2. Architecture of GPS Receiver.

The ephemeris data describe the satellite orbits relative to the center of the earth. Based on the time of signal transmission, the position of satellites on the orbit can be estimated. The pseudorange measurement is obtained from code tracking loop. The raw pseudorange measurement of signal, which is the distance between a satellite and receiver's antenna, is generally calculated by the time difference between signal transmitting and arriving:

$$\rho^j = c(TOT^j - TOA),\tag{1}$$

where ρ^j is the estimated raw pseudorange and its superscript is its satellite index, c is the speed of light, TOT denotes the time of signal transmission described based on satellite's clock and TOA denotes the time of arrival measured by receiver's clock. The geometric relationship between user's position and satellite's position can be linked by the observation of pseudorange as shown in Figure 3.

The linearized observation equation for pseudorange in vector form can be represented as in (2) (Borre et al. 2007).

$$\rho_i^j = g_i^j +$$

$$\left[-\frac{X^j - X_i}{g_i^j} \quad -\frac{Y^j - Y_i}{g_i^j} \quad -\frac{Z^j - Z_i}{g_i^j} \quad 1 \right] \begin{bmatrix} \Delta X_i \\ \Delta Y_i \\ \Delta Z_i \\ cdt_i \end{bmatrix} - cdt^j + T_i^j + I_i^j + e_i^j,$$

$$\tag{2}$$

where (X^j, Y^j, Z^j) is the 3-dimension position of the j-th satellite in the earth-centered, earth-fixed (ECEF) coordinate, (X_i, Y_i, Z_i) is the 3-dimension receiver position at the i-th epoch, dt^j is the satellite clock bias, dt_i is the receiver clock offset with regard to the GPS system time, T_i^j and I_i^j are the tropospheric and ionospheric delay, and e_i^j is the satellite ephemeris bias. g_i^j is the geometrical range, which can be expressed as

$$g_i^j = \sqrt{(X^j - X_i)^2 + (Y^j - Y_i)^2 + (Z^j - Z_i)^2}.\tag{3}$$

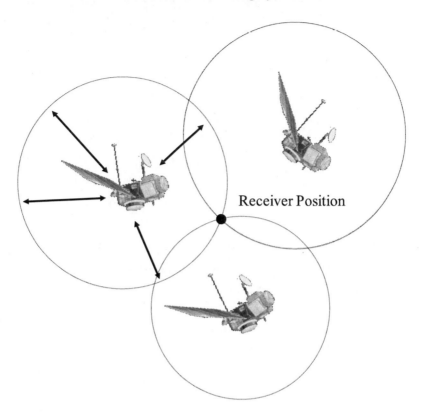

Receiver Position

Figure 3. Illustration of GPS Positioning based on Triangulation.

If the number of satellites is m and assuming $\Delta\rho^j = \rho_i^j - g_i^j + cdt^j - T_i^j - I_i^j - e_i^j$, the equation will form a least square (LS) problem, which is used in a scenario of more equations than unknowns (namely $m > 4$), as shown in (4).

$$\begin{bmatrix} -\dfrac{X^1-X_i}{g_i^1} & -\dfrac{Y^1-Y_i}{g_i^1} & -\dfrac{Z^1-Z_i}{g_i^1} & 1 \\ -\dfrac{X^2-X_i}{g_i^2} & -\dfrac{Y^2-Y_i}{g_i^2} & -\dfrac{Z^2-Z_i}{g_i^2} & 1 \\ & \vdots & & \\ -\dfrac{X^m-X_i}{g_i^m} & -\dfrac{Y^m-Y_i}{g_i^m} & -\dfrac{Z^m-Z_i}{g_i^m} & 1 \end{bmatrix} \begin{bmatrix} \Delta X_i \\ \Delta Y_i \\ \Delta Z_i \\ cdt_i \end{bmatrix} = \begin{bmatrix} \Delta\rho^1 \\ \Delta\rho^2 \\ \vdots \\ \Delta\rho^m \end{bmatrix} \qquad (4)$$

where the matrix of unit line-of-sight (LOS) vector is called observation matrix, $\mathbf{H}$, (ΔX_i, ΔY_i, ΔZ_i) is the 3-dimension position difference between the real receiver position and predicted (or guessed) receiver position. In order to obtain this position difference, the LS approach is used. In this case, the technique of pseudoinverse is used as $\Delta \mathbf{x}_i = [\mathbf{H}^T \mathbf{H}]^{-1} \mathbf{H}^T \Delta \boldsymbol{\rho}$. The superscript ^{1} and ^{T} denote the inverse and transpose of matrix, respectively, $\Delta \mathbf{x}_i = [\Delta X_i \quad \Delta Y_i \quad \Delta Z_i \quad cdt_i]^T$, and $\Delta \boldsymbol{\rho} = [\Delta \rho^1 \quad \Delta \rho^2 \quad \cdots \quad \Delta \rho^m]^T$. To estimate the receiver position, the position difference estimated from (4) above must be used to correct the predicted receiver position as $\mathbf{r}_{a,i,1} = \mathbf{r}_{a,i,0} + \Delta \mathbf{x}_{i,1}$, where $\mathbf{r}_{a,i,1}$ is the estimated receiver position after the first iteration at the i-th epoch, $\mathbf{r}_{a,i,0}$ is the estimated receiver position within the first iteration, and $\Delta \mathbf{x}_{i,1}$ is the position difference for the first iteration. The iteration stops when the position is converged and the last estimated receiver position is declared as the final receiver position.

There are several factors resulting in the positioning error to GPS receiver, including satellite clock and orbit error, ionospheric delay, tropospheric delay, multipath effect, and receiver clock and thermal noise as shown in Figure 4.

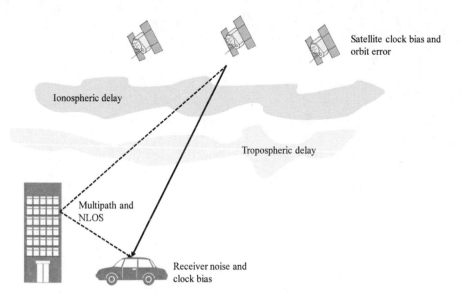

Figure 4. Sources of GPS Measurement Error.

Most of the error sources are eliminable by utilizing the differential GPS (DGPS) technique or sophisticated models (Misra and Enge 2011). The DGPS technique assumes the 'reference station' is not far from the GPS receiver. As a result, the measurement error of a GPS receiver is similar to that of a reference station. In general, DGPS correction can be applied to GPS receiver if the baseline between the reference stations is less than 30 kilometers. The error budget before and after applying the DGPS correction is listed in Table 1. In the open-sky areas, the GPS positioning can easily achieve sub-meter level accuracy if the receiver has applied the DGPS correction. However, it is not the same case if the GPS receiver is used in urban areas.

Table 1. GPS error budget before and after applying DGPS correction. rms denotes root mean square error

Error Source	Potential error using SPP	Error mitigation using DGPS
Satellite clock model	2 m (rms)	0.0 m
Satellite ephemeris prediction	2 m (rms) along the LOS	0.1 m (rms)
Ionospheric delay	2-10 m (zenith) Obliquity factor 3 at 5°	0.2 m (rms)
Tropospheric delay	2.3-2.5m (zenith) Obliquity factor 10 at 5°	0.2 m (rms) + altitude effect
Multipath and NLOS (open sky)	Code : 0.5-1 m Carrier : 0.5-1 cm	Not helpful
Receiver Noise	Code : 0.25-0.5 m (rms) Carrier : 1-2 mm (rms)	Not helpful

Unlike ionospheric, tropospheric, and satellite orbit and clock errors, multipath effect and NLOS reception are not correlated between the two receivers (i.e., one in vehicle and one in reference station). Moreover, it is different in each channel due to the different travelling paths of signals. As a result, the conventional differential observation algorithms are ineffective in multipath mitigation. The radio frequency difficult environments mentioned earlier, such as tunnel, under bridge, dense foliage and urban canyon (are illustrated in Figure 5), might easily attenuate, reflect or even block the GPS signal to reduce the stabilities and performance of GPS receivers. These phenomena of signal reflection and attenuation are known as multipath, scattering effects and non-line of sight (NLOS) reception (Petovello and Groves 2013). Currently, the multipath effects and NLOS receptions are the major bottlenecks of GPS positioning used in vehicular network (Breßler et al. 2016).

Figure 5. Illustrations for radio difficult environments: a) dense foliage, b) urban canyon, c) road tunnel and d) road under bridges.

LiDAR POSITIONING

Due to the rise of autonomous driving, LiDAR becomes an irreplaceable sensor for the future connected autonomous driving vehicle. LiDAR is a state-of-the-art sensor for sensing the surrounding environments with 3D point clouds. The output of 3D LiDAR sensors is the distance from the center of LiDAR to the reflector, which is estimated by the principle of TOA as shown in Figure 6. The LiDAR first transmits a signal, which is reflected by surrounding objects and then received by LiDAR's internal receiver

(Weitkamp 2006). The distance is finally calculated based on triangulation. The 3D LiDAR for autonomous driving purpose usually has multiple channels. Thus, the LiDAR can output ample points at one epoch. From the principle of LiDAR sensor, we can find that the measurements of LiDAR rely highly on environment features. In other words, the LiDAR measurements can be abundant in complicated environments and sparse in open areas. Conversely, GNSS can obtain decent accuracy in open areas and erroneous positioning solutions in complicated dense urban areas. Therefore, GNSS and LiDAR integration can make the positioning more accurate and robust by employing their complementary features.

The main principle of LiDAR positioning is to estimate the pose of vehicle by tracking the transformation between consecutive frames of point clouds. The transformation between two frames (called reference point cloud and input point cloud) is calculated by point cloud registrations as shown in Figure 7.

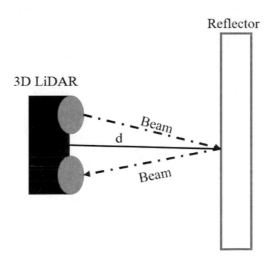

Figure 6. Illustration of the TOA principle used in LiDAR. The *d* represents the distance from the center of LiDAR to the reflector.

The objective of point clouds registration is to obtain the optimal transformation matrix to match or align the reference and the input point clouds. The most well-known method of point cloud registration is the iterative closest point (ICP) (Yang et al. 2016) method. The ICP is a straightforward method to calculate the transformation between two consecutive frames by iteratively searching pairs of nearby points in the two scans and minimizing the sum of all point-to-point distances. The objective function can be expressed as follow:

$$C(\hat{\mathbf{R}}, \hat{\mathbf{T}}) = \arg\min \sum_{i=1}^{N} ||(\mathbf{R}p_i + \mathbf{T}) - q_i||^2, \qquad (5)$$

where N indicates the number of points in one scan. $\mathbf{R}$ and $\mathbf{T}$ indicate the rotation and translation matrixes, respectively, to transform the input point cloud (p) into the reference point cloud (q). The objective function $C(\hat{\mathbf{R}}, \hat{\mathbf{T}})$ indicates the transformation residual error.

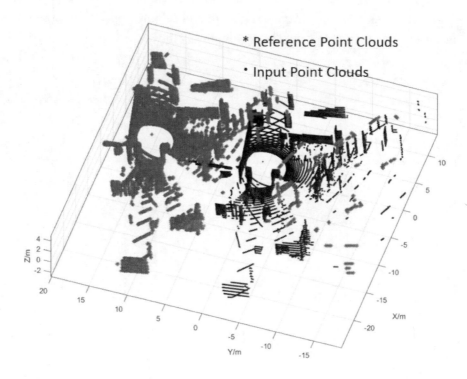

Figure 7. Illustration for point cloud registration between reference and input point clouds.

The normal distribution transform (NDT) (Magnusson 2009), modeling the points based on Gaussian distribution, is another method to align two consecutive point clouds. The NDT innovatively divides the point cloud space into cells. As shown in Figure 8, each cell is continuously modeled by a Gaussian distribution. Hence, the discrete point clouds are transformed into successive continuous functions. Assuming that the transformation between two consecutive frames of point clouds can be expressed as $(\hat{R}, \hat{T}) = [T_x \quad T_y \quad T_z \quad R_x \quad R_y \quad R_z]^T$. The process of calculating the relative pose between the reference and the input point clouds is listed as follows:

1) Normal distribution transform: fetch all the points $x_{i=1...n}$ contained in the 3D cell.

   Calculate the mean among all the points, $q = \frac{1}{n}\Sigma_i x_i$.

   Calculate the covariance matrix μ,

$$\mu = \frac{1}{n}\Sigma_i(x_i - q)(x_i - q)^T \qquad (6)$$

2) The matching score is modeled as:

$$f(p) = -score(p) = \Sigma_i \exp(-\frac{(x_i' - q_i)^T \mu_i^{-1}(x_i' - q_i)}{2}) \qquad (7)$$

where x_i indicates the points in the current frame of the scan. x_i' denotes the point in the previous scan mapped from the current frame using $(\hat{R}, \hat{T})$. q_i and μ_i indicate the mean and the covariance of the corresponding normal distribution to point x_i' in the NDT of the previous scan.

3) Update the pose using the Quasi-Newton method (Shanno 1970) using the objective function to minimize the score $f(p)$.
4) Repeat steps 2) and 3) until the convergence is achieved.

With all the points in one frame of point clouds being modeled as cells, the objective of the optimization for NDT is to match current cells into the previous cells with the highest probability. Therefore, the optimal transformation $(\hat{R}, \hat{T})$ is obtained.

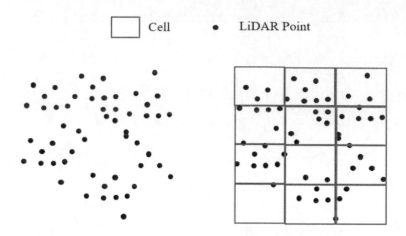

Figure 8. Illustration of transforming point clouds (left) into cells (right). Each cell is represented by a normal distribution using step (1) above.

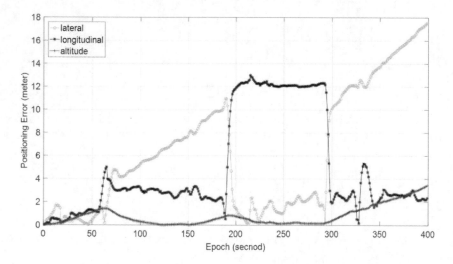

Figure 9. Example of the performance of LiDAR in an urban scenario in lateral, longitudinal and altitude directions, respectively.

The main problem of stand-alone LiDAR positioning is the accumulated error over time. An example is given in Figure 9. As the accuracy of LiDAR odometry is highly related to the environment features and only relative positioning is obtained, the positioning result drifts over time. We can see from the figure that the main trend is that the positioning error accumulates over time.To provide lane-level positioning service for autonomous vehicles, sensor integration by fusing multiple sensors is a promising solution. For example, the GNSS can provide periodic and globally referenced positioning. Therefore, GNSS/LiDAR integration can effectively mitigate the accumulated error.

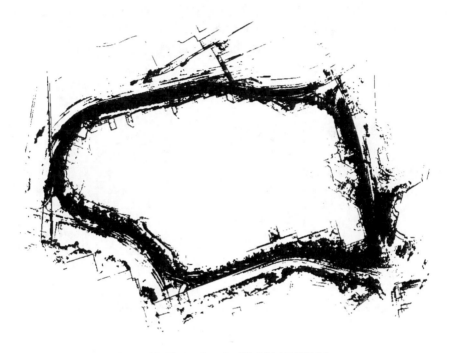

Figure 10. Example of a 3D LiDARHD Map.

The high definition map (HD map) is an offline digital map which contains several layers, usually including points map (Levinson and Thrun 2010). The points map is a discrete representation of environment constituted by organized points. The matching between real-time point clouds from 3D LiDAR and the points map can provide high-frequency and accurate positioning. Moreover, as the points map is globally referenced, there will be no accumulated positioning error. The main problem for the universal application of HD map is its expense of maintenance. The environment can change over time, thus the HD map has to be updated frequently which can introduce immense expense.

MULTI-SENSOR INTEGRATED POSITIONING SYSTEM

For autonomous driving or other vehicular application, it is essential to acknowledge the position and motion of the vehicle. Without the position or motion information, the vehicular control and navigation to the destination cannot be accomplished. To estimate the position and motion of the vehicle, various sensors are used based on different principles, as shown in Figure 11.

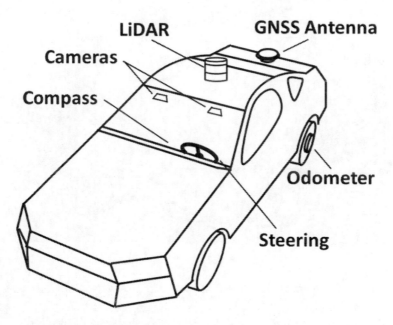

Figure 11. Example of sensors employed for vehicular positioning.

Besides GNSS and LiDAR for positioning, the vehicle is usually equipped with sensors, such as the electronic compass (E-Compass), the steering sensor, and vehicular odometer. The E-Compass measures the angular difference between the vehicle's heading and the north. The steering sensor measures the attitude difference during operation with regarding to the vehicle's body, as the turning angle during operation. The vehicular odometer is a widely used sensor, measuring the relative moving distance in the vehicle's heading direction. Since different sensors are following different operating principles, the characteristic of each sensor is also different, making the sensors redundant or complimentary for the overall system. The characteristic of each sensor is shown in Table 2, including the output, strength and weakness.

Table 2. Comparison between GPS, LiDAR and on-board vehicular sensors

	Output	Strength	Weakness
GNSS receiver	Global positioning in ECEF coordinate	Provide absolute positioning solution	Low frequency, environment sensitive
LiDARodometry	Relative positioning on body-fixed coordinate	Precise positioning solution, high frequency	High computation, environment sensitive
Vehicular odometer	1D Relative positioning on body-fixed coordinate	Environment independent	Low accuracy
E-Compass	Angular difference between ENU coordinate	Absolute attitude measurement	Low accuracy
Vehicular Steering	Angular difference between body-fixed coordinate	Environment independent	Relative measurement, Low accuracy

GNSS measures the absolute position of a vehicle in a global coordinate frame. The introduction of the coordinate systems can be found in the Appendix of this chapter. The solution of GNSS is usually under low frequency and not very precise with around 5 meters of error. Nevertheless, the GNSS is one of the significant sensors that directly measures the absolute positioning of an object on the Earth, making it essential for vehicular positioning. The LiDAR odometry is able to achieve precise relative positioning solution with high frequency based on the consecutive frames of 3D point clouds. The computation load for processing point cloud data is relatively high. Moreover, the performance of LiDAR odometry also relates to the operating environment, the obstacles (other vehicle or buildings) blocking the beams may cause large uncertainty for positioning. For the on-board sensors, they provide less accurate measurements but with less environment dependency. Due to the principles and characteristics of different sensors, no standalone sensor can operate perfectly under all circumstances. An appropriate approach is to integrate all the available sensors together, using their complimentary aspects to optimize the vehicular positioning solution. As shown in the table, it is complimentary that the precise measurements of GNSS and LiDAR are environment dependent, while the on-board vehicular sensors are less accurate but environment independent. Moreover, the GNSS and compass directly obtain the absolute information while the LiDAR, vehicular odometer, and steering obtain relative information. These sensors are complimentary on different aspects, making use of their strengths and mitigating the drawbacks of different sensors. Therefore, multi-sensor integration is a feasible method for vehicular navigation, achieving an overall positioning solution with higher accuracy and robustness.

Loosely-Coupled Integration System Based on Kalman Filter

To integrate different sensors for vehicular navigation, a common approach is the Kalman filter (KF). The Kalman filter is able to estimate the state variables based on the knowledge of prediction and measurement uncertainty. By comparing the process noise and measurement noise covariance, the Kalman gain is calculated to determine the confidence between the prediction and measurement. The final solution is optimized by integrating the predictions and measurements with Kalman gain as the weighting. To deal with different operating conditions, different kinds of Kalman filter are developed, such as the extended Kalman filter (EKF), unscented Kalman filter (UKF) and adaptive Kalman filter (Groves 2013). Here, a basic Kalman filter with loosely coupled integration is introduced as an example for vehicular navigation.

For a basic vehicular navigation application, the operating space can be simplified to a 2-dimensional space, i.e., the East and North direction from the

ENU coordinate system. The vehicular heading direction is also considered in the 2D space using azimuth (the angle between heading and the North). Therefore, the state vector **x** for multi-sensor integrated positioning is given by

$$\mathbf{x} = \begin{bmatrix} x_E \\ x_N \\ \theta \end{bmatrix}, \tag{8}$$

where x_E is the East directional position and x_N is the North directional position in ENU coordinate system. θ is the azimuth angle of the vehicle's heading. During the operation, the LiDAR odometry measurements and the on-board vehicular sensors (vehicular odometer and steering sensor) measurements are sampled at different rate. Therefore, there are two different system models corresponding to LiDAR odometry and vehicular on-board sensor. For the LiDAR odometry during operation, the system model for positioning can be derived as following

$$\hat{\mathbf{x}}_k = \mathbf{F} \cdot \hat{\mathbf{x}}_{k-1} + \mathbf{C} \cdot \mathbf{u}_k + \boldsymbol{\omega}_k \tag{9}$$

$$= \begin{bmatrix} 1 & 0 & 0 \\ 0 & 1 & 0 \\ 0 & 0 & 1 \end{bmatrix} \cdot \begin{bmatrix} x_{E,k-1} \\ x_{N,k-1} \\ \theta_{k-1} \end{bmatrix} + \begin{bmatrix} 1 & 0 & 0 \\ 0 & 1 & 0 \\ 0 & 0 & 1 \end{bmatrix} \cdot \begin{bmatrix} \Delta x_{E,k}^{LiDAR} \\ \Delta x_{N,k}^{LiDAR} \\ \Delta \theta_k^{LiDAR} \end{bmatrix} + \boldsymbol{\omega}_k \tag{10}$$

$\hat{\mathbf{x}}_k$ is the predicted state vector at the k-th epoch. $\hat{\mathbf{x}}_{k-1}$ is the estimated state vector at the $(k-1)$-th epoch. **F** is the transition matrix for the previous epoch's state estimation. **C** is the control matrix for the control vector $\mathbf{u}_k$ at the current epoch. Note that the control vector constructed by LiDAR odometry is in the same domain as the state vector, making both **F** and **C** an identity matrix. $\boldsymbol{\omega}_k$ is the process noise assumed to be Gaussian white noise. $\Delta x_{E,k}^{LiDAR}$ and $\Delta x_{N,k}^{LiDAR}$ are the variation of position along the East axis and North axis, respectively, from LiDAR odometry. $\Delta \theta_k^{LiDAR}$ is the difference of vehicular heading direction measured by LiDAR. Similarly, the system model for vehicular on-board sensor (odometer and steering) can be derived by

$$\hat{\mathbf{x}}_k = \begin{bmatrix} 1 & 0 & 0 \\ 0 & 1 & 0 \\ 0 & 0 & 1 \end{bmatrix} \cdot \begin{bmatrix} x_{E,k-1} \\ x_{N,k-1} \\ \theta_{k-1} \end{bmatrix} + \begin{bmatrix} 1 & 0 & 0 \\ 0 & 1 & 0 \\ 0 & 0 & 1 \end{bmatrix} \cdot \begin{bmatrix} \Delta x_{E,k}^{odometer} \\ \Delta x_{N,k}^{odometer} \\ \Delta \theta_k^{steering} \end{bmatrix} + \boldsymbol{\omega}_k \qquad (11)$$

where $\Delta x_{E,k}^{odometer}$ and $\Delta x_{N,k}^{odometer}$ are the position displacement on the East axis and North axis, respectively, from vehicular odometer. Note that the vehicular odometer is only measuring the 1-D vehicular displacement along the vehicle's heading. Hence, the 1-D displacement from vehicular odometer is converted into ENU coordinate based on vehicle's heading in advance. $\Delta \theta_k^{steering}$ is the difference of vehicular heading direction, related to the steering angle of a vehicle.

The implementation of the Kalman filter follows several steps. Firstly, the state vector estimation is predicted based on the knowledge of the system model, using

$$\hat{\mathbf{x}}_{k-1}^k = \mathbf{F} \cdot \hat{\mathbf{x}}_{k-1}^{k-1} + \mathbf{C} \cdot \mathbf{u}_k, \qquad (12)$$

where $\hat{\mathbf{x}}_{k-1}^k$ is the predicted state estimation at the k-th epoch. $\hat{\mathbf{x}}_{k-1}^{k-1}$is the updated state estimation at the $(k-1)$-th epoch. In this example, the measurements from different sensors are obtained at different time, resulting into two different system models based on the availability of the measurements. The prediction of state vector is also following different system models corresponding to the availability of LiDAR odometry measurements or vehicular on-board sensor measurements. Afterwards, the error covariance matrix is propagated based on the previous error covariance matrix, transition matrix, and the process noise covariance as follows.

$$\mathbf{P}_{k-1}^k = \mathbf{F} \cdot \mathbf{P}_{k-1}^{k-1} \cdot \mathbf{F}^{\mathrm{T}} + \mathbf{Q}, \qquad (13)$$

where $\mathbf{P}_{k-1}^k$ is the error covariance matrix predicted by previous epoch's error covariance matrix $\mathbf{P}_{k-1}^{k-1}$. $\mathbf{Q}$is the process noise covariance matrix, determined by the behavior of process noise. At this point, the prediction process is accomplished. Without an observation, the static vector can be iteratively predicted based on the control vector and system model. Since GNSS has a much lower frequency, the standalone prediction based on LiDAR and steering sensor is common during the GNSS measurement interval. Once the observation is available, the update part is engaged for integration.

To integrate the observations with the predicted state, the observation model should be defined based on the output characteristic of the sensors. In this case, the GNSS measurement as absolute position and E-compass as absolute heading azimuth are used for observation. The observation model can be further derived as

$$\mathbf{z}_k = \mathbf{H} \cdot \mathbf{x}_k + \boldsymbol{\upsilon}_k \tag{14}$$

$$\begin{bmatrix} x_{E,k}^{GNSS} \\ x_{N,k}^{GNSS} \\ \theta_k^{compass} \end{bmatrix} = \begin{bmatrix} 1 & 0 & 0 \\ 0 & 1 & 0 \\ 0 & 0 & 1 \end{bmatrix} \cdot \begin{bmatrix} x_{E,k} \\ x_{N,k} \\ \theta_k \end{bmatrix} + \boldsymbol{\upsilon}_k, \tag{15}$$

where $\mathbf{z}_k$ is the observation vector and $\mathbf{H}$ is the matrix of observation model, converting the state vector into the observation vector domain. Here, the GNSS measurement is converted from the ECEF coordinate system to the ENU coordinate system in advance, making $\mathbf{H}$ become an identity matrix. $\boldsymbol{\upsilon}_k$ is the observation noise assumed to be Gaussian white noise. $x_{E,k}^{GNSS}$ and $x_{N,k}^{GNSS}$ are the GNSS positioning solution along East axis and North axis, respectively. $\theta_k^{compass}$ is the current azimuth of the vehicle with respect to the North direction.

For the update process of the Kalman filter, the measurement innovation $\tilde{\tau}_k$ is computed based on the observation model, using

$$\tilde{\tau}_k = \mathbf{z}_k - \mathbf{H} \cdot \hat{\mathbf{x}}_{k-1}^k. \tag{16}$$

After that, the Kalman gain $\mathbf{K}_k$ is derived based on the preceding error covariance matrix, observation matrix, and the measurement noise covariance as follows.

$$\mathbf{K}_k = \mathbf{P}_{k-1}^k \mathbf{H}^T (\mathbf{H} \mathbf{P}_{k-1}^k \mathbf{H}^T + \mathbf{R})^{-1}, \tag{17}$$

where $\mathbf{R}$ is the measurement noise covariance matrix determined by the error characteristic of the measurements. Then, the state vector can be estimated by the prediction and observations with Kalman gain, which is the weighting matrix that evaluates the confidence between prediction and observation. The estimation of the state vector $\hat{\mathbf{x}}_k^k$ is computed by

$$\hat{\mathbf{x}}_k^k = \hat{\mathbf{x}}_{k-1}^k + \mathbf{K}_k \cdot \tilde{\tau}_k, \tag{18}$$

where $\hat{\mathbf{x}}_k^k$ denotes the integrated positioning solution at the k-th epoch. The remaining step is to update the estimate covariance matrix $\mathbf{P}_k^k$ using

$$\mathbf{P}_k^k = (\mathbf{I} - \mathbf{K}_k \cdot \mathbf{H}) \cdot \mathbf{P}_{k-1}^k. \tag{19}$$

For the following epoch, the notation k is substituted with $k-1$ and we repeat the same procedures to estimate the state vector for an integrated positioning solution. It is worth mentioning that the Kalman gain as the weighting between prediction and measurement is determined by the process noise covariance matrix $\mathbf{Q}$and measurement noise covariance matrix $\mathbf{R}$. The design of $\mathbf{Q}$and $\mathbf{R}$greatly influences the performance of Kalman filter integration. It is essential to determine $\mathbf{Q}$and $\mathbf{R}$appropriately based on the error characteristic and knowledge of each involved sensor. By applying the Kalman-filter-based loosely-coupled multi-sensor integration, an accurate and robust vehicular positioning solution can be achieved.

Loosely-Coupled Integration System Based on Graph Optimization

In the past several decades, filtering algorithm, such as Kalman filter, is the major sensor integration method. The filter-based method can obtain optimal estimate of the state on the condition that all the noise models of measurements are subject to Gaussian distribution. The Kalman filter-based sensor integration optimally estimates current state by considering previous state and observation measurements at the current epoch. Despite of the Kalman filter's popularity and capability of incorporating measurements from different asynchronous sensors operating at different frequencies, it fails to fully make use of all the previous states and measurements when estimating the current states. The other smoothing-based sensor integration method, graph-based sensor integration, takes all the historical and current sensor inputs as constraints and construct the graph based on measurements (Gutjahr 2000). Then, the state estimation transfers to a non-linear optimization problem. Using graph-based integration allows coping with different sensors inputs at different frequencies in an intuitive and simple manner. More importantly, the graph-based sensor integration framework provides a plug and play capability (Chiu et al. 2014). New inputs from sensors are simply new constraints added into the graph. In some cases, the signals may be unavailable due to signal loss, for example, the satellite navigation signal in GPS-denied areas. The graph fusion framework simply refrains from adding the associated constraints.

This section presents the graph-based sensor integration (Grisetti et al. 2010). In this section, the constraints are provided by the GNSS positioning, LiDAR odometry, vehicular odometer, E-compass, and vehicular steering. Two steps are needed to implement the graph-based integration and generation, and the graph optimization.

Graph Generation

The graph is constituted of edges and nodes. Edges are provided by the observed measurements including GNSS, LiDAR odometry, vehicular odometer, E-compass, and vehicular steering as shown in Figure 12. The nodes represent the estimated states. Similar to the previous section, the estimated state (2-D state) is represented by x. For each node, the state is denoted by x_i. As the objective of the graph optimization is to minimize the error between 'all' the measurements and the estimated states, the error function construction is one of the key parts for the graph optimization for each measurement from sensors. Note that the measurements from sensors are the same as those in the previous Kalman-filter-based integration. The error function for the GNSS observation is expressed as follows:

$$e_k^{GNSS} = ||H_{GNSS}(x_k) - z_k^{GNSS}||_{\Omega_{GNSS}}^2, \tag{20}$$

where $H_{GNSS}(*)$ is the measurement function, relating the GNSS measurement z_i^{GNSS} to state x_i. Ω is the covariance matrix of the corresponding GNSS measurement.

LiDAR odometry can provide continuous state estimation and the corresponding covariance. The error function for the LiDAR odometry is expressed as:

$$e_{k-1,k}^{LiDAR} = ||x_k - x_{k-1} - z_k^{LiDAR}||_{\Omega_{LiDAR}}^2, \tag{21}$$

where z_i^{LiDAR} is the measurement from the LiDAR odometry. The state for the LiDAR odometry is the same as that in the previous Kalman-filter-based integration. Ω is the covariance matrix of the corresponding LiDAR odometry.

Vehicular odometer can provide relative transitional and orientational difference between epochs. The error function for vehicular odometer is expressed as:

$$e_{k-1,k}^{vo} = ||x_k - x_{k-1} - z_k^{vo}||_{\Omega_{vo}}^2, \tag{22}$$

where z_k^{vo} is the measurement from vehicular odometer. E-Compass can provide the globally referenced heading information at each epoch. The error function for E-Compass is expressed as:

$$e_k^{compass} = ||H_{compass}(x_k) - z_i^{compass}||_{\Omega_{compass}}^2, \tag{23}$$

where $z_i^{compass}$ is the measurement from E-Compass.

The vehicular steering can provide the relative heading difference between two epochs. The error function for vehicular steering is expressed as:

$$e_{k-1,k}^{vs} = ||H_{vs}(x_k) - H_{vs}(x_{k-1}) - z_k^{vs}||_{\Omega_{vs}}^2. \tag{24}$$

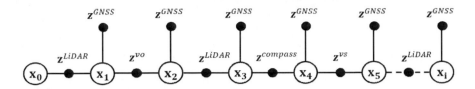

Figure 12. Demonstration of graph generation based on multiple sensors.

Graph Optimization

The graph optimization is straightforward that takes all the constraints into a non-linear optimization problem. The optimization for the sensor integration problem is shown as follows:

$$F(x) = \sum_{k=0}^{n}(||H_{GNSS}(x_k) - z_k^{GNSS}||_{\Omega_{GNSS}}^2 + ||x_k - x_{k-1} - z_k^{LiDAR}||_{\Omega_{LiDAR}}^2 + ||x_k - x_{k-1} - z_k^{vo}||_{\Omega_{vo}}^2 + ||H_{compass}(x_k) - z_i^{compass}||_{\Omega_{compass}}^2 + ||H_{vs}(x_k) - H_{vs}(x_{k-1}) - z_k^{vs}||_{\Omega_{vs}}),$$

$$(25)$$

where $F(x)$ is the objective function which is the sum errors of all the edges. Ω with different subscripts is the error covariance matrix indicating the importance of each constraint in the global graph optimization. The final solution of this optimization is the x^* satisfying the following function:

$$x^* = argminF(x). \qquad (26)$$

Thus, the optimization lies in solving the equation above to obtain the optimal state estimation x^*. Some existing packages, such as G2O (Grisetti et al. 2011) and GTSAM (Dellaert 2012), can be applied to solve the optimization problem. Comparing with the Kalman filter-based sensor integration presented in the previous section, the graph-based sensor integration transfers the filtering problem into an optimization problem. All the measurements are considered to optimize the state set from the first epoch to the current epoch.

APPENDIX

Coordinate Systems for Positioning Systems

The principles of different sensors and applications vary, thus different coordinate systems are employed. In general, the GNSS positioning uses the earth-centered earth-fixed coordinate system. The LiDAR odometry, vehicular on-board odometer and steering sensor use the body-fixed coordinate system. The vehicular on-board compass uses the local tangent plane (LTP) coordinate system which aligns with east, north, and up. Usually, the multi-sensor integrated solution is described in the LTP coordinate system such as the ENU frame. For positioning visualization in the map, the final positioning solution is always converted into the geodetic coordinate system with latitude, longitude, and height. By applying translation and rotation, the measurements and solutions can be converted among different coordinate systems.

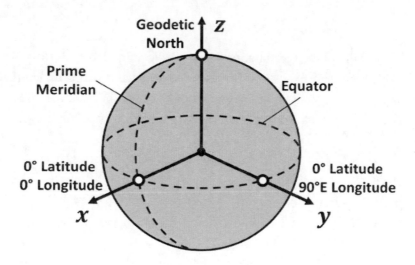

Figure A1. Example of the ECEF coordinate system.

ECEF Coordinate System

GNSS positioning includes the satellite positions in space and vehicular position on Earth. Since the Earth is rotating, a more appropriate approach is to employ the ECEF coordinate system for GNSS positioning, which is rotating and remains fixed with regard to the Earth. For the ECEF coordinate system, the z-axis is pointing to the geodetic north, vertical to the equatorial plane. The x-axis points to the intersection of the equator and the prime meridian, which are 0° latitude and 0° longitude respectively. The y-axis is perpendicular to the x-axis on the equatorial plane, pointing to the 90° East longitude. The axes of the ECEF coordinate system are shown in Figure A1.

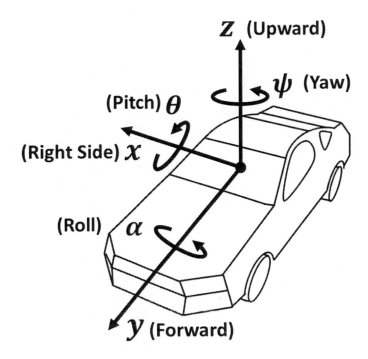

Figure A2. Example of the body-fixed coordinate system.

Body-Fixed Coordinate System

The body-fixed coordinate system is commonly employed to the on-board sensors related to vehicle's motion. The body-fixed coordinate system is a local coordinate system fixed to the vehicle. The origin and directions of the axes may vary due to different sensors' location, operation principles or applications. For vehicular applications, the body-fixed coordinate can be defined based on the motion characteristic of the vehicle and the right-hand rule. The origin of the body-fixed coordinate system is defined as the center of the vehicle, convenient for applying sensor fusion. The *z*-axis is pointing upward from the center of vehicle. The y-axis is pointing forward with regarding to the vehicle, which is the usual moving direction. The *x*-axis is following the right-hand rule, pointing to the right side of the vehicle and perpendicular to the *x*-axis. The attitude of the vehicle can be illustrated based on the Euler angle. The vehicular rotation around *x*, *y* and *z*-axis are the pitch angle θ, roll angle α and yaw angle ψ respectively. The example of the body-fixed coordinate system is shown in Figure A2. As an object has six degrees of freedom (DOF), the motion of a vehicle can be fully described in the body-fixed coordinate system.

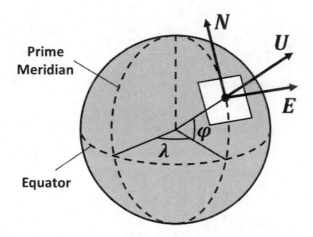

Figure A3. Example of the local tangent plane coordinate system.

Local Tangent Plane Coordinate System

To fuse different sensors for an integrated navigation solution, the measurements or solutions are usually converted into a common coordinate system. A popular approach is the ENU coordinate frame, one of the local tangent plane coordinate systems. The ENU coordinate frame may vary depending on the origin's location and it is related to the geographical system. The E axis is tangent to parallels and pointing to the East, while the N axis is tangent to meridians and pointing to the North. The U-axis is vertical to the

Earth's ellipsoid and pointing upwards. Example of the local tangent plane coordinate system is shown in Figure A3. The φ and λ are the latitude and longitude of the origin of the ENU coordinate, respectively. The ENU coordinate assumes the operating region is relatively small and flat regarding to the size of the Earth, making it convenient to evaluate the motion and operation of a vehicle.

Geographic Coordinate System

To describe a vehicle's location, a widely used and easily understandable method is the geographic coordinate system, by latitude, longitude, and elevation. The geographic coordinate system varies for different geodetic datum. For GPS positioning, the world geodetic system (WGS84) is used as a standard (Malys 1996). The latitude of a specific vehicle denotes the angle between the meridian crossing the vehicle and the prime meridian. By linking the vehicle and the center of the earth with a line, the longitude of the vehicle is the angle between that line and the equator plane. The elevation is usually based on the geoid (Smith and Milbert 1999), describing the vehicle's height above the mean sea level. Example of the geographic coordinate system is shown in Figure A4. By using latitude, longitude and elevation, the location of an object on Earth can be easily identified.

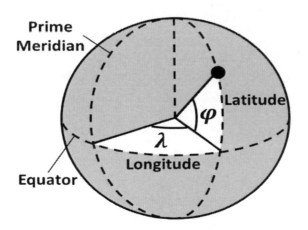

Figure A4. Example of the geographic coordinate system.

Coordinate System Transformation

The measurements from different sensors may use different coordinate systems, converting all the measurements into the same coordinate system is required for sensor fusion. An effective way to convert variables from a specific coordinate system to another is to use the coordinate transformation matrix. The coordinate transformation matrix is a 3-by-3 matrix, each component is the product of the corresponding unit vectors from two different coordinate systems:

$$C_A^B = \begin{pmatrix} i_{B,x} \cdot i_{A,x} & i_{B,x} \cdot i_{A,y} & i_{B,x} \cdot i_{A,z} \\ i_{B,y} \cdot i_{A,x} & i_{B,y} \cdot i_{A,y} & i_{B,y} \cdot i_{A,z} \\ i_{B,z} \cdot i_{A,x} & i_{B,z} \cdot i_{A,y} & i_{B,z} \cdot i_{A,z} \end{pmatrix} \tag{I}$$

C_A^B is the coordinate transformation matrix from coordinate system A to coordinate system B, $i_{B,x}$ is the unit vector of x-axis from B coordinate system and $i_{A,x}$ is the unit vector of x-axis from A coordinate system. Therefore, the product of unit vectors from different coordinate systems can be further compute with trigonometric functions. To convert a set of variables (such as positions or velocities) from one to another coordinate system, the process can be done by multiplying the transformation matrix using:

$$X_B = C_A^B X_A, \tag{II}$$

where X_A is the original variables from coordinate system A, and X_B is the corresponding variables in coordinate system B converted from A. By using the coordinate transformation matrix, the corresponding variables can be computed with regard to different coordinate systems. Moreover, the coordinate transformation matrix can also be used to illustrate the attitude rotation of an object with regard to a specific coordinate system. A common example is using the transformation matrix to describe the roll, pith, and raw of a vehicle with respect to its body-fixed coordinate system.

REFERENCES

Borre, K., Akos D. M., Bertelsen N., Rinder P. and Jensen S.H. 2007. *A Software-Defined GPS and Galileo Receiver - A Single-Frequency Approach*. New York, NY: Birkhäuser Boston.

Breßler, J., Reisdorf P., Obst M. and Wanielik G. 2016. "GNSS positioning in non-line-of-sight context - A survey." *2016 IEEE 19th International Conference on Intelligent Transportation Systems (ITSC)*, 1-4 Nov. 2016.

Chiu, H., Zhou X. S., Carlone L., Dellaert F., SamarasekeraS. and Kumar R. 2014. "Constrained optimal selection for multi-sensor robot navigation using plug-and-play factor graphs." *2014 IEEE International Conference on Robotics and Automation (ICRA)*, 31 May-7 June 2014.

Dellaert, Frank. 2012. *Factor graphs and GTSAM: A hands-on introduction*. Georgia Institute of Technology.

Grisetti, Giorgio, Rainer Kümmerle, Hauke Strasdat and Kurt Konolige. 2011. "g2o: A general Framework for (Hyper) Graph Optimization." *Tech. Rep.*

Grisetti, Giorgio, Rainer Kummerle, Cyrill Stachniss and Wolfram Burgard. 2010. "A tutorial on graph-based SLAM." *IEEE Intelligent Transportation Systems Magazine* 2 (4):31-43.

Groves, Paul. D. 2013. *Principles of GNSS, Inertial and Multi-Sensor Integrated Navigation Systems (GNSS Technology and Applications)*. 2nd ed: Artech House Publishers. Reprint.

Gutjahr, Walter J. 2000. "A graph-based ant system and its convergence. "*Future generation computer systems* 16 (8):873-888.

ICD, GPS. 2013. IS-*GPS-200 Revision H. IRN-200H-001: Navstar Global Positioning*.

Kaplan, Elliott and Christopher Hegarty. 2005. *Understanding GPS: principles and applications*: Artech house.

Levinson, Jesse and Sebastian Thrun. 2010. "Robust vehicle localization in urban environments using probabilistic maps." *2010 IEEE International Conference on Robotics and Automation (ICRA)*.

Magnusson, Martin. 2009. *The three-dimensional normal-distributions transform: an efficient representation for registration, surface analysis and loop detection*. Örebro universitet.

Malys, S. 1996. *The WGS84 Reference Frame.* National Imagery and Mapping Agency.

Misra, Pratap, and Per Enge. 2011. *Global Positioning System: Signals, Measurements, and Performance.* Lincoln, MA 01773 Ganga-Jamuna Press.

Petovello, Mark G. and Paul. D. Groves. 2013. "Multipath vs. NLOS signals." *Inside GNSS* 8 (6):40-42.

Shanno, David F. 1970. "Conditioning of quasi-Newton methods for function minimization." *Mathematics of computation* 24 (111):647-656.

Smith, Dry A. and Dennis G. Milbert. 1999. "The GEOID96 high-resolution geoid height model for the United States." *Journal of Geodesy* 73 (5):219-236.

Weitkamp, Claus. 2006. *Lidar: range-resolved optical remote sensing of the atmosphere.* Vol. 102: Springer Science & Business.

Yang, Jiaolong, Hongdong Li, Dylan Campbell, and Yunde Jia. 2016. *"Go-ICP: a globally optimal solution to 3D ICP point-set registration."* arXiv preprint arXiv:1605.03344.

In: Vehicular Networks   ISBN: 978-1-53615-978-3
Editors: P. H. J. Chong and I. W-H. Ho © 2019 Nova Science Publishers, Inc.

Chapter 3

VEHICLE TRAJECTORY PROCESSING AND BIG DATA MINING

Zhu Xiao[1,], Dong Wang[1,†] and Keqin Li[1,2]*
[1]College of Information Science and Engineering,
Hunan University, Changsha, China
[2]Department of Computer Science,
State University of New York, New York, US

ABSTRACT

Intelligent transportation system (ITS) is an advanced application which aims to provide innovative services relating to different modes of transport and traffic management and enable users to be better informed and make safer, more coordinated, and 'smarter' use of transport networks (Cai et al. 2010). ITS improves traffic efficiency and reduces traffic congestion, traffic accidents, energy consumption, and environmental pollution through harmony and close cooperation among people, vehicles and roads. Among them, perception, prediction (Xiao et al. 2018) and knowledge extraction are the key issues of ITS. Therefore, the following sections will introduce vehicle location awareness, traffic flow prediction, and private car trajectory data mining.

---

[*] Corresponding Author's E-mail: zhxiao@hnu.edu.cn.
[†] Corresponding Author's E-mail: wangd@hnu.edu.cn.

Conventional localization techniques mostly rely on global navigation satellite system (GNSS) or global positioning system (GPS) technologies which are however not suitable to establish accurate locations under poor conditions of satellites visibility due to high buildings, tunnels and mountains, multi-path reflections, and bad weather conditions (Xiao et al. 2016), (Havyarimana et al. 2018), (Georges et al. 2016). To cope with this issue, an alternative multi-sensor integrated navigation system that fuses GPS and inertial navigation system (INS) has been introduced and widely applied to many navigation fields as INS/GPS integrated system.

Accurate traffic flow prediction could estimate the congestion level of the road, therefore leading the driver to choose the best route to reach the destination and providing more effective guidance to traffic authorities. Among the numerous branches of ITS, short-term traffic flow prediction plays a fundamental role and also a challenging task to be calculated due to a lot of influencing factors. Therefore, short-term traffic flow forecast in recent decades has attracted the attention of many researchers. Traffic flow at a fixed point is influenced by many factors and has great variability, the prediction of traffic flow is quite complex. That is a typical nonlinear time series forecasting problem.

Recent development of ITS has significantly improved our ability to collect, store (Chen et al. 2018), and analyze large-scale dataset, which enables studying trajectory of vehicle at a wide range of spatial and temporal scales. For private cars, its trajectories have a certain regularity (Wang et al. 2018), namely, its travel is often concentrated in the commute time and specified areas such as residence and workplace, and it has an obvious impact on the urban traffic, for example, the acute increasing of traffic flow congestion. Regularity is an important property of private cars travel behavior, its regularity trajectory reflects individual's different sociodemographic attributes. The trajectories of private cars reflect individual subjective traveling demands of private car users who have repeated travel behaviors, like 'driving to work'. Understanding private car travel regularity can contribute to solving urban sustainability challenges significantly, such as urban planning, traffic management, reality mining, and opportunistic networks. Therefore, there is a severe need to exploit effective method to discover travel behavior of private cars.

INTRODUCTION

Vehicles play important roles in modern urban transportation system, especially those in megacities. With the economic development and people's increasing demand for convenient transportation, the number of vehicles in cities has experienced fast-growth in recent years (Xiao et al. 2018), which brings tremendous traffic pressure for limited road resources. Although providing essential amenities, the ever-increasing number of vehicles has significantly contributed to a number of urban problems such as urban energy consumption, environmental pollution, and traffic congestion (Xiao et al. 2018). Among the numerous branches of Intelligent Transportation System (ITS), short-term traffic flow prediction plays a fundamental role and is also a challenging task to be resolved due to a lot of influencing factors. Good traffic flow prediction (Zheng et al. 2016) could accurately estimate the congestion level of the road, therefore assisting the driver to choose the best route to reach the destination and providing more effective guidance to traffic authorities (Xu, Kong and Liu 2013). Therefore, short-term traffic flow forecast in recent decades has attracted the attention of many researchers. Moreover, vehicle state determination is another fundamental issue in various fields related to intelligent transportation systems (ITS) like vehicle localization, navigation, and target tracking, where many researchers are widely interested. For instance, in order to avoid fatal accidents or collisions between vehicles, vehicle information should be accurately provided and hence drivers and pedestrians can be warned by the in-vehicle systems at the earliest possible moment.

Nowadays, private cars are becoming more and more popular in our daily livings. Despite the fact that they have brought a lot of convenience to people, many problems have also emerged accordingly. To improve urban mobility, and quality of living, understanding how individuals travel has been the major focus of city and transportation planners and geographers (Jiang, Ferreira and Morikawa 2016). Owing to the large population of private cars (a class of small motor vehicles usually registered by individual and for personal use), the use of private cars is a major cause of congestion and air pollution (Li, Miwa and Morikawa 2016). Taking China as an example, by the end of 2017, the number of automobiles had reached 217 million, more than 83 percent of them are private cars (Bureau 2011-2017). The ownership of private cars per one hundred families has exceeds 70 in some cities such as Shenzhen, Chengdu and Suzhou. In addition, the possession of private cars has exhibited a growing trend from 2011 to 2017 (Guangdong Province Bureau 2011-2017).

Various types of vehicles, especially the large number of private cars, driving in the city produce large-scale trajectory data (Giannotti, Nanni and Pedreschi 2011), which are of special significance to understand individual travel activities and traffic flow evolution. In most cases, it reflects the individual travel demand for people with the long-term use of vehicles, there are frequent driving modes, showing the characteristics of regular travel. Their travel is often concentrated to specified areas such as residential areas, workplaces and hotspots, such regularity reflects individual's different sociodemographic attributes (Goulet-Langlois et al. 2017). Such trajectories offer us unprecedented information to understand moving objects' locations, and foster a broad range of applications in location-based social networks, intelligent transportation systems, and urban computing (Zheng 2015). The knowledge generated through trajectory data is useful in different application areas under urban environment (Mazimpaka and Timpf 2016), such as path discovery, movement behavior analysis and transportation safety. In recent years, mining and understanding trajectory data of moving objects have gained extensive attentions in the area of internet of vehicles (IoV) and intelligent transportation systems (ITS) (Li et al. 2010; Zhang et al. 2016; Yuan et al. 2016). What is more, the travel regularity of private cars has considerable impacts on the urban traffic, which in turn leads to the formation of the urban hot zones.

VEHICLE LOCALIZATION AND TRAJECTORY DATA ACQUISITION

In this part we will introduce three methods for vehicle positioning and trajectory data collection. Firstly, we introduce a two-task hierarchical method to estimate the vehicle's movement information where process and measurement noises are first optimized separately. Secondly, we present a hybrid approach named non-Gaussian square root-unscented particle filtering (nGSR-UPF) to improve the accuracy of vehicle's movement information. Lastly, we highlight a Bayesian-sparse random Gaussian prediction (B-SRGP) approach to predict vehicle position in challenging environments. These methods are described in detail below.

A TWO-TASK HIERARCHICAL CONSTRAINED TAR-OBJECTIVE OPTIMIZATION APPROACH FOR VEHICLE STATE ESTIMATION

In this method, process and measurement noises are first optimized separately and then, based on the obtained optimal solutions, the upper bound for the state estimation error is addressed. These noises are assumed to follow a generalized error distribution (GED) and the maximum likelihood estimation (MLE) model is adopted with the intention of estimating sample parameters; thus, reducing the computational burden of the proposed method.

In order to estimate the vehicle state such as the position (latitude and longitude), the velocity as well as the acceleration, the proposed state estimation method is supposed to follow the nonlinear system given by the following state and measurement equations:

$$(S) \equiv \begin{cases} X_t = \varphi_t(X_{t-1}) + \alpha_{t-1} \\ Z_t = \psi_t(X_{t-1}) + \beta_t \end{cases}, \tag{1}$$

where $X_t \in IR^{n \times 1}$ describes the vehicle state vector and $Z_t \in IR^{p \times 1}$ represents the measurement vector at time t, $t = 0, \ldots, T$. (1) represents the state or process equation and the measurement or observation equation. Throughout this chapter, the estimate of X_t is denoted by $\hat{X}_t$. The linearization of the state equation around the estimated state $\hat{X}_t$ is provided by:

$$(S) \equiv \begin{cases} X_t = \varphi_t X_{t-1} + \alpha_{t-1} \\ Z_t = \psi_t X_t + \beta_t \end{cases}, \tag{2}$$

where the state transition matrix $\Phi_t \in IR^{n \times n}$ and the measurement matrix $\Psi_t \in IR^{p \times n}$ ($p \geq n$) are defined as $\Phi_t = \dfrac{\partial \phi_t}{\partial X_t}\bigg|_{\hat{X}_t}$ and $\Psi_t = \dfrac{\partial \psi_t}{\partial X_t}\bigg|_{\hat{X}_t}$ respectively.

We assume that the initial state X_0 is such that:

$$\left(X_0 - \hat{X}_0\right)\left(X_0 - \hat{X}_0\right)^T \leq G_0, \tag{3}$$

where $\hat{X}_0$ is an estimate of X_0 which is also supposed to be known and $G_0 = G_0^T \in IR^{n \times n}$ is a known positive matrix. The superscript (T) stands for the transposition operator. In (2), α_{t-1} and β_t represent the additive process noise and measurement noise sequences respectively. Moreover, the filter for the system which is based on the current observation such that $\hat{Z}_{t-1} = \Psi_{t-1} \hat{X}_{t-1}$ is defined as:

$$\hat{X}_t = \Phi_t \hat{X}_{t-1} + L_t \left(Z_{t-1} - \hat{Z}_{t-1} \right)$$
$$= \Phi_t \hat{X}_{t-1} + L_t \left(\Psi_{t-1} X_{t-1} + \beta_{t-1} - \Psi_{t-1} \hat{X}_{t-1} \right), \tag{4}$$

where L_t is the gain matrix to be determined. We assume the following:

Assumption 1. Assume that the process noise α_t and the measurement noise β_t are non-Gaussian distributed and follow the generalized error distribution (GED).

The GED is particularly adopted as an approximation to non-Gaussian densities with the intention of addressing the non-Gaussian noises. The main advantage of GED relies on some important properties that are related to shape parameter which, when varying, provides for instance other different distributions(Zhang 2013).The probability density functions (PDF) of these noise sequences are given by:

$$p_{\alpha_t}(g) = M(g) \sigma_t^{-1} exp \left[-J(g) \left| \frac{\alpha_t - \mu_t}{\sigma_t} \right|^{\frac{2}{1+g}} \right] \tag{5}$$

$$p_{\beta_t}(g) = M(g) \sigma_t^{-1} exp \left[-J(g) \left| \frac{\beta_t - \mu_t}{\sigma_t} \right|^{\frac{2}{1+g}} \right], \tag{6}$$

where $M(g) = \dfrac{\{\Gamma[3(1+g)/2]\}^{\frac{1}{2}}}{(1+g)\{\Gamma[(1+g)/2]\}^{\frac{3}{2}}}$, $J(g) = \left\{\dfrac{\Gamma[3(1+g)/2]}{\Gamma[(1+g)/2]}\right\}^{\frac{1}{1+g}}$ and $\Gamma(\cdot)$ is the

gamma function.

Besides, μ_t and σ_t are location and scale parameters respectively and σ_t represents the standard deviation of the sample. The variable g is a shape parameter that is related to the kurtosis of the distribution that characterizes the "non-normality" of the sample. The mean and variance of the GED are given by $E(\alpha_t) = \mu_\alpha$ (or $E(\beta_t) = \mu_\beta$) and $var(\alpha_t) = \sigma_\alpha^2$ (or $var(\beta_t) = \sigma_\beta^2$) respectively for all $\alpha_t, \beta_t, \mu_t \in [-\infty, +\infty]$, $\sigma_t \in [0, +\infty]$ and $g \in [-2, +\infty]$.

Proposition 1. The generalized error distribution approaches the normal or Gaussian distribution when the shape parameter g tends to zero and is given by:

$$p(\alpha_t, g = 0, \sigma_t, \mu_t) = \frac{1}{\sqrt{2\pi}} \sigma_t^{-1} exp\left[-\frac{1}{2}\left|\frac{\alpha_t - \mu_t}{\sigma_t}\right|^2\right] \tag{7}$$

Proof. In particular, letting $g = 0$ reveals that (5) becomes:

$$p(\alpha_t, g = 0, \sigma_t, \mu_t) = M(0)\sigma_t^{-1} exp\left[-J(0)\left|\frac{\alpha_t - \mu_t}{\sigma_t}\right|^2\right], \tag{8}$$

where

$$M(0) = \frac{\{\Gamma[3/2]\}^{1/2}}{\{\Gamma[1/2]\}^{3/2}} = \frac{\left(\frac{1}{2}\sqrt{\pi}\right)^{1/2}}{(\sqrt{\pi})^{3/2}} = \frac{1}{\sqrt{2\pi}} \text{ and } J(0) = \left\{\frac{\Gamma[3/2]}{\Gamma[1/2]}\right\} = \frac{\frac{1}{2}\sqrt{\pi}}{\sqrt{\pi}} = \frac{1}{2}.$$

Then, by plugging these results into (3.7) leads to the following Gaussian distribution:

Zhu Xiao, Dong Wang and Keqin Li

$$p(\alpha_t, g = 0, \sigma_t, \mu_t) = \frac{1}{\sqrt{2\pi}} \sigma_t^{-1} exp\left[-\frac{1}{2}\left|\frac{\alpha_t - \mu_t}{\sigma_t}\right|^2\right] \quad \text{Q.E.D.} \quad (9)$$

Figure 1 demonstrates the proposition in a graphical representation. We plot the curves showing different shape values where when the shape value vanishes ($g = 0$), the non-Gaussian distribution, GED, approaches the Gaussian distribution and is represented in green color. On the other hand, the tail distribution gets thinner as g increases positively and gets thicker as g increases negatively.

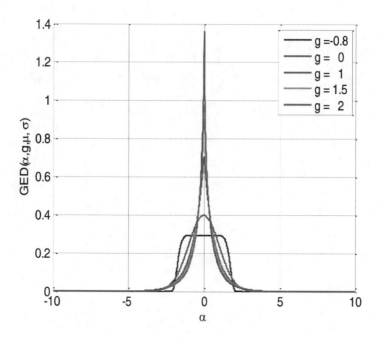

Figure 1. The generalized error distribution with $\mu = 0$, $\sigma = 1$ and different values of the shape g. The curve ($g = 0$) represents the Gaussian distribution of the process noise α in $[-10,10]$, for example.

In general, comparing to Gaussian distribution, the non-Gaussian distributions do not have an analytically tractable solution (Yang et al. 2008). Therefore, for better handling these non-Gaussian distribution difficulties, we need to estimate its parameters such as the variances σ_α^2 and σ_β^2 as well as the means μ_α and μ_β related to the process and measurement noises respectively.

Our goal is to estimate the vehicle state vector by minimizing the process noise, the measurement noise and then the matrix *Gt* is defined in the update state of (3) as follows:

$$\left(X_t - \hat{X}_t\right)\left(X_t - \hat{X}_t\right)^T \leq G_t. \tag{10}$$

Assumption 2. Assume that the problem satisfies the least square formulation is $\Theta = \|\alpha_t\| + \|\beta_t\| + \|G_t\|$ such that the symbol $\|\bullet\|$ stands for the Euclidean norm and the matrices *R* and *Q* are also assumed to be positive definite noise covariance matrices and are relative to the system and measurement models respectively.

Based on (10) and Assumption 2, the resulting state estimation problem can be formulated as a nonlinear programming problem (NLP):

$$\hat{\Theta} = \min_{\{\alpha_t, \beta_t, X_t\}} \|\alpha_t\| + \|\beta_t\| + \|G_t\| \tag{11}$$

$$s.t. \quad \left(X_t - \hat{X}_t\right)\left(X_t - \hat{X}_t\right)^T \leq G_t, t = 0,...,T-1 \tag{12}$$

$$tr(R_{t-1}) \leq \gamma, t = 1,...,T, \gamma \in IR_0^+ \tag{13}$$

$$tr(Q_t) \leq \gamma, t = 0,...,T-1, \gamma \in IR_0^+, \tag{14}$$

where the positive scalar γ is the weight constraint associated with the noises α_t and β_t respectively. The function $tr(A)$ represents the trace of *A* and is equal to the sum of the diagonal entries of *A*. One could also use the determinant of *A* instead of trace since the solution of the trace problem coincides with the solution to the determinant problem for small γ (William, Yong and Tan 2006)(i.e., $\gamma \in [1,10]$). Here, the constrained view leads us to forcing the trace of the noise covariance matrix to the boundary, γ . Moreover, (12) represents geometrically the ellipsoid where for instance, $\hat{X}_t$ is the center of the ellipsoid and the matrix G_t includes its shape and size parameters. The problem (11) refers to as NLP with multiple sub-objective functions and this stands for the multi-objective optimization problem (MOP) (Barolli et al. 2011).

In this section, we focus on the tri-objective optimization problem (TOP), i.e., MOP with three objective functions where the hierarchical method to achieve this tri-objective optimization is adopted. The hierarchical multi-objective optimization (HMO) efficiently solves problems with a hierarchical structure among the objectives, thus a Pareto front is not needed because tradeoff information is not required (Louie and Strunz 2006). In case of two objectives for example, the second objective is optimized while keeping the optimized value of the first objective fixed as presented in the following formulation (Fonseca, Leeuwenburgh and VandenHof 2014):

$$\min_{X_{1:T}} / \max \Xi_2(X_{1:T}) \text{ subject to } \begin{cases} f_t(X_{t-1}, X_t) = 0, t = 1,\dots,T \\ h_t(X_t) \le 0, t = 0,\dots,T-1 \\ \Xi_1^* - \Xi_1(X_{1:T}) \le \lambda \end{cases}, \qquad (15)$$

where the parameter $\lambda > 0$ has the small value compared to Ξ_1^* which is, in turn, the optimized value of Ξ_1 computed from the primary objective optimization. In case of multiple objective functions (i.e., more than two), the optimization problem can be presented in this way: firstly, the optimizers of the first objective function are found; and then the optimizers of the second most important objective are searched for, and so on, until all the objective functions have been optimized on smaller sets (Caramia and Dell'Olmo 2008).

Based on the previously stated Assumptions 1 and 2, the hierarchical method consists of minimizing the global problem (11) which is divided into three smaller sub-problems: $\Theta_1 = \|\alpha_t\|$, $\Theta_2 = \|\beta_t\|$, and $\Theta_3 = \|G_t\|$. These sub-problems are solved separately under a particular priority as presented in the following system:

$$min \ \Theta = \underset{,\alpha,\beta,X}{min} \left[\Theta_1, \Theta_2, \Theta_3\right] \tag{16}$$

$$\left\{\breve{\alpha}_{1:T}\right\} = min \ \Theta_1\left(\alpha_{1:T}\right) = min \left\|\alpha_t\right\| \ \text{s.t. (13)} \tag{17}$$

$$\left\{\breve{\beta}_{1:T}\right\} = min \ \Theta_2\left(\beta_{1:T}\right) = min \left\|\beta_t\right\| \ \text{s.t. (14)} \tag{18}$$

$$\left\{\hat{G}_{1:T}\right\} = min \Theta_3\left(G_{1:T}\right) = \underset{G_t>0}{min} G_t \tag{19}$$

s.t.

$$\left(X_t - \hat{X}_t\right)\left(X_t - \hat{X}_t\right)^T \leq G_t \tag{20}$$

$$\breve{a}_t - a_t \leq \lambda, a_t \in \alpha_t \subseteq IR^n \tag{21}$$

$$\breve{b}_t - b_t \leq \lambda, b_t \in \beta_t \subseteq IR^p \tag{22}$$

In order to achieve the optimal solution of our global problem (Θ), we need to find the optimal solution of each sub-problems (Θ_1, Θ_2, and Θ_3) and then, through an effective procedure, all these solutions are aggregated. Indeed, this technique allows us to first minimize the process noise represented by $\Theta_1 = \|\alpha_t\|$ and then the measurement noise given by $\Theta_2 = \|\beta_t\|$ subject to (13) and (14), and lastly Θ_3 will be considered. By computing the sequence of G_t ($0 < t \leq T-1$) in Θ_3, we want to find $\hat{X}_t$, the optimal solution of our main problem. As one can see, in order to complete the characteristics of the hierarchical method, the constraints (21) and (22) which are defined based on the obtained optimal solutions of Θ_1 and Θ_2 are added to the objective function Θ_3.

The considered three levels (L_1 , L_2 , and L_3) of the hierarchical optimization problem for the two main tasks is summarized in Figure 2. This importance order is motivated by the observation that the accuracy of state estimator is largely influenced by the process noise and the measurement covariance matrices.

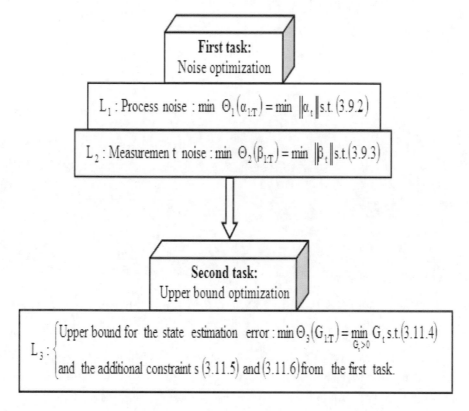

Figure 2. A two-task multi-objective with three-level hierarchical optimization problem.

Since the considered non-Gaussian distribution does not have an analytically tractable solution, the weighting matrices R and Q are estimated in this subsection via the maximum likelihood estimation (MLE) method. See the appendix for the process of estimating the noise sequence and the complexity analysis using MLE and ML estimates.

Our proposal aims to estimate the vehicle state using the optimization of the process and measurement noises as well as the error state via the hierarchical constrained tri-objective optimization (HCTO) algorithm. Moreover, the input to HCTO is the initial set of values including different parameters related to the noises and the state error optimization problems as well as the initial vehicle state that comprises the longitude, latitude, velocity, and acceleration provided by sensors embedded in the smartphone.

In order to experimentally validate the effectiveness of our proposed HCTO method, the vehicle state was estimated in real-setting experiments. Indeed, the test vehicle was driven along different roads in Hunan University area (an open air environment) with different velocities for about 5 minutes. A smartphone, Samsung Galaxy S4, on board of the vehicle was with Android OS v4.2.2 as operating system. This device does not only comprise an Assisted-Global Positioning System (A-GPS) support and GLONASS, but also includes the usual accelerometer, gyroscope, proximity, compass and ambient light sensors for improving urban navigation performance. Data from smartphone were uploaded to a Laptop computer and converted to excel spreadsheets.

Moreover, although the device comprises two navigation systems, data from different satellites in view were collected using only A-GPS during the road experiments. This new advanced technology based on mobile computing system has gained a large popularity nowadays in various applications such as in target localization (Lee et al. 2013) and tracking systems (Benavoli et al. 2007). Other benefits of choosing the sensors embedded in smartphone over the on-board ones for vehicle positioning can also be found in (Almazan 2013; Walter et al. 2013).

First, we compare and analyze the results. In this experiment, at each time $t = 1, \cdots, T$ ($T = 295s$), the input measurements to the adopted methods come from two different sensors, i.e., GPS and accelerometer; both embedded in the smartphone. GPS produces the vehicle position (latitude, longitude) and velocity whereas the accelerometer provides the acceleration. Besides, although the velocity measured by GPS and the acceleration measured by the accelerometer are inherently three-dimension (i.e., v_x, v_y, v_z and a_x, a_y, a_z), one-dimension (i.e., v_x and a_x) was used in our experiments, for simplicity.

The test was then started with $X_0 = [112.9415, \ 28.1827, 3.4885, 0.8200]$ as initial values which represent respectively the initial longitude [deg], latitude [deg], velocity [m/s], and acceleration [m/s2].

This implies that the dimension of the state is $n = 4$. To achieve better accuracy using the proposed method, different parameters are set as follows: the interval time Δt is set to 1s, $\mu_\alpha^0 = \mu_\beta^0$ to $[0.1, 0.1, 0.1, 0.1]$, R_0 to $diag(0.02^2, 0.01^2, 1.0^2, 1.0^2)$, Q_0 to $diag(0.1^2, 1.0^2, 0.02, 0.02^2)$, G_0 to $diag(1.0, 1.0, 0.0, 1.0)$ and the weight constraints associated with the noises γ is set to 1 (William et al. 2006). The gain matrix L_t developed in (Guo et al. 2006) is used to design the filtering system as stated in (4).

The proposed method is tested under the assumption that the shape parameter $g = 2$ and $g = 0$ for noises which are non-Gaussian and Gaussian distributed and this method is therefore called HCTO (non-gn) and HCTO (gn) respectively, where "non-gn" stands for "non-Gaussian noise" and "gn" for "Gaussian noise". We also compared the performance of HCTO method by taking as references the most nonlinear estimation methods extensively used in the literature such as particle filter (PF) (Read Jet al. 2014) which does not require the noise to be Gaussian and unscented Kalman filter (UKF) (Zhang et al. 2013) which is assumed to successfully approximate a Gaussian distribution of the system. Figure 3 and Figure 4 present a comparison of the state estimation methods from the two alternatives as well as the PF and UKF. For simplicity, the experiments were conducted only for PF and UKF when noises are non-Gaussian distributed and Gaussian distributed in order to make better comparison with HCTO (non-gn) and HCTO (gn) respectively.

From Figure 3 and Figure 4, one can see that defining the process and measurement noises as non-Gaussian model in HCTO ($g=2$) increases notably the vehicle state accuracy, because the estimated covariance matrix based MLE which represents the noise weight become smaller in this case. In addition, even though UKF can favorably tackle the Gaussian noises, HCTO (gn) presents better vehicle state accuracy. In fact, the constraints used for dealing the process and measurement noises makes HCTO (gn) well-conditioned since the constrained view leads us to forcing the trace of the estimated noise covariance matrices to the boundary, $\gamma = 1$.

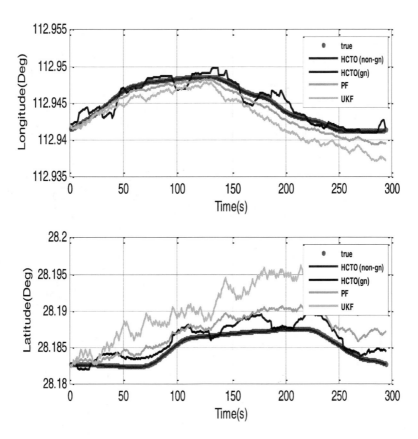

Figure 3. The actual and the estimated vehicle state in terms of latitude and longitude using HCTO (non-gn), HCTO (gn), PF, and UKF.

This allows it to increase the state accuracy whereas UKF suffers from larger process and measurement noise variances (Prakash et al. 2008). Also, PF is less accurate than HCTO (non-gn) although both are fed with non-Gaussian noises in this experiment. This is because HCTO has the proper statistics of the process and measurement noise sequences α_t and β_t, with the addition of the inequality constraints and the used method to optimize the upper bound for the state estimation error. Hence, the constrained estimation problem formulated through HCTO accurately models the non-Gaussian variables α_t and β_t compared to PF.

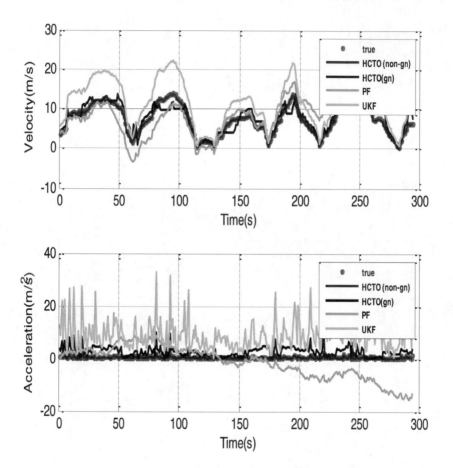

Figure 4. The actual and the estimated vehicle state in terms of velocity and acceleration using HCTO (non-gn), HCTO (gn), PF, and UKF.

We then conduct statistical evaluation to obtain a quantitative comparison. A statistical evaluation of the state errors is conducted based on the root mean-square errors (RMSE) as the metric of estimation performance. The performance in terms of RMSE of the adopted methods is illustrated in Figure 5 and Figure 6.

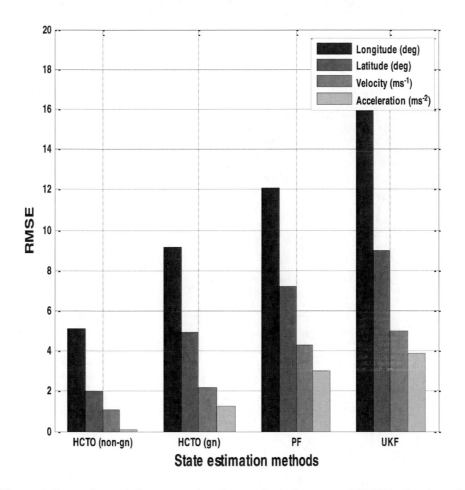

Figure 5. Comparison of the state estimation methods in terms of RMSE related to the vehicle state.

Figure 5 highlights the performance of different algorithms used in this work in terms of RMSE whereas Figure 6 illustrates the comparison of the vehicle state estimation based on HCTO with different values of the shape parameter of GED. Figure 5 indeed plots the RMSE for all adopted estimation methods based on the components of the vehicle position (latitude and longitude) as well as its velocity and acceleration.

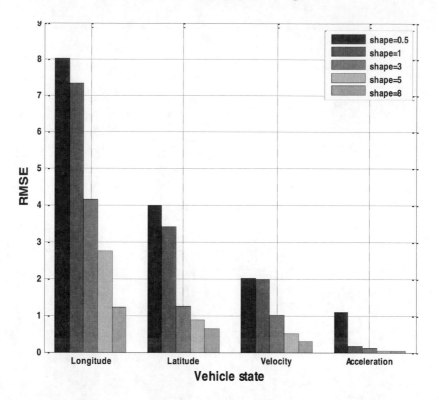

Figure 6. Comparison of the vehicle state estimation in terms of RMSE based on HCTO with different values of the shape.

Recall that low RMSE imply the high confidence for the state estimation methods. It is noticeable that the HCTO method has smaller RMSE than PF and UKF. This is mainly due to the way that HCTO addressed the problem related to the noises by imposing the constrained conditions as well as the implementation of the upper bound for the state estimation error.

The presence of constraints in PF could increase its performance (Kung et al. 2010), since they are crucial for an accurate state estimate in practical applications. On the other hand, PF performs better than UKF. In fact, given sufficient number of samples (1500 in our case), PF can successfully handle the process and measurement noise variance and this decreases the RMSE. It should be specified however that in terms of computational time, the UKF is a considerably faster tool than the PF technique, given that the latter requires an important amount of samples to be more accurate and this makes it more computational-intensive (Kun et al. 2010). Furthermore, the difference between HCTO (gn), $g = 0$ and HCTO (non-gn), $g = 2$ in terms of RMSE is related to the estimated large process and measurement noise variance (or covariance matrix) of HCTO (gn) which makes the method inefficient and therefore produces the large value of RMSE. What's more, notice that RMSE becomes smaller as the shape parameter value increases.

To determine whether this conclusion is consistent across different values, we analyzed how the experimental results vary when tackling other different values. More precisely, the behavior of HCTO by setting the shape parameter value $g \in \{0.5,1,3,5,8\}$ was studied as illustrated in Figure 6. Outstandingly, the performance improvements of the proposed method in terms of RMSE for the vehicle state are particularly important when handling larger shape parameter values which in turn decrease the estimated weight (covariance matrix) of the process and measurement noises implemented in the first two objective functions of HCTO.

Finally, we perform computational complexity analysis. The influence of the generalized error distribution (GED) on the HCTO algorithm is finally evaluated based on the time complexity of MLE.

Thanks to MLE, the computation cost of the original GED is reduced from $O(n^2 * N)$ to $O(n * N)$, where $N = 500$ represents the number of samples and n is the sample dimension.

Figure 7 illustrates the average execution time (in terms of CPU time) for estimating the vehicle state using HCTO (non-gn) and HCTO (gn) in the presence and absence of MLE for different number of samples. From this comparison, two observations are made: The execution time associated to both HCTO (non-gn) and HCTO (gn) without MLE is more computational-intensive than HCTO in the presence of MLE; In the presence of MLE, the execution time using HCTO (non-gn) where the shape parameter $g = 2$ is less computational-intensive than HCTO (gn) where the shape parameter $g = 0$.

This implies that the weight of the process and measurement noise expressed in terms of the estimated covariance (using MLE) influences the execution time of the proposed method.

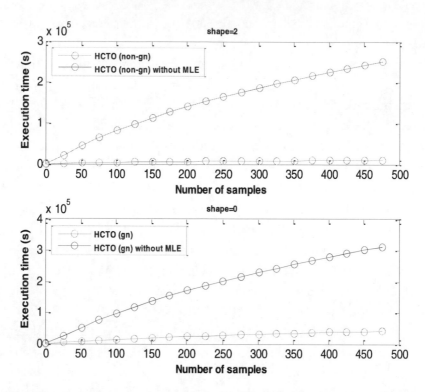

Figure 7. Influence of MLE on the HCTO algorithm in terms of execution time for $g = 2$ (non-Gaussian distribution) and $g = 0$ (Gaussian distribution).

We find that the aforementioned results from the comparison study clearly demonstrate the practicability for taking into account the process and measurement noises as non-Gaussian model and the use of different constraints to achieve a near-optimal vehicle state accuracy.

A HYBRID APPROACH-BASED SPARSE GAUSSIAN KERNEL MODEL FOR VEHICLE STATE DETERMINATION DURING THE FREE AND COMPLETED GPS OUTAGES

This is a hybrid approach taking into account the measurement noise as non-Gaussian distributed and thus providing a better vehicle state accuracy during both free and complete GPS outages using multi-sensor system. To achieve this, we propose an algorithm named non-Gaussian square root-unscented particle filtering (nGSR-UPF). This technique is based on the improved version of PF and combines UKF and PF for the integration of GPS and INS. Moreover, the sparse Gaussian–kernel density estimation (SG-KDE) is taken into consideration to approximate the non-Gaussian probability density whereas the least absolute shrinkage and selection operator (LASSO) technique is introduced with the intention of reducing the computational burden of nGSR-UPF caused by the kernel weight. This technique optimizes the non-Gaussian probability density in general by rendering most of elements of the weight vector to zero.

In this framework, a dynamic model is used to predict the vehicle state information and is given by:

$$X_t = f(X_{t-1}) + \varphi_t.$$

(23)

Here, φ_t indicates the process noise sequence and $f_t(\cdot)$ is the system transition function. Moreover, $\{X_t ; X \in IR^{m_x} ; m,t \in IN\}$ represents the vehicle state vector and m_X is the state dimension. In most situations, the system noise φ_t which is a tuning parameter depends especially on the filter designer and can be considered as a Gaussian process. At discrete time, when measurements Z_t are available, they are provided by:

$$Z_t = h(X_t) + \gamma_t,$$

(24)

where $h(\cdot)$ is the nonlinear function and γ_t stands for the measurement noise sequence. In our present scenario, the measurement (or observation) noise γ_t is assumed to be non-Gaussian distributed and will be taken as finite Gaussian kernel mixture(Chen, Cheng, Gan 2013; Hamid, Baker, Aziz 2014). When GPS signals are available, the measurements $\{Z_t ; Z \in IR^{p_z} ; p,t \in IN\}$ are such that $Z_t = [Z_{GPS}]$, where Z_{GPS} stands for the GPS measurements and p_z is the measurement vector dimension. Meanwhile, when complete GPS outages occur, the technique uses the available measurements provided by the accelerometer and in this case, $Z_t = [Z_{acc}]$ where Z_{acc} represents the accelerometer output signal.

Our structure works as a GPS aided INS system, where GPS position and velocity data are used to determine the vehicle position and velocity respectively and INS (accelerometer) information is used to predict the vehicle position and the velocity during the complete GPS outages. Indeed, acceleration measurements are integrated once and twice to establish the velocity and the position respectively. We limit the scope of this study to state determination using these two sensors (GPS and accelerometer) to demonstrate the efficiency of the proposed positioning and velocity solutions.

We introduce briefly the sparse Gaussian–kernel density estimation (SG-KDE) method which is utilized to approximate the measurement noises, considered as finite Gaussian kernel mixture and then the proposed technique for vehicle state determination will be discussed later. Referring to the nonlinear dynamic state model described in (23) and (24), the density probability $p(\gamma_t)$ related to measurement noise is approximated by general Gaussian kernel density estimation as follows (Han et al. 2011):

$$\hat{p}_L(\gamma_t \mid Z_t, \rho) = \sum_{j=1}^{L} \varpi_j K_t(\gamma_t, \gamma_{tj}, \rho),$$

(25)

subject to $\varpi_j \geq 0$, $1 \leq j \leq L$ and $\varpi^T 1_L = 1$; 1_L is the L-dimensional unit vector, L and ϖ_j are the size of samples and the kernel weights respectively such that $\varpi_L = [\varpi_1 \varpi_2 \ldots \varpi_L]^T$ is the kernel weight vector. Here, $K_t(\gamma_t, \gamma_{tj}, \rho)$ indicates the Gaussian kernel function and ρ represents the kernel bandwidth (or smoothing constant). Indeed,

$$K_t\left(\gamma_t, \gamma_{tj}, \rho\right) = \frac{1}{\left(2\pi\rho^2\right)^{\frac{1}{2}}} \, exp\left(-\frac{\left\|\gamma_t - \gamma_{tj}\right\|^2}{2\rho^2}\right). \tag{26}$$

Obviously, from (26), γ_{tj} can be taken as the mean and will be denoted as μ_{tj} hereinafter. Let assume $\Lambda = \rho^2 I_L$ to be the covariance matrix related to bandwidth, and then (25) can be expressed as:

$$\hat{p}_L\left(\gamma_t \mid Z_t, \rho\right) = \sum_{j=1}^{L} \varpi_j K_t\left(\gamma_t, \mu_{tj}, \Lambda\right), \text{ where } \mu_j = \left[\mu_{j1} \mu_{j2} \ldots \mu_{jm}\right]. \tag{27}$$

The main purpose is to optimize sensibly the kernel weight until most of the elements in ϖ_j become zeros. Note that the kernel method without sparse property becomes very slow and needs a large memory space to store the sample data. This motivates us to sparsify the Gaussian kernel weight and the process is therefore called sparse Gaussian–kernel density estimation (SG-KDE). In this chapter, the constant value presented in(Hong et al. 2010) as the bandwidth which determines the "width" of the weighting function will be considered. For the weight sparsification, there are a variety of methods in the literature such as multiplicative nonnegative quadratic programming (MNQP) algorithm (Chen et al. 2008), sparse probability density function estimation based on the minimum integrated square error (MISE)(Hong et al. 2013), and sparse kernel density construction using orthogonal forward regression(Hong et al. 2013). This chapter refers to the least absolute shrinkage and selection operator (LASSO), which is one of the suitable estimators widely used to handle the variable selection problem(Iturbide et al. 2013).

Indeed, assume that (27) can be equivalently expressed in the matrix form as:

$$d = \varpi_j K, \tag{28}$$

where $d \equiv \hat{p}_L\left(\gamma \mid Z, \rho\right) = \left[d_1 \, d_2 \ldots d_m\right]^T$ and

$$K = [K_1 \ K_2 \ldots K_l] = \begin{bmatrix} K(\gamma, \mu_{11}, \Lambda) & \cdots & K(\gamma, \mu_{l1}, \Lambda) \\ \vdots & \ddots & \vdots \\ K(\gamma, \mu_{1m}, \Lambda) & \cdots & K(\gamma, \mu_{lm}, \Lambda) \end{bmatrix}.$$

Given the regularization parameter ν and threshold parameter ε, the weight optimization based on (LASSO) method is defined as follows:

$$\tilde{\varpi}_j = arg\,min_{\varpi} \left\| K\varpi_j - d \right\|_F^2 + \nu \sum_i^l \left\| \varpi_i \right\|_1 , \qquad (29)$$

such that $B = \left\{ b : \left\| K_b \varpi_b' \right\|_F^2 \leq \varepsilon \left\| d \right\|_F^2 \right\}$. The matrix $K \in IR^{l \times m}$ will be updated following the sparse property $\breve{K}_B := 0_{l \times card(B)}$. The symbol $\left\| \cdot \right\|_F$ represents the Frobenius norm of a matrix and $card(B)$ is the cardinality of the index set B. Finally, the kernel weight will be computed based on the normal equation definition (Arioli et al. 2012) and hence most of its elements become zeros:

$$\tilde{\varpi}_{newj} = \left[\left(\breve{K}_b' \breve{K}_b \right)^{-1} \breve{K}_b' d \right]. \qquad (30)$$

Given the dimensions of the matrices K, $\breve{K}_b$ and d, the total time complexity of the kernel weight $\tilde{\varpi}_{newj}$ is $O(Nb^2 c_*)$ where N is the number of training samples and c_* is the number of non-zero variables in matrix K. Moreover, the total time complexity of the original kernel weight before the sparsification is given by $O(Nm^3 l)$ where $m > b$ and $l \times m > c_*$.

Recall that this updated kernel weight which speeds up the computation will also be used in the measurement process given that at the first step $t = 0$, the prior knowledge X_0 is defined by the probability density function (PDF) and is assumed to be known. Furthermore, referring to (24), if the first measurement Z_1 and X_1 are known at time $t = 1$, the current measurements using Bayes' formula is as follows (Morelande et al. 2005):

$$p(X_1 \mid Z_1) = \left(\int p(Z_1 \mid X_1) p(X_1) dX_1 \right)^{-1} p(Z_1 \mid X_1) p(X_1)$$

$$= \left(\int p(Z_1 \mid X_1) p(X_1) dX_1 \right)^{-1} \sum_{j=1}^{L} \widetilde{\varpi}_{newj} p_j (Z_1 \mid X_1) p_j(X_1) \quad , \tag{31}$$

where

$$p_j(X_1 \mid Z_1) \propto p_j(Z_1 \mid X_1) p_j(X_1). \tag{32}$$

This process continues up to the tth measurement ($t = 1, \ldots, T$).

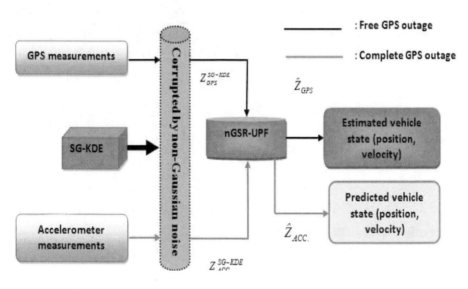

Figure 8. The estimation and prediction procedure of nGSR-UPF.

During the GPS signals availability (free GPS outage), vehicle information such as position and velocity are provided by GPS. As shown in Figure 8, the accelerometer and GPS are combined as a data fusion system using the proposed nGSR-UPF. Based on this new method, the determination of the vehicle state consists of predicting and estimating the vehicle information during the complete GPS outage and the free GPS outage respectively.

In the present algorithm, SR-UKF contribution is to highlight the parameters from which the sampling strategy is computed and therefore deals with the proposal distribution challenge caused by PF. Indeed, for each particle, $s = 1, \cdots, M$, one step ahead of particles $\{X_t^s\}_{s=1}^M$ is predicted according to the state equation (23) and samples of the system noise (Gaussian distributed), and then the estimated mean in the previous step $\hat{X}_{t|t-1}$ and the covariance matrix $P_{t|t-1}$ are computed using SR-UKF.

In this method, sensors measurements denoted $Z_{GPS/ACC}^{SG-KDE}$ are assumed to be corrupted by non-Gaussian noise and the latter is taken as finite Gaussian kernel mixture where the sparse Gaussian–kernel density estimation (SG-KDE) is adopted for its approximation. With the intention of decreasing the computational complexity during the process and thus providing the reliable predicted measurements $\hat{Z}_{GPS/ACC}$, SR-UKFs are used instead of UKFs for each particle. During the free GPS outage, the updated mean and covariance matrix computed using SR-UKF, are estimated based on the GPS observations updating. On the other hand, since the accelerometer sensor suffers from the large drift during the complete GPS outage, SR-UKF-based importance density operates in prediction mode and is responsible for shifting the weighted particles X_t^s toward the high-likelihood regions and consequently the information can accurately be predicted. Furthermore, based on (32), the weights updating of different particles can be computed as follows:

$$\hat{\omega}_t^s \propto \omega_{t-1}^s \frac{p\left(Z_t^{SG-KDE} \mid X_t^s\right) p\left(X_t^s \mid X_{t-1}^s\right)}{\pi\left(X_t^s \mid X_{1:t-1}^s, Z_t^{SG-KDE}\right)}, \tag{33}$$

where $p\left(Z_t^{SG-KDE} \mid X_t^s\right) \propto p\left(X_t \mid Z_t^{SG-KDE}\right) p^{-1}\left(X_t\right)$; the function $\pi(\cdot)$ and $\hat{\omega}_t^s$ represent the importance sampling distribution for each propagated particle and the un-normalized weights respectively. The normalization of weights in

(33) can be defined as $\omega_t^s = \dfrac{\widehat{\omega}_t^s}{\sum_{s=1}^{M} \widehat{\omega}_t^s}$ such that the sum of all weights will be equal to 1. In the measurement update, the new measurements are used to assign a probability represented by the normalized importance weight to each particle.

Table 1. Specifications of the used Smartphone sensors

Sensor Name	Sensor Type	Outputdata rate	Scale factor	Range	Noise (RMS)
GPS receiver	BCM 4752	4-8000 Hz	<3%	About 3 meters	1 (m)
Accelerometer	MPU 6500	4-8000 Hz	<3%	±2g/4g/8g (g=ms-2)	6.1 (mg)

Then we do the simulation setup, the performance of the proposed method is also evaluated with respect to real-world data collected using Smartphone-based vehicular sensing model. The technical specifications of the used Smartphone sensors are highlighted in Table 1.

Throughout the test, even though the imbedded GPS receiver can detect signals from several satellites, its design is limited to the demodulation of signals from at most six satellites and no natural GPS outages were detected. Moreover, at each time; at least four satellites were detected except for some negligible cases where less than four satellites were detected. As supported by Kaplan E. and Hegarty D. (Kaplan et al. 2005) and Mok E. et al. (Mok et al. 2012), the GPS measurement or the GPS accuracy is reliable if the signals are coming from at least four GPS satellites.

The performance of the nGSR-UPF method is then evaluated by comparing its output to that of the GPS and accelerometer, which were considered as a reference. Moreover, for testing purposes, nine short and long complete GPS outages (Figure 9) are intentionally introduced to compare the performance of the proposed method under various conditions (i.e., free and complete GPS outage). Indeed, these complete outages are from 73 to109, from 268 to 307, from 532 to 562, from 602 to 643, from 699 to 748, from 780 to 827, from 991 to 1041, from 1111 to 1163, and from 1290 to 1345 seconds with lengths of 36, 39, 30, 41, 51, 47, 50, 52 and 55 seconds respectively.

Although the used sensors provide vehicle information in three-dimension system, that is, $pos\left(p_k^x, p_k^y, p_k^z\right)$, $v\left(v_k^x, v_k^y, v_k^z\right)$, and $a\left(a_k^x, a_k^y, a_k^z\right)$ expressed in terms of East-North-Up (ENU) coordinate system, a two-dimension system (East-North) for vehicle position, velocity, and acceleration is considered in this experiment for simplicity. Hence, the state vector is composed of six elements such that $X_t = \left[\, p_t^x,\ p_t^y,\ v_t^x, v_t^y, a_t^x, a_t^y \,\right]$.

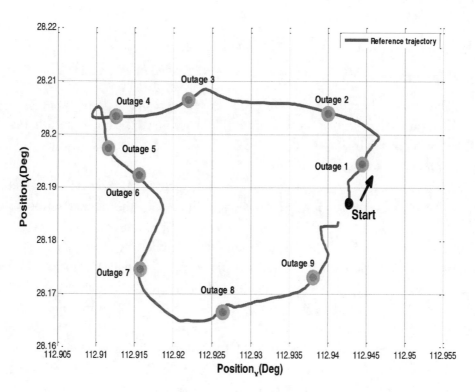

Figure 9. Test trajectory and the nine simulated (artificial) complete GPS outages.

Different parameters are used in order to evaluate the performance of the proposed algorithm. Indeed, the number of Gaussian kernels and the constant kernel bandwidth are set to $L = 5$ and $\rho = 1.0$ respectively according to (Hong et al. 2010). Moreover, in our case, five is considered as the optimum number guaranteeing that all mixtures are statistically independent respectively. The mean μ_j in 6-D is given by:

$$\mu_1 = \begin{bmatrix}1.0,1.0,1.0,1.0,1.0,1.0\end{bmatrix}^T,$$
$$\mu_2 = \begin{bmatrix}0.0,1.0,1.0,0.0,0.0,0.0\end{bmatrix}^T,$$
$$\mu_3 = \begin{bmatrix}1.0,0.0,0.0,1.0,1.0,1.0\end{bmatrix}^T,$$
$$\mu_4 = \begin{bmatrix}-1.0,-1.0,1.0,1.0,1.0,1.0\end{bmatrix}^T, \text{ and}$$
$$\mu_5 = \begin{bmatrix}0.0,0.0,0.0,1.0,1.0,1.0\end{bmatrix}^T$$

whereas Λ is the unit covariance matrix defined based on the bandwidth value. For sparse kernel weight based on the LASSO technique, the regularization and threshold parameters were set to $v = 0.1$ and $\varepsilon = 0.2$ respectively.

Concretely, for better implementation (Woo et al. 2014), 1000 particles were drawn for the bootstrap PF with resampling after each measurement, and the times of Monte Carlo runs are 100.

The expectations were computed using UT with $2*m+1$ sigma points, where m indicates the state dimension. The proposed nGSR-UPF solutions are compared with the classic estimation methods such as Gaussian sum particle filtering (GSPF) (Yukihiro et al. 2008), EKF and UPF where process noise and measurement noise are assumed to be Gaussian distributed (i.e., $\varphi_t^i \sim N(0.05;1)$) and non-Gaussian distributed (i.e., using SG-KDE) respectively. Figure 10 highlights the comparison of the vehicle state errors obtained using the aforementioned estimation methods run over 1410 iterations.

Based on the positioning and velocity results presented below, we can conclude that during the free GPS outages, the contribution of the proposed nGSR-UPF and GSPF are significant. The main reason is related to the fact that GSPF and nGSR-UPF can overcome degeneracy and have good performance for state estimation in non-Gaussian environment. Indeed, the introduction of the square root in nGSR-UPF reduces not only the computational cost, but also the state error covariance and thus increases numerical stability when compared to the standard UPF (Li et al. 2010).

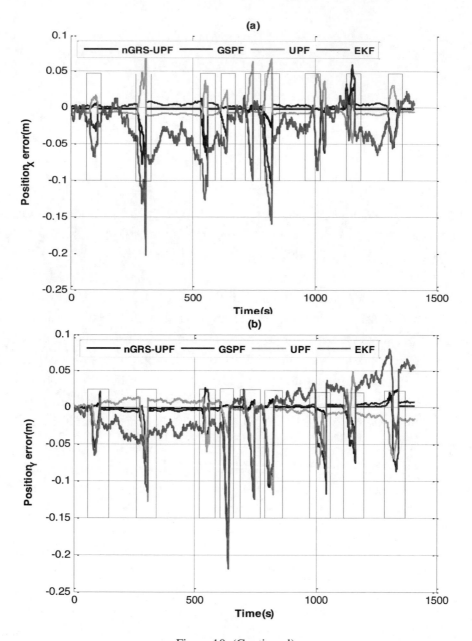

Figure 10. (Continued)

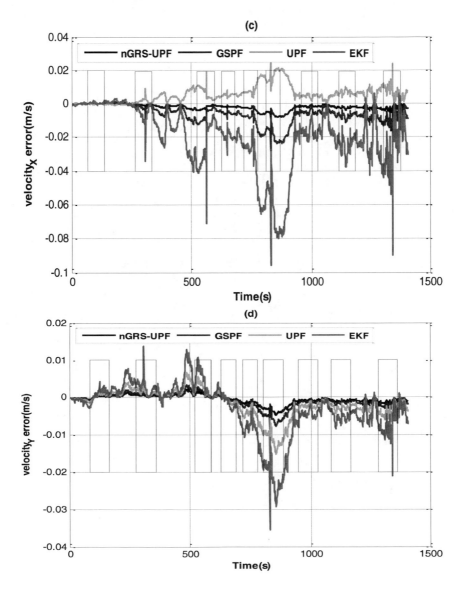

Figure 10. Vehicle positioning (a)-(b) and velocity (c-d) errors plot depicting the performance for various estimation methods where the rectangular symbols indicate the location of the simulated nine complete GPS outages.

During the complete GPS outage where the accelerometer inertial sensor is used to provide vehicle positioning and velocity, one can see that nGSR-UPF and UPF based on SR-UKF and UKF respectively perform much better than EKF and GSPF. Indeed, since the accelerometer sensor suffers from the large drift during this challenging case, SR-UKF (resp.UKF)-based importance density operates in prediction mode and is responsible for shifting the weighted particles toward the high-likelihood regions, and this decreases notably the vehicle positioning and velocity prediction error.

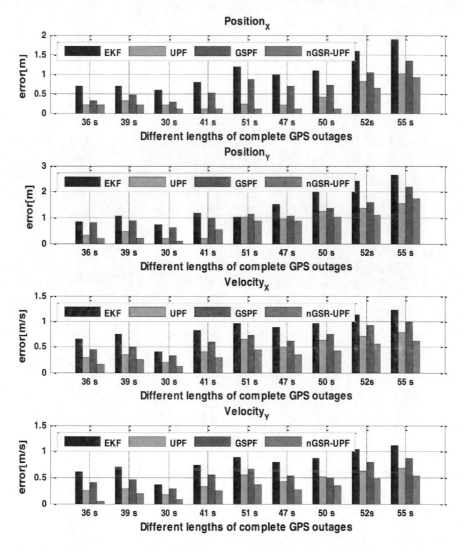

Figure 11. Average of the maximum error (in %) for different estimation methods during complete GPS outages.

Figure 11 shows the averages of the maximum state errors expressed in percentage (%) and it can be observed that the average of maximum state error increases as the length of the outages increases.

On the other hand, although EKF is moderately easier to implement and is reliable in many practical situations, it is the worst estimator and predictor among the adopted ones during both the free and complete GPS outages. In fact, this is due to the strong non-linear state equations that may bring on fickleness problems (Feng et al. 2011) especially in non-Gaussian environments.

Indeed, let's consider for instance the three last outages on position (X) with 50, 52, and 55 seconds of lengths respectively.

The averages of maximum positioning error are 0.1179, 0.6459, and 0.9069 m respectively for nGSR-UPF; 0.709, 1.034, and 1.349m respectively for GSPF; 0.424, 0.807, and 1.004 m respectively for UPF and 1.1, 1.6, and 1.9 m respectively for EKF. These results are consistent because the outage lengths where only data from accelerometer inertial sensor are used to replace GPS information (position and velocity) are not extremely large. This observation is also supported by authors in (Yuan W et al. 2016)who demonstrated that, in general, bridging by inertial sensors can be applied for only very short time.

Moreover, based on for instance the shortest and longest complete GPS outages, Figure 11 shows that in comparison with EKF, nGSR-UPF enhances the state accuracy during the complete GPS outages (shortest, 30 s) by 49.8%, 61.4%, 28.5%, and 22.3% in position (X), position (Y), velocity(X), and velocity (Y) respectively. However, compared with GSPF, the solution improvements are only 18.5%, 50.2%, 20%, and 18.7% in position (X), position (Y), velocity (X), and velocity (Y), respectively. In addition, during the complete GPS outages (longest, 55 s), one can remark that nGSR-UPF enhances the state accuracy by 99.3%, 91.5%, 60.2%, and 58.9% when compared with EKF in position (X), position (Y), velocity (X), and velocity (Y) respectively. With GSPF, the solution improvements are only 44.2%, 44.0%, 37.2%, and 31.4% in position (X), position (Y), velocity(X), and velocity (Y) respectively. Although in general, nGSR-UPF and UPF present good positioning results in all four state components, nGSR-UPF is more accurate than UPF due to the use of square root method which decreases significantly the state error covariance and thus increases numerical stability.

In sum, the use of nGSR-UPF scheme allows to improve significantly the accuracy of the vehicle's movement information such as the position and velocity during both the free and complete GPS outages.

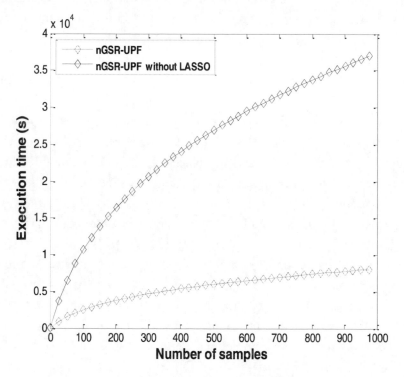

Figure 12. Influence of LASSO on our proposed nGSR-UPF algorithm in terms of execution time.

The computational cost related to the LASSO technique is given by $O(Mm^3l)$ for the original kernel weight and $O(Mb^2c_*)$ with $m > b$ and $l \times m > c_*$ for the sparsified weight kernel where M is the total number of the particles and c_* is the number of nonzero variables in matrix $K_{l \times m}$. Figure 12 illustrates indeed, the average execution times (in terms of CPU time) for determining the vehicle state using nGSR-UPF in presence and absence of LASSO for different number of particles. In short, nGSR-UPF without

LASSO is slower than nGSR-UPF in presence of LASSO due to the complexity of the kernel weight.

A Novel Probabilistic Approach for Vehicle Position Prediction in Free, Partial, and Full GPS Outages

In the statistical signal processing framework, one can predict the values of a continuous dependent variable x from a set of independent variables y using the following nonlinear model:

$$Y_i = f(X_i) + \xi_i, \ i = 1,\ldots,n, \tag{34}$$

where Y_i represents the $n \times 1$ response or measurement vector. The variable $X_i \in IR^p$ indicates the $p \times 1$ input to be predicted. Here, ξ_i stands for the $n \times 1$ error vector and is supposed to be non-Gaussian distributed whereas $f(\cdot): IR \to IR$ is an unknown prediction function. This function can be transformed as:

$$Y_i = FX_i + \xi_i, \ i = 1,\ldots,n, \tag{35}$$

where F stands for the $n \times p$ measurement matrix or predictor matrix, with $n < p$. The crucial task here is how to design the predictor matrix F to guarantee that it preserves the information X_i. To achieve this, we assume that F is a sparsified random Gaussian matrix whose entries F_{ij} are given by(Wang et al. 2010):

$$F_{ij} = \begin{cases} N\left(0, \dfrac{1}{\lambda}\right) & w.p. \ \lambda \\ 0 & w.p. \ 1-\lambda, \end{cases} \tag{36}$$

where $\lambda \in [0,1]$ is the measurement sparsification parameter. Moreover, since there are more unknowns than the number of equations ($n < p$), the measurement matrix F becomes singular and leads (35) to an ill-conditioned system. Therefore, for better prediction, F should satisfy the restricted isometry property (RIP) (Tillmann et al.2014). Indeed, the matrix F satisfies the (s, δ_s) -RIP with restricted isometry constant (RIC) $\varepsilon_s \in [0,1]$ if $(1-\varepsilon_s)\|X_i\|_2^2 \le \|F_s X_i\|_2^2 \le (1+\varepsilon_s)\|X_i\|_2^2$ where s ($n \le s \le n \times p$) represents the non-vanishing entries of the sparse matrix F. This property is also used to evaluate the quality of the measurement matrix.

Moreover, according to(Richard et al.2008), the sparsified random Gaussian matrix F satisfies the RIP with high probability if $p\big((1-\varepsilon_s)\|X_i\|_2^2 \le \|F_s X_i\|_2^2 \le (1+\varepsilon_s)\|X_i\|_2^2\big) \ge r$ where the constants $r = 1 - 2(12/\varepsilon_s)^k \exp(-q(\varepsilon_s/2)n)$ and $q(\varepsilon_s/2) = \varepsilon_s^2(1-\varepsilon_s/48)$. The variable k represents the dimension of the subspace. After the proof, it is shown that the matrix F obeys the RIP with the probability as follows.

$$p\big((1-\varepsilon_s)\|X_i\|_2^2 \le \|F_s X_i\|_2^2 \le (1+\varepsilon_s)\|X_i\|_2^2\big) \ge 1-\varepsilon_s. \qquad (37)$$

The choice of the sparsified random Gaussian matrix over the deterministic matrix is due to the fact that it is very hard to get the latter matrix with $n \times p$ size that satisfies the RIP because it requires the larger size of n and smaller sparsity level (Bourgain et al. 2010; Haupt et al. 2010). More benefits of choosing the random matrix as the measurement matrix can be found in (Foucart et al.2013).

In this chapter, we assume that the measurement device comprises both the global positioning system (GPS) and the inertial navigation system (INS). Based on (35), the measurements of GPS and INS are given by Y_t^{GPS} and Y_t^{INS} where $Y_t^{GPS} = F X_t^{GPS} + \xi_t^{GPS}$ and $Y_t^{INS} = F_t X_t^{INS} + \xi_t^{INS}$ respectively; where F_t is the s -sparse predictor matrix constructed based on (36). The variable X_t^{GPS} indicates the position in terms of latitude and longitude over the sample time t for example, whereas X_t^{INS} represents data provided by INS such as the acceleration, direction, angle and angular velocity. Moreover, variables ξ_t^{GPS} and ξ_t^{INS} are the GPS and INS measurement noises which show the dependence of Y_t^{GPS} and Y_t^{INS} on the variables other than predictor variables X_t^{GPS} and X_t^{INS}. These noises are considered as non-Gaussian distributed and follow the generalized error distribution (GED)(Zhang. 2013). The probability density function (PDF) related to ξ_t^{GPS} and ξ_t^{INS} is therefore defined as:

$$P_{GPS/INS}\left(\xi_t \mid g\right) = M(g)\sigma_{GPS/INS}^{-1} \, exp\left[-N(g)\left|\frac{\xi_t - \mu_{GPS/INS}}{\sigma_{GPS/INS}}\right|^{\frac{2}{1+g}}\right], \qquad (38)$$

where $M(g) = \dfrac{\{\Gamma[3(1+g)/2]\}^{\frac{1}{2}}}{(1+g)\{\Gamma[(1+g)/2]\}^{\frac{3}{2}}}$, $N(g) = \left\{\dfrac{\Gamma[3(1+g)/2]}{\Gamma[(1+g)/2]}\right\}^{\frac{1}{1+g}}$ and $\Gamma(\cdot)$ is the gamma function.

The quantities $\mu_{GPS/INS}$ and $\sigma_{GPS/INS}$ are location and scale parameters respectively and $\sigma_{GPS/INS}$ represents specifically the standard deviation of the sample. The variable g is a shape parameter. If the shape parameter g is zero, the generalized error distribution (GED) becomes the normal or Gaussian distribution as follows:

$$P_{GPS/INS}\left(\xi_t \mid g=0\right) = \frac{1}{\sqrt{2\pi}}\sigma_{GPS/INS}^{-1} \, exp\left[-\frac{1}{2}\left|\frac{\xi_t - \mu_{GPS/INS}}{\sigma_{GPS/INS}}\right|^2\right]. \qquad (39)$$

We consider also that the response variable Y which depends on both Y_t^{GPS} and Y_i^{INS} is defined as $Y = A_{GPS} Y_t^{GPS} + A_{INS} Y_t^{INS}$ where A_{GPS} and A_{INS} stand for the weight related to GPS and INS respectively. Hereafter, we suppose that A_{INS} also depends on the GPS weight in order to regulate the contribution of GPS for the accurate navigation solution in the system. The GPS weight denoted as α_{GPS} is assumed to be Gaussian distributed and is computed based on the Gaussian PDF (Bhatt et al. 2014) as follows:

$$\alpha = \left[(2\pi)^{1/2} |D|_{GPS} \right]^{-1} exp\left[-\frac{1}{2}(GPS - \mu_{GPS})^T D_{GPS}^{-1} (GPS - \mu_{GPS}) \right] \qquad (40)$$

where D_{GPS} and $|D|_{GPS}$ indicate the covariance matrix of GPS and its determinant respectively whereas μ_{GPS} represents the mean value of the GPS measurement. Moreover, we assume that the estimated response $\hat{Y}$ is given by:

$$\hat{Y} = A_{GPS} \hat{Y}_t^{GPS} + A_{INS} \hat{Y}_t^{INS} \text{ subject to } (A) \equiv \begin{cases} A_{GPS} = \alpha_{GPS} \\ A_{INS} = 1 - \alpha_{GPS} \end{cases}, \qquad (41)$$

where $\hat{Y}_t^{GPS} = F_s X_t^{GPS}$ and $\hat{Y}_t^{INS} = F_s X_t^{INS}$ are the estimated measurements provided by GPS and INS respectively. Since the GPS weight is defined using Gaussian PDF, its values vary from 0 to 1 (i.e., $\alpha_{GPS} \in [0,1]$) (Bishop 2006). Indeed, the GPS weight α_{GPS} is calculated by integrating the PDF α where the random variable varies from negative infinity to a certain limit d, i.e., $[-\infty, d]$. In this case, $A_{(\cdot)}$ is equal to $\vee \alpha_{GPS}$ where '$\vee$' denotes the logical inclusive OR. This is due to the fact that information can come at the same time from both the GPS and INS but monitored by the GPS weight α_{GPS}.

During the process, if $\alpha_{GPS} = 1$, that is, when the number of available satellites is at least four (Boucher et al. 2004), it is clear that the system ignores the INS contribution and GPS will be solely taken into account at 100% (see (41) and Figure 4). Then, no GPS outage occurs. In this case, the system uses only the GPS measurements to predict the state of $\hat{Y}$ ($\hat{Y}_t = \hat{Y}_t^{GPS}$). Therefore, a predictive distribution for an unknown data can then be obtained by conditioning on the known data as $p(\hat{Y}_t \mid Y) = p(\hat{Y}_t^{GPS} \mid Y)$ and the likelihood related to the GPS measurement noise is proportional to:

$$L_{\xi^{GPS}}\left(\hat{Y}_t \mid Y\right) \sim \left(\hat{Y}_t^{GPS} - Y^{GPS}\right)^T \left(\hat{R}_t^{GPS}\right)^{-1} \left(\hat{Y}_t^{GPS} - Y^{GPS}\right), \tag{42}$$

where $\hat{R}_t^{GPS}$ is the estimated covariance matrix. In this dissertation, $\hat{R}_t^{GPS}$ is estimated via the maximum likelihood estimation (MLE) (Fisher 1912) and is given by $\hat{R}_t^{GPS} = diag\left(\hat{\sigma}_{GPS}^2 / n, 2\hat{\sigma}_{GPS}^4 / n\right)$. In addition, n represents the sample size and $\hat{\sigma}_{GPS}^2$ is the estimated variance defined in terms of shape parameter g as follows:

$$\hat{\sigma}_{GPS}^2 = \frac{2N(g)\sum_{i=1}^{n}\left|\xi_i^{GPS} - \hat{\mu}_{GPS}\right|^{\frac{2}{1+g}}}{n(1+g)}, \text{ for } g \neq -1. \tag{43}$$

Similarly, if $\alpha_{GPS} = 0$, that is, when GPS signals are absent (full GPS outage), the system assigns the 100% confidence to the INS (see (41) and Figure 4) and is used to estimate the state of $\hat{Y}$ ($\hat{Y} = \hat{Y}^{INS}$). Therefore, $p(\hat{Y}_t \mid Y) = p(\hat{Y}_t^{INS} \mid Y)$ and the likelihood related to the INS measurement noise is proportional to:

$$L_{\xi^{INS}}\left(\hat{Y}_t \mid Y\right) \sim \left(\hat{Y}_t^{INS} - Y^{INS}\right)^T \left(\hat{R}_t^{INS}\right)^{-1} \left(\hat{Y}_t^{INS} - Y^{INS}\right), \tag{44}$$

where $\hat{R}_t^{INS}$ stands for the estimated covariance matrix. Its variance in terms of the shape parameter g is given by:

$$\hat{\sigma}_{INS}^2 = \frac{2N(g)\sum_{i=1}^n \left|\xi_i^{INS} - \hat{\mu}_{INS}\right|^{\frac{2}{1+g}}}{n(1+g)}, \text{ for } g \neq -1. \qquad (45)$$

In (43) and (45), $\hat{\mu}_{(\bullet)}$ represents the estimated mean (via MLE) related to the GPS and INS measurement noises respectively and is defined as:

$$\hat{\mu}_{(\bullet)} = \sum_{i=1}^n \left|\xi_i^{(\bullet)} - \mu_{(\bullet)}\right|^{\frac{1-g}{1+g}}, \text{ for } g \neq \{-1,1\}. \qquad (46)$$

This particular situation happens if $\alpha_{GPS} \in [0,1]$, i.e., if the number of available satellites is less than four or if the geometry of the four selected satellites is not adequate (a greater angle between satellites provides a better measurement and therefore the good position accuracy(Srilatha et al. 2009)). In this case, there is interaction between the dependent variables X_t^{GPS} and X_t^{INS}. The selection of these local variables is made based on (40) which affects different values to $\alpha_{GPS} \in [0,1]$.

In the case of partial GPS outages, the basic idea is to use the available information from both X_t^{GPS} and X_t^{INS}. To achieve this, the Bayesian inference is applied in order to optimally detect which information is more accurate for good position prediction. Indeed, assuming that the prior probabilities $p(X_t^{GPS})$ and $p(X_t^{INS})$ for X_t^{GPS} and X_t^{INS} respectively are known and based on (41), the Bayes' theorem provides the following conditional probabilities:

$$p(X_t^{GPS} \mid \hat{Y}_t, \alpha_{GPS}) = \frac{p(\hat{Y}_t \mid X_t^{GPS})p(X_t^{GPS} \mid \alpha_{GPS})}{p(\hat{Y}_t \mid \alpha_{GPS})} \qquad (47)$$

$$p\left(X_t^{INS} \mid \hat{Y}_t, \alpha_{GPS}\right) = \frac{p\left(\hat{Y}_t \mid X_t^{INS}\right) p\left(X_t^{INS} \mid \alpha_{GPS}\right)}{p\left(\hat{Y}_t \mid \alpha_{GPS}\right)},$$ (48)

where $p\left(X_t^{GPS} \mid \hat{Y}_t\right)$ and $p\left(X_t^{INS} \mid \hat{Y}_t\right)$ are the posterior probabilities related to the prior probabilities $p\left(X_t^{GPS}\right)$ and $p\left(X_t^{INS}\right)$ whereas $p\left(\hat{Y}_t \mid X_t^{GPS}\right)$ and $p\left(\hat{Y}_t \mid X_t^{INS}\right)$ are the probability densities from which the training data were drawn.

Recall that the denominators in (47) and (48) can be expressed in terms of the numerators as

$$p\left(\hat{Y}_t \mid \alpha_{GPS}\right) \approx p\left(\hat{Y}_t \mid X_t^{GPS}\right) p\left(X_t^{GPS} \mid \alpha_{GPS}\right) + p\left(\hat{Y}_t \mid X_t^{INS}\right) p\left(X_t^{INS} \mid \alpha_{GPS}\right)$$

which acts as a normalization factor. Now the main problem is how to decide which information either coming from the GPS or INS to assign to the new output $\hat{Y}_t$. Based on (Bishop 2006), one can consider that $\hat{Y}_t$ is assigned to the data with larger posterior probability that is, the response $\hat{Y}_t$ is for instance assigned to GPS data if $p\left(X_t^{GPS} \mid \hat{Y}_t\right) > p\left(X_t^{INS} \mid \hat{Y}_t\right)$. This condition is verified if

$$p\left(\hat{Y}_t \mid X_t^{GPS}\right) > \frac{p\left(\hat{Y}_t \mid X_t^{INS}\right) p\left(X_t^{INS} \mid \alpha_{GPS}\right)}{p\left(X_t^{GPS}\right)}.$$ (49)

Otherwise, the response is assigned to INS data. This method can be practical for detecting new data coming from the GPS or INS that have low probability during the process and for which the predictions may be of low accuracy. However, under the condition with which $\alpha_{GPS} \in [0,1]$, this cannot provide the accurate position prediction since the GPS or INS weight is still insufficient.

To overcome this weakness, we adopt the combination of data from both INS and GPS by summing (47) and (48) to get the following predictive distribution:

$$p\left(\hat{Y}_t^{GPS \wedge INS}\right) = \sum_{k=1}^{K} p\left(X_t^k \mid \hat{Y}_t\right) \text{ such that } \left\|\hat{Y}_t^{GPS \wedge INS}\right\|_1 \geq \delta, \tag{50}$$

where $K = 2$ stands for GPS and INS respectively, $\|\bullet\|_1$ represents the 1-norm function. The $GPS \wedge INS$ notation indicates that information is from both GPS and INS where '$\wedge$' is the AND logical operator. In this case, as the measurements form GPS and INS are received at the fusion center, the K-scan sliding window approach is adopted to update the tracks and control the flow data generated by both INS and GPS which are required for the prediction accuracy (Boucher et al. 2004). The value $\delta = (\theta - \tau)K$ is a regulation parameter where θ is the predefined support threshold and τ is the bound parameter error. The block diagram during the free, partial, and full GPS outages is presented in Figure 13.

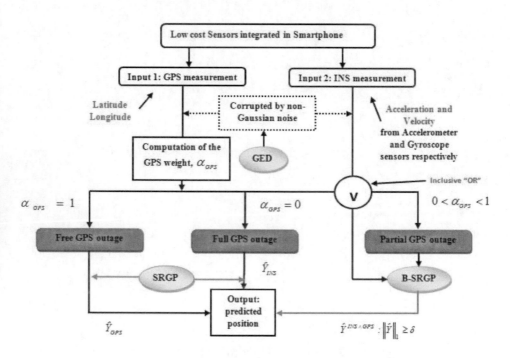

Figure 13. Block diagram during the free, partial, and full GPS outages.

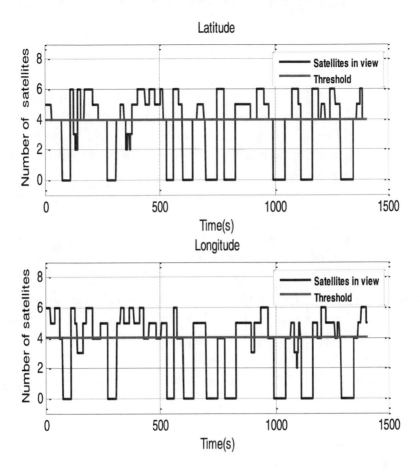

Figure 14. Number of satellites in view during the road test. The plot shows the number of satellites available at each time (second) where four (4) satellites are taken as minimum threshold for vehicle position accuracy.

With the intention of effectively predicting the vehicle position in free, partial, and full GPS outages based on the proposed method, the real-world data were collected using Smartphone-based vehicular sensing model along different roads in Hunan University area for about 25 minutes. Although the device comprises two navigation systems, data from different satellites in view were collected using only A-GPS during the road experiments. Moreover, for the purpose of computing the vehicle position (latitude and longitude), the Earth-centered Earth Fixed (ECEF) system was utilized. This system was then changed into the coordinate system based on the Universal Transverse Mercator projection (UTM) system which is the most commonly method used in China.

In order to show the location of the full and partial GPS outages, the number of satellites in-view system was used. The geometric dilution of precision (GDOP) technique can also be adopted since even though several satellites are available, the smaller angle between the four selected satellites leads to inaccurate position. This case is also regarded as the partial GPS outage (Boucher et al. 2004).However, due to the technical limitations, the strategy related to the recorded satellites in-view is preferred instead of using GDOP in order to detect different types of outages. The number of satellites in-view which determines the free, partial and full GPS outages during the road experiments is shown in Figure 14.

As can be seen from Figure 14, like in the previous chapter, nine full GPS outages have been intentionally introduced in different periods on both the latitude and longitude from 73 to 109, from 268 to 307, from 532 to 562, from 602 to 643, from 699 to 748, from 780 to 827, from 991 to 1041, from 1111 to 1163, and from 1290 to 1345 seconds respectively with the lengths of 36, 39, 30, 41, 51, 47, 50, 52, and 55 seconds.

Even though the imbedded GPS receiver can detect signals from several satellites, its design is limited to the demodulation of signals from at most six satellites. Beside the nine artificial full GPS outages, the used system shows five natural partial outages distributed on latitude and longitude. It should be noted that the two natural partial GPS outages were detected on latitude from 123 to 140 and from 351 to 378 seconds respectively with the lengths of 17 and 27 seconds and three were detected on longitude from 135 to 159, from 893 to 907, and from 1081 to 1101 seconds with lengths of 24, 14, and 30 seconds respectively.

In this experiment, at each time $t = 1, \cdots, T$ ($T = 1410s$), different values related to the vehicle position (latitude, longitude), were provided by GPS integrated in Smartphone. The test was started with $X_0 = [490659.0, \ 2219445.0]$ as initial values which represent respectively the latitude [m] and longitude[m]. To achieve the better accuracy using the proposed method, the measurement matrix F_t defined the sparse random Gaussian (SRG) matrix of size $n = 4$ and $p = 6$ with only $s = 14$, non-zero coefficients was randomly generated after $M = 18$ iterations. For satisfying the RIP, the fixed RIC $\delta_s = 0.41$ (Candes 2008) is considered which permits the canonical convex optimization problem for sparse approximation as well as to guarantee the high probability. When the GPS signals are considerably available (the weight parameter $\alpha_{GPS} = 1$), the GPS error covariance matrix and the mean are estimated based on (43) and (46) respectively where the scale parameter is set to $g = 2$ (for non-Gaussian measurement noise). In this case, the vehicle position was predicted using all available GPS information.

During the full GPS outage (the weight parameter $\alpha_{GPS} = 0$), the system assigns the 100% confidence to INS which means that all available INS data (from gyroscope and accelerometer sensors) are used for bridging the vehicle position prediction. Similarly, the INS error covariance matrix and the mean are estimated based on (45) and (46) respectively. Finally, during the partial GPS outage (the weight parameter $\alpha_{GPS} \in [0,1]$), the available GPS information is completed by the INS data coming from both the gyroscope and accelerometer sensors in order to successfully provide the reliable vehicle position prediction.

We have compared the performance of our proposed B-SRGP algorithm by taking KF (Linzhouting et al. 2014) and MARS (Martinez et al. 2015) as references which were the most prediction algorithms extensively used in the literature. Moreover, the effect of measurement noise on our proposed method B-SRGP is tested by considering the measurement noise to be non-Gaussian distributed (following GED) on one hand and Gaussian distributed on the other hand. This latter distribution was determined by zeroing the scale parameter, $g = 0$. In this case, for simplicity, the proposed method is denoted as 'B-SRGP (gn)' and 'B-SRGP (non-gn)' respectively where 'gn' stands for 'Gaussian noise' and 'non-gn' represents 'non- Gaussian noise' as shown in Figure 15.

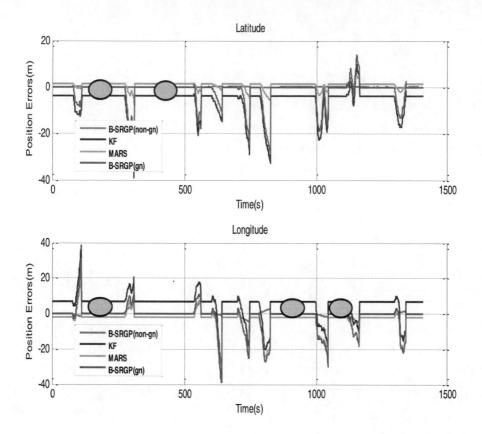

Figure 15. Vehicle position prediction in terms of longitude and latitude errors using the adopted methods KF, MARS, B-SRGP (non-gn) and B-SRGP (gn) in free, partial, and full outages. The black circle symbols show the detected partial outages on the latitude and longitude respectively.

This assessment was conducted based not only on different free outages but also on nine artificial simulated full outages as well as five natural partial outages of different durations as shown in Figure 9 and Figure 10. A comparison of KF, MARS, B-SRGP (non-gn) and B-SRGP (gn) was performed for both the longitude and latitude which constitute the vehicle position.

The vehicle position error-based latitude and longitude coordinates is computed by comparing the predicted vehicle position observed from the measurement with the corresponding *true* vehicle position. Figure 15 indicates the longitude position and the latitude position error curves of the four methods mentioned above.

To achieve the reliable results, the regulation parameter is set such that the support threshold $\theta = 0.5$ and the bound parameter error $\tau = 0.05$ (Loo K K et al. 2005). Moreover, 2-scan sliding window is used as $K = 2$ systems (INS and GPS).

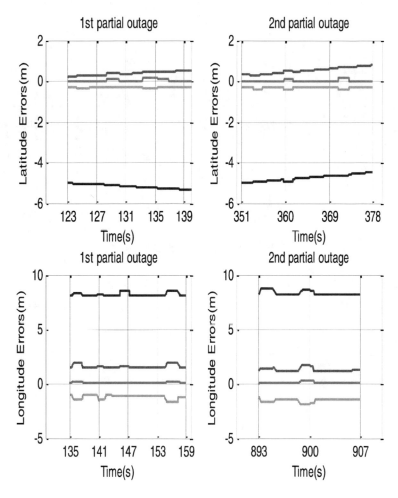

Figure 16. Highlighting the position prediction errors in different partial outages distributed on the latitude and longitude under the adopted methods: Red for B-SRGP (gn), Magenta B-SRGP (non-gn), Blue for KF, and Green for MARS.

Zhu Xiao, Dong Wang and Keqin Li

Through the zoom of the four out of the five partial GPS outages plotted in Figure 16, one can see that the proposed method also provides the good performance in terms of vehicle position prediction. The aforementioned comparison analysis about the adopted methods is relatively identical for partial GPS outages. Generally, based on B-SRGP (non-gn), the prediction accuracy during the partial GPS outages is better than the prediction accuracy during the full GPS outages.

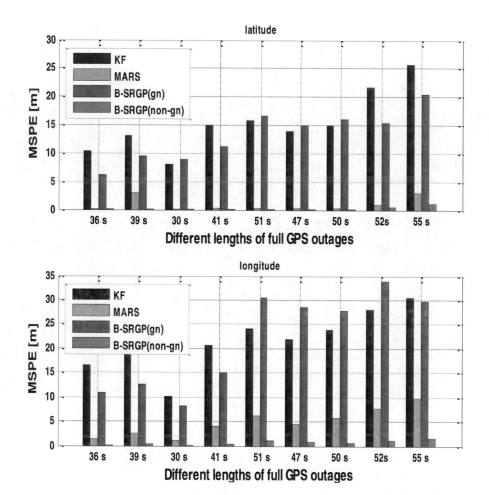

Figure 17. Comparison of the adopted methods in terms of MSPE related to the vehicle position prediction during the nine full GPS outages detected on latitude and longitude respectively.

Indeed, during the partial GPS outages, the INS and GPS data are complemented and the Bayesian inference uses prior distributions which allow the usage of more information. Besides, the selection of the sliding window also contributes to increasing the vehicle position prediction. For all the simulated free, partial, and full GPS outages considered in this study, the proposed B-SRGP algorithm is more efficient than other adopted methods for the vehicle position prediction when the measurement noises are non-Gaussian distributed.

Figure 17 plots the MSPE for all the adopted prediction methods based on the components of the vehicle position (latitude and longitude) during the full GPS outages taking into account the length of each outage.

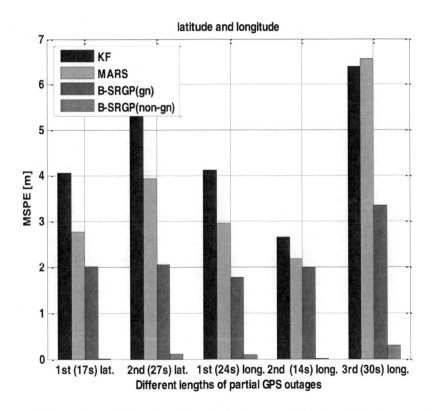

Figure 18. Comparison of the adopted methods in terms of MSPE related to the vehicle position prediction during the two partial GPS outages and the three partial GPS outages detected on latitude and longitude respectively.

Recall that low MSPE implies the high confidence for the prediction method. Specifically, the difference between B-SRGP (gn) and B-SRGP (non-gn) in terms of MSPE is related to the large measurement noise variance of B-SRGP (gn) which produces the large value of MSPE. The same observations are applied on the partial outages plotted in Figure 18. In addition, the MSP errors increase as the lengths of the outages increase. Indeed, let us consider for instance the three last full outages on longitude (see Figure 12) with 50, 52, and 55 seconds of length respectively. The MSP longitude errors are 0.55, 1.14, and 1.49 m respectively for B-SRGP (non-gn); 27.69, 33.90, and 29.8 m respectively for B-SRGP(gn); 5.70, 7.72, and 9.61 m respectively for MARS, and 23.91, 28.14, and 30.55 m respectively for KF.

Table 2. MSP position errors average during full GPS outage and partial GPS outage [m]

		B-SRGP (non-gn)	MARS	KF	B-SRGP (gn)
Full GPS outage	latitude	**0.26**	0.96	15.42	13.25
	longitude	**0.68**	4.78	21.64	21.90
Partial GPS outage	latitude	**0.07**	3.35	5.0	2.05
	longitude	**0.13**	3.89	4.39	2.37

These results are consistent because the full outage lengths where only data from INS are used to replace GPS information are not extremely large. This observation is also supported by authors in (Bauer 2013)who demonstrated that, in general, bridging by inertial sensors can be applied for only very short time.

In terms of averages, as it is stated in Table 2, it can be seen that the B-SRGP (non-gn) has the lower average of MSPE than other adopted prediction methods based on the nine full outages and five partial outages located on both the latitude and longitude. Although B-SRGP (gn) outperforms MARS in free and partial GPS outages (see Figure 18), we can notice from Table 1 that MARS is rather better than B-SRGP (gn) in terms of MSPE in full GPS outages. The main reasons are due to the good characteristics of MARS that has already been explained while B-SRGP (gn) suffers from the drawbacks related to the Gaussian measurement noise, especially when the measurement data are from INS only.

In sum, the above experimental results reveal that B-SRGP (non-gn) presents higher accuracy prediction and lower mean-squared prediction error (MSPE) for vehicle position when compared to the other adopted methods. Although our proposed method is reliable for predicting the vehicle position even in challenging environments, it faces some limitations.

Indeed, if the size of the measurement matrix tends to infinity, that is, $p \to \infty$ (or $n \to \infty$), this leads to the higher computational complexity of our proposed method which was not treated in this study. In other words, while MARS is suitable for handling fairly large dataset (Kayri 2010), the proposed B-SRGP is still not applicable to very large-scale problems due to its computational complexity. This implies that MARS would become better than our proposed method when large amount of data are taken into account.

SHORT-TERM TRAFFIC FLOW PREDICTION

Under non-stationary traffic condition including traffic peak or breakdown traffic point, short-term traffic flow data fluctuates greatly. The relationship among variables is mutual independent, time-varying, and non-linear which requires a well generalization method to fit the time-varying data in limited time. Near-future traffic flow data should be predicted timely based on historical and current time-varying data. Through the mining and learning of the changing trend of traffic flow and combing the current traffic flow data to predict the future traffic flow, a traffic flow forecast model is constructed.

Formally, given a traffic flow time sequence $\{X_1,...,X_t\}$ and some observed vehicle information (such as speed or lane occupancy) at a major road node, the goal for traffic forecasting is to predict the traffic flow $X_t + \Delta$ at the moment $t + \Delta$. There is no clear definition of short-term traffic flow. In general, Δ is less than fifteen minutes. Several traffic flow prediction methods are described in detail below.

ENSEMBLE REAL-TIME SEQUENTIAL EXTREME LEARNING MACHINE

A novel short-term traffic flow prediction method called Ensemble Real-time Sequential Extreme Learning Machine (ERS-ELM) with simplified single layer feed-forward networks (SLFN) structure under freeway peak traffic condition and non-stationary condition is proposed.

In ELM, weights connecting input layer and the hidden layer, as well as the bias values of hidden layer do not need to be tuned and can be randomly generated before learning, whereas the output weights are analytically determined using the least-square method, thus allowing a significant training time reduction (Wang et al. 2014).The structure of ELM is simple and the correctness has been verified in (Lan et al.2009; Huang et al. 2006).

In ELM, assume that there are N separately training sample data(X_i,T_i), where $X_i=[x_{i1},x_{i2},...,x_{in}]T \in R_n$ and $T_i=[t_{i1}, t_{i2},..., t_{im}]T \in R_m.x_{in}=[f_{k+1}, f_k, s_k, o_k, f_{k-1}]$ indicates a vector that represents the traffic variables including next moment traffic flow, current moment traffic flow, average traffic speed, traffic occupancy, and pre-moment traffic flow. And t_{im} represents the actual observed traffic data. The number of hidden nodes is $\tilde{N}$ and the activation function $g(x)$is defined as follow:

$$\sum_{i=1}^{\tilde{N}} \beta_i g_i(X_j) = \sum_{i=1}^{\tilde{N}} \beta_i g_i(w_i x_j + b_i) = f_i , \qquad (51)$$

where $w_i=[w_{i1},w_{i2}, ..., w_{in}]T$ denotes the weight vector between the input nodes and the hidden nodes, $\beta_i=[\beta_{i1},\beta_{i2},...,\beta_{im}]T$ represents the weight vector between the i-th hidden node and the output nodes, and $b_i$is the bias value of i-th hidden node.

In ERS-ELM, weights connecting the input layer and the hidden layer.The bias values of hidden layer do not need to be tuned and can be randomly generated before learning, whereas the output weights are analytically determined using the least-square method, thus reducing the training time in traffic flow prediction and optimizing the original ELM algorithm(Yibin et al.

2013). Three phases are included: the initialization phase, sequential learning phase, and predicting phase.

Initialization Phase

In ERS-ELM initialization phase, assuming that a small chunk of data $Z_0 = \{(x_t, t_i)\}_{i=1}^{N_0}$ is used to initialize the training phase. In ELM, the input parameter should also be assigned randomly including w_i(the weight vector between the input nodes and hidden nodes) as well as b_i(the bias value of the i-th hidden node). So, the initial hidden layer output matrix H_0in ERS-ELM can be calculated as

$$H_0 = \begin{bmatrix} g(w_1 x_1 + b_1) & \cdots & g(w_{\tilde{N}} x_1 + b_{\tilde{N}}) \\ \vdots & \ddots & \vdots \\ g(w_1 x_{N_0} + b_1) & \cdots & g(w_{\tilde{N}} x_{N_0} + b_{\tilde{N}}) \end{bmatrix}_{N_0 \times \tilde{N}}. \tag{52}$$

Considering the $rank(H) = \tilde{N}$ is required to ensure that ERS-ELM can receive the same learning performance as ELM, and $T_0 = [t_1, ..., t_{N_0}]_{N_0 \times m}^T$. Theory in (Yibin et al. 2013) have verified that $\beta = H^+T$ and $H^+ = (H^T H)^{-1} H^T$, so the initial output weight $\beta(0)$ can be estimated as follows:

$$\beta^{(0)} = (H_0^T H_0)^{-1} H_0^T T_0 = P_0 H_0^T T_0 \tag{53}$$

where $P_0 = (H_0^T H_0)^{-1}$ and $M_0 = H_0^T H_0 = P_0^{-1}$. We use K to indicate the number of chunks of data that is presented to the network.

Sequential Learning Phase

Then in the sequential learning phase, once the chunk of new traffic flow data arrived, the partial hidden layer output matrix H_{k+1} can be calculated by

$$H_{k+1} = \begin{bmatrix} g(w_1 x_{(\sum_{j=0}^{k} N_j)+1} + b_1) & \cdots & g(w_{\tilde{N}} x_{(\sum_{j=0}^{k} N_j)+1} + b_{\tilde{N}}) \\ \vdots & \ddots & \vdots \\ g(w_1 x_{\sum_{j=0}^{k+1} N_j} + b_1) & \cdots & g(w_{\tilde{N}} x_{\sum_{j=0}^{k+1} N_j} + b_{\tilde{N}}) \end{bmatrix}_{N_{k+1} \times \tilde{N}},$$ (54)

where the arrived and observed traffic flow are described as follows:

$$Z_{k+1} = \{(x_i, t_i)\}_{i=(\sum_{j=0}^{k} N_j)+1}^{\sum_{j=0}^{k+1} N_j}$$ (55)

$$T_{k+1} = \left[t_{(\sum_{j=0}^{k} N_j)+1}, \ldots, t_{\sum_{j=0}^{k+1} N_j} \right]^T_{N_{k+1} * m}$$ (56)

$$M_{k+1} = M_k + H_{k+1}^T H_{k+1}.$$ (57)

Then the output weight $\beta^{(k+1)}$ can be obtained by

$$\beta^{(k+1)} = \beta^{(k)} + K_{k+1}^{-1} H_{k+1}^T (T_{k+1} - H_{k+1}\beta^{(k)}),$$ (58)

and P_{k+1} can be deduced from P_0 as follows

$$P_{k+1} = P_k - P_k H_{k+1}^T (I + H_{k+1} P_k H_{k+1}^T)^{-1} H_{k+1} P_k.$$ (59)

Considering the equation

$$M_{k+1}^{-1} = (M_k + H_{k+1}^T H_{k+1})^{-1}$$
$$= M_k^{-1} - M_k^{-1} H_{k+1}^T (I + H_{k+1} M_k^{-1} H_{k+1}^T)^{-1} H_{k+1} M_k^{-1},$$ (60)

and set k = k+1 for the next chunk of new arriving data.

Predicting Phase

In the predicting phase, the number of ERS-ELM networks is L, with the same number of hidden nodes and same activation function for each hidden node. They train new arrival traffic flow data in each incremental step at the same time. For each ERS-ELM, the new next predicted flow data f_{k+1} should be put into the training dataset as the current training data and use it to predict f_{k+2} at the next moment, this process is repeated until there is no new data arrived. The final output of ERS-ELM is equal to the average of outputs of each ERS-ELM network which can be defined as follows

$$f(x_i) = \frac{1}{L} \sum_{j=1}^{L} f^{(i)}(x_i)$$

(61)

ERS-ELM reduces the distinction caused by randomly generated parameters since different individual ERS-ELM has different adaptive capacity to the new data. ERS-ELM could be more stable when number of ELM is larger.

Table 3. Information of each selected detectors

	ID	*LAT*	*LON*	*ABS PM*	*LANE*
I880S	400312	37.677442	-122.118925	0.32	123456
SR120E	1004510	37.783152	-121.233897	3.83	12
US101N	769346	34.156793	-118.407014	14.88	12345
I5N	1122528	32.897689	-117.225386	30.1	123456

EXPERIMENTS AND RESULTS

The proposed ERS-ELM method was applied to the dataset collected from the Caltrans Performance Measurement Systems (PeMS version 14.0) database, and traffic flow data from the PeMS were collected every 30 seconds from over 15000 individual detectors, which were deployed statewide in freeway systems across California. Table 3 shows the information of four randomly selected detector stations. The two non-stationary traffic scenarios are listed as follows:

- *Scenario one:* non-stationary traffic peak data from 2014-11-24 to 2014-12-1 aggregated all the lanes for each detector station were chosen. The first seven days data were selected as the training dataset, the remaining data on Monday were selected as the testing dataset, mainly used for predicting the two peak periods flow including 5:00-10:00AM and 5:00-10:00PM, the predicted interval is 5 minutes.
- *Scenario two:* non-stationary traffic flow data with breakdown or missing data points. For example, traffic flow data at detector SR120E with breakdown data during 5:20-6:05AM, 6:55-7:10PM and 8:45-9:00PM were chosen. The dataset is kept the same with scenario one setting.

The methods used for comparison include traditional MLP-NN, Wave-NN and ELM. As for MLP-NN, the number of hidden layers is set to three. The network training method is gradient descent with momentum adaptive learning back propagation algorithm, the learning rate is set to 0.3. As for the Wave-NN algorithm, the learning rate is set to 0.01.The number of iterations is limited to 100, and parameters are the same as in the MLP-NN algorithm. As for ELM, the number of hidden nodes is 20, the active function is sigmoid. Results are calculated by the mean function. Current flow, average speed and occupancy data as well as pre-flow data are evaluated. The size of sliding window is set to three. As for ERS-ELM, the number of hidden nodes is also 20, and the initial node is 15, the block is set as one, which means that once getting new arrived data it will update the ERS-ELM model to predict the traffic flow data at the next moment. The RBF activation function can map non-literary relationship and its stability is better. The number of ensemble times is set to 50. The size of sliding window is set to three. The training time consumption, absolute percentage error (APE), mean absolute percentage error (MAPE) and, test root mean square error (RMSE) are chosen to evaluate the performance of the proposed method (Jeong et al. 2013).

Table 4. Overall performance of each method in Scenario 1

	Detectors	MAPE(%)				RMSE			
		WAVE-NN	*MLP-NN*	*ELM*	*ERS-ELM*	*WAVE-NN*	*MLP-NN*	*ELM*	*ERS-ELM*
Peak 1	I880S	8.7933	9.5002	6.667	5.9757	57.0334	65.0806	42.9002	49.4
	SR120E	39.8126	59.2904	36.7602	27.4255	21.9608	22.0752	17.1771	15.3798
5:00-	US101N	7.1428	15.5685	11.8276	3.0448	52.5779	130.2714	78.5658	41.6985
10:00	I5N	13.6519	9.3961	8.5825	4.1345	40.19	37.4345	35.7999	35.2037
AM	*Average*	**17.35015**	**23.4388**	**15.959325**	**10.145125**	**42.940525**	**63.715425**	**43.61075**	**35.405**
Peak 2	I880S	0.1466	0.1583	0.111	0.0996	60.5215	57.262	45.4516	43.8701
	SR120E	0.6635	0.9882	0.6127	0.4571	15.6099	10.4343	9.4229	11.2517
5:00-	US101N	0.119	0.2595	0.1971	0.0507	58.1651	77.0903	61.7954	45.1576
10:00	I5N	0.2275	0.1566	0.146	0.0686	37.4555	36.8314	25.496	31.9461
PM	*Average*	**0.28915**	**0.39065**	**0.266725**	**0.169075**	**42.938**	**45.4045**	**35.541475**	**33.056375**

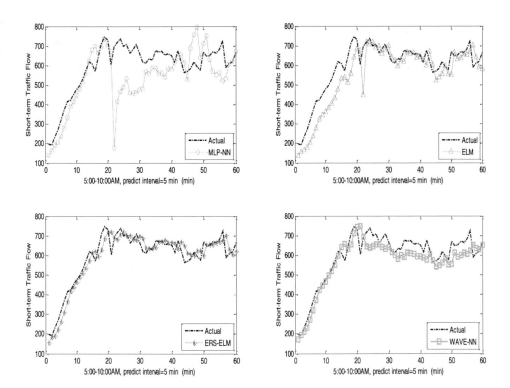

Figure 19. Actual and predicted value during peak1 5:00-10:00AM without breakdown data at detector US101N, Scenario 1.

Table 4 shows the MAPE value and RMSE value calculated by different prediction methods at the four detectors in scenario one after 50 times of running. Firstly, for each method at each detector, the smaller the MAPE value and RMSE value, the higher the prediction accuracy of the method. The MAPE value calculated by ERS-ELM is lowest and is nearly half of WAVE-NN's. The RMSE value calculated by ERS-ELM is lowest, except for detectors SR120E and I5N during peak 2. ERS-ELM's RMSE value is a little bit larger than ELM's. Secondly, we calculate the average MAPE value and RMSE value of the four detectors. ERS-ELM achieves the smallest error in both peak periods. Due to the random choice of bias, the performance of ERS-ELM may fluctuate sometime, but the average value of RMSE is acceptable.

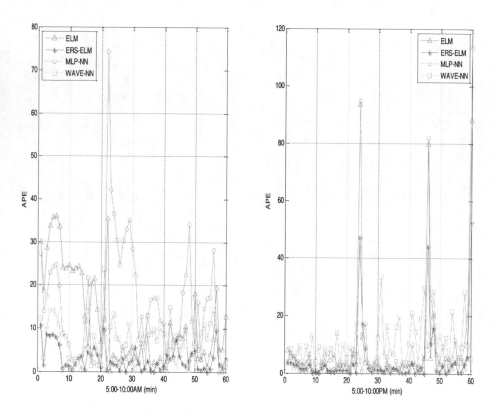

Figure 20. APE during peak1 at detector US101N and peak 2 with breakdown data at detector SR120E.

Figure 19 shows the actual and predicted value during peak 1. Figure 20 shows the APE value at detector US101N and peak 2 with breakdown data at detector SR120E. The predicted value calculated by ERS-ELM is relatively close to the actual traffic flow data trend, even during the fluctuated period such as 6:10-7:00AM, so the APE error is relatively small. ELM is the one with the next best performance. During 6:00AM to 7:30AM, the predicted values calculated by the WAVE-NN algorithm are far from the actual traffic flow data.

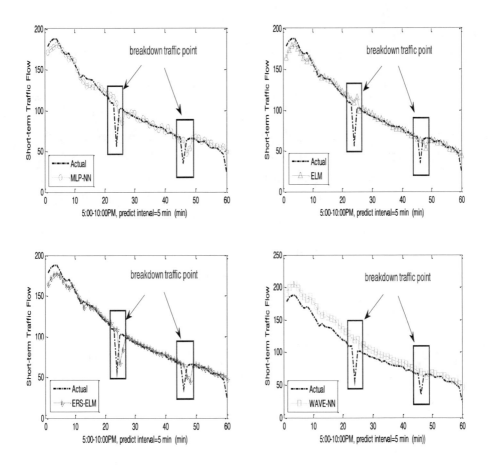

Figure 21. Actual and predicted value at detector SR120E with breakdown data during 6:55-7:10PM and 8:45-9:00PM, Scenario 2.

Figure 21 shows the actual and predicted values at detector SR120E with breakdown data such as 6:55-7:10PM and 8:45-9:00PM. According to the experiments, the proposed algorithm can learn the historical traffic flow data quickly and correctly. They get the predicted breakdown data by changeable slide-window and incrementally append predicted traffic data to make the next time prediction. For example, in Figure 21, the predicted value calculated by ERS-ELM is the only method that can adequately indicate the traffic breakdown points, while other three algorithms cannot reconstruct the traffic trend well. ELM is also the one with the next best performance. The WAVE-NN and MLP-NN algorithms can tell the trend, but are not adapted in a fluctuating condition.

Except for the prediction accuracy, the time consumption is another crucial factor that should be taken into account when the number of training data is large or the data suffering from non-stationary condition. The data quality also influences the number of iterations needed in MLP-NN. The MLP-NN method needs to be iterated thousands of time before reaching the required prediction accuracy. From Table 5, ELM and ERS-ELM algorithms are faster than MLP-NN when they get similar prediction accuracy. By training traffic data incrementally, ERS-ELM with simple prediction structure can further reduce the amount of time consumption.

Table 5. Time consumption of each method during training phase

	Time Consumption (s)			
	WAVE-NN	*MLP-NN*	*ELM*	*ERS-ELM*
I880S	58.2236	80.2	0.00284	0.0555
SR120E	56.0356	27.5	0.0225	0.0409
US101N	60.78826	134	0.0284	0.0605
I5N	60.1914	20.8	0.0203	0.0518
Average	**58.809715**	**65.625**	**0.0249**	**0.052175**

A NOVEL INCREMENTAL REGRESSION FRAMEWORK UNDER THE CONCEPT DRIFTING ENVIRONMENT

Method Overview

A novel incremental regression framework under the concept drifting environment is proposed, with ensemble learning as the major solution for updating the distribution representation. A great number of ensemble learning methods are designed for the classification problem. One such example is Learn++, which cannot be directly applied to regression due to the classification error rate computation process. Inspired by (Gao et al. 2010), we propose a regression to classification (R2C) framework that can train any ensemble algorithm on linear and non-linear SVRs. Then, R2C is integrated with Learn++ to solve the incremental learning, non-linearity, and non-stationarity problems of traffic volume prediction. Since distribution changes would cause the parameters of the seasonal model and other predictive models to shift, the proposed framework focuses on the real-time adjustment of the model parameters. There are three steps in the proposed framework. The first step is to construct classification datasets from the regression datasets. Then, by integrating them with the Learn++ algorithms, we can achieve an integration of classifiers. Finally, we construct a regression model upon the classifiers, which is updated incrementally. In the following, we detail the proposed general framework for learning the concept drift from non-stationary environments.

By moving the values of the response variables up and down within a small distance δ, a sample can be split into two. δ is an adaptive parameter, and the value is selected automatically and randomly between 0 and 1. Then, by assigning the two values with different labels, i.e., 1 and -1, a regression dataset can be transformed into a classification dataset. Assume that explanatory variables X are n-dimensional input features and y is the corresponding response variable involved in the regression problem.

The original regression samples are divided into a series of training datasets, such as $\mathbf{S}_R = \{(X_i, y_i) \mid X_i \in \mathcal{R}^n, y_i \in \mathcal{R}, i = 1, 2, ...\}$. Based on the parameter δ, each block regression sample is transformed as follows:

$$S^t = \{([X_i^T, y_i \pm \delta]^T, y_i^t) \mid [X_i^T, y_i \pm \delta]^T \in X, y_i^t \in Y, i = 1, 2, ..., m^t\} . \quad (62)$$

It is obvious that the classification hyperplane generated by dataset $\mathbf{S}_C$ is the same as the regression hyperplane generated by $\mathbf{S}_R$. By rewriting the norm vector as $W = [W_X^T, w_y]^T$ to separate the explanatory and response variables, the classifier separation hyperplane becomes

$$W_X^T X + w_y y + b = 0.$$

(63)

Then we train an ensemble learning algorithm with SVC as the base classifier on the generated dataset. The error rate to evaluate the prediction in each example (a block) is calculated as follows.

$$\varepsilon = \sum_{i=1}^{m} D(i)[h(X_i) \neq y_i]$$

(64)

The predictors with high error rates are discarded in the process. The regression plane (or a plane in the kernel space) is constructed incrementally with the remaining predictors and their weights $\omega \propto 1/\varepsilon$ of the ensemble learning. That is, the predictors in $\{h\}$ are weighted less if the error on the current block is large. The historical predictors are weighted in a manner to best fit the current data block as follows

$$\sum_k \omega_k W_{Xk} X + \sum_k w_{yk} \omega_k y + b = 0$$

$$\Leftrightarrow y = \frac{\sum_k \omega_k W_{Xk} X + b}{-\sum_k w_{yk} \omega_k}.$$

(65)

It is obvious that with the above framework, only linear regression models can be constructed. For non-linear regression, we propose adopting the polynomial kernel, RBF kernel, and sigmoid kernel. Unfortunately, the nonlinear kernel in traditional SVMs cannot be directly applied to our framework, as we need to solve an equation to obtain the response variables in the kernel space in the R2C framework. The details are given below.

When there is a kernel function, the ensemble separate planes are as follows:

$$\sum_k \omega_k C_k^T K(X_k^S, X) + b = 0 \text{,} \tag{66}$$

where K is the kernel function, and C is a dual coefficient calculated by quadratic programming in SVM trainings, and X^S are the support vectors obtained in each step of SVM trainings. Taking the polynomial example $K(X^S, X) = (\gamma(X^S)^T X + r)^d$, Eq. (67) can be transform into the following:

$$\sum_k \omega_k C_k^T (\gamma(X^S)^T X + r)^d + b = 0 \text{.} \tag{67}$$

By separating the explanatory and response variables, and denoting $X(i)$ as the i-th element of array X and $X^S(i, j)$ as the j-th element of the i-th support vector, with m as the length of C, we have

$$\sum_k \omega_k C_k^T \begin{pmatrix} (\sum_j X_k^S(1, j)X(j) + r)^d \\ \dots \\ (\sum_j X_k^S(n, j)X(j) + r)^d \\ (\sum_j X_k^S(n+1, j)y + r)^d \end{pmatrix} + b = 0 \tag{68}$$

$$\Leftrightarrow \sum_k \omega_k \left[(\sum_l C_k(l) \sum_j^{m-1} X_k^S(l, j)X(j) + r)^d) + (C_k(m) \sum_j X_k^S(n+1, j)y + r)^d) \right] + b = 0 \tag{69}$$

Both (68) and (69) are equivalent and can be solved analytically, and the final estimated value y is derived as follows.

$$y = \frac{\sqrt[d]{\frac{-b}{\sum_k \omega_k} - (\sum_l C_k(l) \sum_j X_k^S(l,j)X(j) + r)^d) - r}}{C_k(m)\sum_j X_k^S(n+1,j)} . \qquad (70)$$

Following the same reasoning, (67) can also be solved for the RBF kernel of $K(X^S, X) = \exp(-\gamma(X^S)^T X + r)$ or sigmoid kernel $K(X^S, X) = \tanh(\gamma(X^S)^T X + r)$.

The R2C-SVR algorithm is a passive drift detection algorithm. It can be solved in an environment that may change at any time orchange continually. It also allows for automatic concept drift and learns continually by constructing and organizing the knowledge base.

Experiments and Results

We performed experiments to validate our predictive model. The datasets were collected from the PeMS. In our experiments, we selected 4 detectors located on 4 freeways, as shown in Figure 22. Node 1 is a freeway that is infamous for its large-scale traffic jams. Node 2 is selected because its location is near crossing roads. Node 3 is a main road, and Node 4 is on a bridge. The time range selected is from 2016-11-6 to 2016-12-3, and the reason for this selection is that there was a serious traffic jam on 2016-11-23, which is a representative example of concept drift. The comparison metrics are the root mean squared error (RMSE) and the mean absolute percentage error (MAPE).

Inspired by the SARIMA model (Kumar et al. 2015), we perform the following preprocessing. Denote v_i as the traffic volume at time index i, where there are *week* time indexes in one week and *day* time indexes in one day, the dataset is constructed as

I405-N @ CA PM .11 (Abs PM 24.1)
District 7, Los Angeles County , City of Long Beach

(a) Note 1

I710-N @ CA PM 6.8 (Abs PM 1.8)
District 7, Los Angeles County , City of Long Beach

(b) Node 2

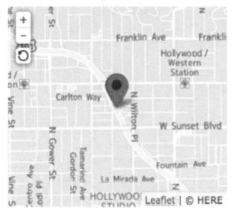

US101-N @ CA PM 6.37 (Abs PM 7.7)
District 7, Los Angeles County , City of Los Angeles

(c) Note 3

I80-E @ CA PM 6.33 (Abs PM 2.8)
District 4, San Francisco County , City of San Francisco

(d) Node 4

Figure 22. Traffic flow collection sites selected.

$$\{(X,y)\,|\,X=[v_{i-1}, v_{i-1}-v_{i-2}, v_{i-week}, v_{i-week}-v_{i-week-1}, v_{i-day}, v_{i-day}-v_{i-day-1}]^T, y=v_i\}.$$

For the purpose of evaluating the performances of the proposed methods under a concept drift and non-stationary environment, we select the day after the large traffic jam on 2016-11-23. Since traffic volume forecasting is based on the historical changes of traffic volume, the ability to recover from abnormal historical traffic volume is a direct representation of the ability to handle concept drift. The compared methods include the classical time series forecasting method SARIMA(Williams et al. 2003), the incremental learning method passive aggressive regression (PAR) (Geurts et al. 2016)and the ensemble learning method with extra trees (ET)(Arnold et al. 2015).

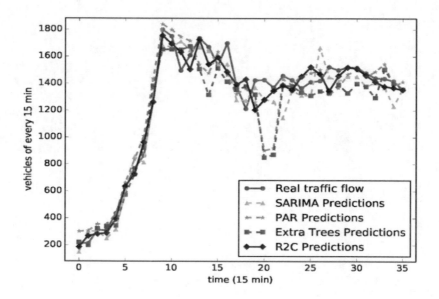

Figure 23. Comparisons of traffic volume prediction on 2016-11-24from 3:00 to 12:00.

On the previous day, i.e., 2016-11-23, there was a serious traffic jam beginning at 8:00 (time index 20). As time progresses to the next day, the statistical characteristics of the traffic volume data begin to change gradually, that is, concept drift occurs. The prediction results of the compared methods and the proposed method at 2016-11-24 from 3:00 to 12:00 are shown in Figure 23 and Figure 24. Figure 23 shows the comparison between the predicted values of the predictive models and real flow, and Figure 24 displays their real difference.

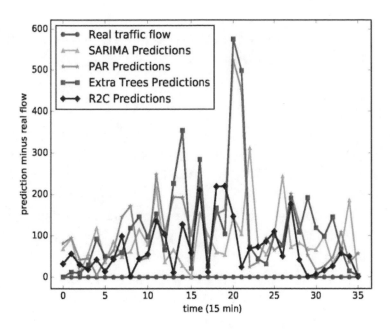

Figure 24. The difference between the prediction and the real traffic volume on 2016-11-24 from 3:00 to 12:00.

As shown in Figure 23 and Figure 24, the proposed method is more accurate than others in traffic volume forecasting under the non-stationary environment, and it is probable that concept drift occurs near time index 20. First, the proposed method can detect the drift and update the model adaptively to the current distribution, so the experimental results show that its values are closer to the true values than those of other methods. It is clear that both SARIMA and ET are influenced by this event, so their prediction from time index 20 decreases a lot (away from the actual flow). The main cause of this phenomenon is that the two methods cannot train the new data and do not update the models, which is due to their lack of ability to address abnormal data. Finally, because PAR is an incremental method, it can train the new data to update the training model, but it is not as powerful in detecting distribution changes. However, the effects of PAR are better than those of SARIMA and

ET based on Figure 23 and Figure 24. Additional qualitative comparisons are presented in the next subsection.

A NOVEL REGRESSION FRAMEWORK FOR SHORT-TERM TRAFFIC FLOW PREDICTION

Method Overview

A novel regression framework for short-term traffic flow prediction with automatic parameter tuning is proposed, with the SVR being the primary regression model for traffic flow prediction and the Bayesian Optimization being the major method for parameter selection. In training the SVR model, the traffic flow data collected in the past is used as input value, and the traffic flow at the current moment is regarded as the output value. For parameter settings, in traditional support vector regression, manual tuning usually cannot achieve good results. To improve this, we propose an efficient Bayesian optimization based method that selects parameters automatically.

There are two major parts that must be discussed when introducing Bayesian optimization. First, prior distribution expresses assumptions about the function being optimized, so it must be discussed in detail. Because of the flexibility and tractability of the Gaussian process, here we choose it as prior over functions. The second point is the acquisition function, which is used to construct a utility function to determine the next point to evaluate. Next, we review the Gaussian process prior and acquisition function.

Gaussian process (GP) offers a convenient and powerful prior distribution over the space of smooth functions. A Gaussian process is a set of infinite number of random variables, where any finite number of random variables are subject to a joint Gaussian distribution (Williams et al. 2016). The sampling points on an unknown function can be treated as random variables of GP, so it can be assumed that the function conforms to Gaussian process. The formula is expressed as

$$f(x) \sim GP(\mu(x), k(x, x^*))_.$$

(71)

The support and properties of Gaussian process are determined by its mean function $\mu(x)$ and covariance function $k(x,x^*)$. By selecting some of the sampling points of the unknown function as priori, we assumed that these points are part of the GP. That is to say, they are subject to multivariate Gaussian distributions. By using the properties of the multivariate Gaussian distribution, the mean and variance can be calculated. In particular, the squared exponential covariance function

$$k(x,x^*) = \exp\left(-\frac{1}{2}\|x-x^*\|^2\right) \tag{72}$$

is a popular choice for Gaussian process. Matérn kernel is another popular choice of the covariance function (Joy et al. 2017).

Let us initialize the sample points from the objective function. We would get $\{x_1, x_2, \ldots, x_t\}$ and the corresponding function values $\{y_1, y_2, \ldots, y_t\}$, where $y_{1:t} = f(x_{1:t})$. One could view that these data pairs $\{x_{1:t}, y_{1:t}\}$ are sampled from the prior Gaussian process with its mean value being zero and the covariance function $k(x_i, x_j)$. The function values $y_{1:t}$ thus follow a joint Gaussian distribution $N(0,K)$, and the covariance matrix is given by:

$$K = \begin{bmatrix} k(x_1,x_1) & \cdots & k(x_1,x_t) \\ \vdots & \ddots & \vdots \\ k(x_t,x_1) & \cdots & k(x_t,x_t) \end{bmatrix}, \tag{73}$$

where the diagonal values are 1 and this matrix is the positive definite matrix. Note that we are considering a noise-free environment. Also, recall that we have chosen the zero-mean function for simplicity.

In each iteration of our optimization task, we use the sampled data to fit the GP and obtain a posterior distribution from an external model. For each iteration, we use acquisition function combining the posterior distribution to decide the point x_{t+1} should be evaluated next. It has been proved that optimal optimization results can be obtained by using as little iteration as possible(Lin et al. 2008). For this arbitrary point, let us denote the value of the function as $y_{t+1} = f(x_{t+1})$. Likewise, $y_{1:t}$ and y_{t+1} also subject to a joint Gaussian distribution, by the properties of Gaussian processes we could get:

$$\begin{bmatrix} y_{1:t} \\ y_{t+1} \end{bmatrix} \sim N\left(0, \begin{bmatrix} K & k \\ k^T & k(x_{p+1}, x_{p+1}) \end{bmatrix}\right), \tag{74}$$

where $k = \begin{bmatrix} k(x_1, x_{t+1}) k(x_2, x_{t+2}) \cdots k(x_t, x_{t+1}) \end{bmatrix}$. Using the Sherman-Morrison-Woodbury formula (Rasmussen and Williams 2005), the posterior distribution of the objective function can be written as:

$$P(y_{t+1} | x_{1:t}, y_{1:t}) \sim N\left(\mu_t(x_{t+1}), \sigma_t^2(x_{t+1})\right) \tag{75}$$

Where

$$\mu_t(x_{t+1}) = k^T K^{-1} y_{1:t} \tag{76}$$

$$\sigma_t^2(x_{t+1}) = k(x_{t+1}, x_{t+1}) - k^T K^{-1} k. \tag{77}$$

So far, we have discussed the Gaussian process priors over the objective function, and how to update these prior knowledges according to the new observation.

The acquisition function is used to determine the next point to evaluate, thus it guides the search to the optimum. In Bayesian optimization, the acquisition function could be viewed as a surrogate function, which is easy to evaluate, to optimize the expensive functions. Maximizing the acquisition function is used to determine the next point at which to evaluate the objective function. That is, we wish to sample f at $\text{argmax}_x u(x|D)$, where $u(\cdot)$ is the generic symbol of the acquisition function.

There are several popular choices of acquisition function, which either using improvement based criteria or using confidence based criteria. The following are introduced separately. In the following, $\varphi(\cdot)$ and $\Phi(\cdot)$ represent the PDF and CDF of the standard normal distribution respectively. $x_{best} = \arg\max_{x_i \in x_{1:t}} f(x_i)$ denotes the current best observation. $\mu(x)$ and $\sigma(x)$ indicate the predictive mean function and predictive variance function of the objective function respectively.

PROBABILITY OF IMPROVEMENT(PI)

$$a_{PI}(x) = \Phi(\gamma(x)), \qquad \gamma(x) = \frac{f(x_{best}) - \mu(x)}{\sigma(x)}. \tag{78}$$

The strategy of PI is to maximize the probability of improving over the best current value (Kushner and Harold 1964). The attendant drawback is that this formulation is pure exploitation without exploration. As a result, an alternative acquisition function is Expected Improvement (EI), which chooses to maximize the expected improvement over the current best.

EXPECTED IMPROVEMENT(EI)

$$a_{EI}(x) = \begin{cases} \left(\mu(x) - f(x_{best})\right)\Phi(\gamma(x)) + \sigma(x)\varphi(x) & if \quad \sigma(x) > 0 \\ 0 & if \quad \sigma(x) = 0 \end{cases} \tag{79}$$

Another acquisition function is GP-UCB (Yee, Matthias, and Michael 2005), which uses the upper confidence bound of the GP predictive distribution.

GP UPPER CONFIDENCE BOUND(GP-UCB)

$$a_{UCP} = \mu(x) + k\sigma(x), \tag{80}$$

where k is used to balance exploitation against exploration. We will focus on the EI criterion, as it has been shown to be better-behaved than PI, but unlike GP-UCP, it does not require its own tuning parameter. In each iteration, we use the acquisition function to determine whether to exploit or to explore in next sampling. Eventually, the global maximum of the objective function can be obtained instead of the local maximum.

In addition, the objective of the SVR can be formulated by the expression below.

$$\min_{\omega,b,\xi_i,\xi_i^*} \frac{1}{2}\|\omega\|^2 + C\sum_{i=1}^{n}(\xi_i + \xi_i^*) \tag{81}$$

$$s.t \begin{cases} f(x)_i - y_i \le \varepsilon + \xi_i \\ y_i - f(x_i) \le \varepsilon + \xi_i^* \\ \xi_i \ge 0, \xi_i^* \ge 0, i = 1,2,...,n. \end{cases} \tag{82}$$

where ξ_i is the lower slack variable (ξ_i^* is the upper) subjecting to the ε-insensitive tube $y - f(x) \le \varepsilon$, the first term $1/2\|\omega\|^2$ is called the regularization term which can improve generalization of model. The second item is the experiential error. Parameter C is the regularization constant that determines the trade-off between believing risk and experiential error.

As mentioned above, it is difficult to achieve the optimal learning results by manually adjusting the SVR parameters. To improve this, we propose an effective support vector regression approach based on Bayesian optimization (BO-SVR) for short-term traffic flow prediction. SVR has three tuning parameters (C,ε,σ). The penalty coefficient C reflects the degree of penalty for the sample data beyond the pipe ε, and its value affects the complexity and stability of the model. The insensitive loss coefficient ε controls the width of the regression function's insensitive region of the sample data. C and ε determine the learning accuracy and generalization of this model. σ is the kernel parameter gamma. The larger the σ value, the smaller the structural risk, the smoother the function curve, but the greater the experiential risk. If the value of σ becomes smaller, the situation changes to the opposite. Thus, if the appropriate (C, ε, σ) combination can be selected, the exact and stable regression model can be obtained.

In order to optimize these parameters automatically, we could view such tuning as the optimization of an unknown black-box function $f(x)$. Specifically, we view such parameters (C, ε, σ) as independent variables of the function and view the generalization ability of SVR as dependent variables of the function. Here, the prediction accuracy (m) of traffic flow is regarded as a representation of generalization. Now, the objective function has been defined and satisfies the Bayesian optimization conditions. Combined with the Gaussian process and the acquisition function, the optimal combination of the parameters can be found after several iterations, thus the short-term traffic flow prediction modeled by SVR can be optimized.

Experiments and Results

In the experiments, the datasets are collected from the PeMS. In our experiment, we further aggregate the data into 15-min periods. Then, we select 4 typical detectors for the study since roads in these cases attract more attention for transportation research. As shown in Figure 25, Node 1 is a busy road section with large traffic flow, Node 2 is selected for its location being near cross roads, Node 3 is the main road, and Node 4 is on the bridge. The time range selected is from 2017-9-25 to 2017-10-9, from 2017-6-25 to 2016-7-9, and from 2017-9-25 to 2017-10-9. We use the data of the first two weeks as the training set and the remaining data as the testing set, mainly used for predicting the two peak periods flow including 5:00-10:00AM and 5:00-10:00PM, the predicted intervals are 5 minutes and 15 minutes.

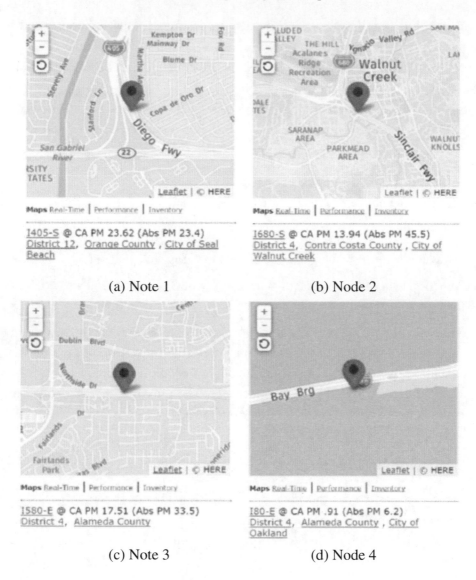

(a) Note 1

(b) Node 2

(c) Note 3

(d) Node 4

Figure 25. Select 4 typical detectors for study.

Evaluation Metrics: The conduction of time series forecasting is typically using error measures. To evaluate the effectiveness of our proposed model, we use three performance indexes, which are the mean absolute percentage error (MAPE), root mean square error (RMSE), mean absolute error (MAE). MAPE is a measure of prediction accuracy of a forecasting method. It usually expresses accuracy as a percentage, and we can get the prediction accuracy(m) by $m = 1 - MAPE$, which is also the optimization objective of the Bayesian Optimization in our model. The concept of MAPE is very intelligible and convincing, but the drawback is that it will cause serious distortion when the observation value is equal to zero or close to zero. Therefore, RMSE and MAE are chosen to measure the performance of the model in this chapter. RMSE is the square root of the average of squared errors. The effect of each error on RMSE is proportional to the size of the squared error, thus, larger error has a disproportionately large effect on RMSE. Consequently, RMSE is sensitive to outliers. MAE is relatively simple, which is mainly used to calculate the absolute average error of the prediction model.

Experimental Design: The performance of the proposed traffic flow forecast method (BO-SVR) is examined with two parts. The first set of experiments is designed to verify the effectiveness of the Bayesian Optimization for parameter selection of the traffic flow method based on support vector regression. The second group will be compared to other classical traffic flow prediction methods, with an aim of verifying the overall effectiveness of our proposed method.

As mentioned above, there are three parameters needed to be optimized in the SVR model we proposed, which are C, ε, and σ. The experiment is as follows: There are four pairs of experiments. Using the Bayesian Optimization to choose parameters of SVR and choose zero parameter at first, namely, without Bayesian Optimization, and then increase one parameter each time. As to the parameters which are not optimized, the parameter of C is set as 1 acquiescently. The ε is set as 0.1 and the σ is set as $1 / n\_features$. These models are trained and tested using the same traffic flow data set and the data is collected from the detector in point 4. The time range selected is from 2017-9-25 to 2017-10-9. We use the data of the first 2 weeks as the training set and the remaining day as the testing set, the predicted interval is 15 minutes. The prediction accuracy of these experiments is shown in Figure 26. In Figure 26, the abscissa represents the traffic flow forecasting model with different optimization parameters. The ordinate represents the prediction accuracy of each model. We can see in the last column, which represents that the model of all parameters is optimized, is over90% which outperforms all other models obviously. At the same time, we can also see that with the increase of optimization parameters, the accuracy of the model increases significantly. Therefore, it can be concluded that Bayesian optimization is effective for parameter selection of SVR-based short-term traffic flow prediction.

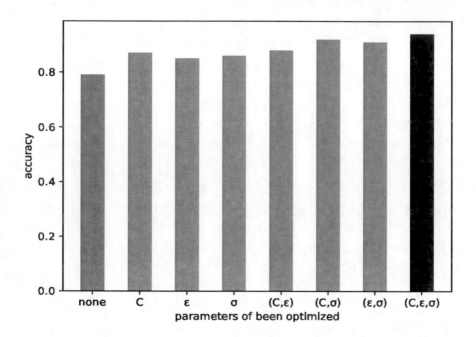

Figure 26. Performance comparison of using default parameters and using parameters selected by Bayesian optimization.

For the purpose of evaluating the performances of the proposed method, we compare the proposed method with other methods. The comparing methods include the classical time series forecasting method SARIMA, the ensemble learning method ERT and Adaboost, and Multi-Layer Perceptron (MLP-NN). As for MLP-NN, the number of hidden layers is set to five. The network training method is gradient descent with the momentum adaptive learning back propagation algorithm, the learning rate is set to 0.3. For all experiments, same training set and test set are used. Figure 27 to Figure 30 show the 15-minute flow forecast results of the proposed algorithm compared with other algorithms at peak hours 5:00 AM to 10:00 PM on node 1.

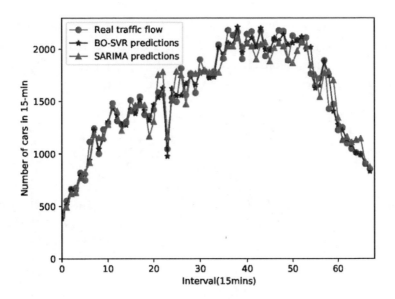

Figure 27. The 15-minute flow forecast results of the proposed algorithm compared with the SARIMA algorithm at peak hours 5:00 AM to 10:00 PM on Node 1.

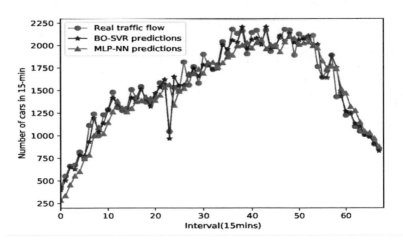

Figure 28. The 15-minute flow forecast results of the proposed algorithm compared with the MLP-NN algorithm at peak hours 5:00 AM to 10:00 PM on Node 1.

From the line chart, we can see that the real traffic flow value has a lowest point at time index 24. There may be a traffic jam at this point. It is obviously that only the proposed BO-SVR and SARIMA have predicted this sudden drop. Other methods including MLP-NN, ERT, and Adaboost are affected by this incident, so they deviate from the actual flow. SARIMA offsets a lot of real values at adjacent moments. Only the proposed method BO-AVR is capable of eliminating this influence.

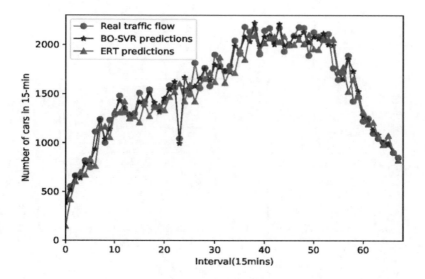

Figure 29. The 15-minute flow forecast results of the proposed algorithm compared with the ERT algorithm at peak hours 5:00 AM to 10:00 PM on Node 1.

In terms of the prediction accuracy, SARIMA forecasts are very unstable during peak periods. This is because that the SARIMA model parameters are fixed. The predicted value of MLP-NN has a significant backward relative to the true value. This may be the reason that inappropriate parameters have been chosen so that the model is not well informed of trends in the traffic flow time series. ERT apparently has a trend below the true value at the peak stage. Adaboost is also the case, and the effect is more unstable. The predictions of BO-SVR are the best, and it can see that the model has learned the inherent tendency of the traffic flow time series changes.

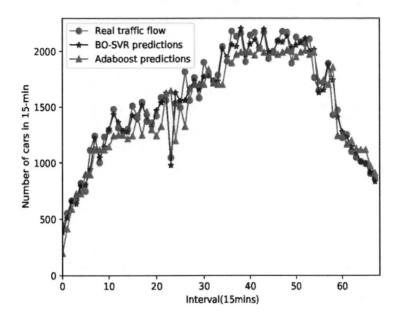

Figure 30. The 15-minute flow forecast results of the proposed algorithm compared with the Adaboost algorithm at peak hours 5:00 AM to 10:00 PM on Node 1.

Table 6. Performance Comparison of the MAPE for SARIMA, MLP-NN, ERT, Adaboost, and the proposed BO-SVR

		MAPE				
	Detectors	SARIMA	MLP-NN	ERT	Adaboost	BO-SVR
	Point 1	91.25	89.58	110.42	179.43	83.33
Peak time 5:00AM-10:00	*Point 2*	27.38	23.17	25.86	57.85	24.47
PM interval 5mins	*Point 3*	401.85	347.85	344.39	988.89	330.54
	Point 4	20.96	21.09	20.70	26.43	20.29
	Point 1	16.84	17.33	16.38	31.04	15.79
Peak time 5:00AM-10:00	*Point 2*	19.70	16.33	14.40	46.02	15.52
PM interval 15mins	*Point 3*	647.45	117.75	100.39	981.63	59.56
	Point 4	6.89	6.29	5.92	9.87	6.21

Table 6 to Table 8 show the MAPE, RMSE value and MAE value calculated by different prediction methods at four detectors after running 5 times. The forecast range is the peak time of October 9, 2017. The forecast period is divided into 5 minutes and 15 minutes. From the previous introduction of the evaluation metrics, we know that MAPE is the representative of the relative error of the predicted values, RMSE and MAE represent the absolute error. Since the test data set contained midnight time period, the number of vehicles at this time is almost zero. Therefore, the overall relative error of MAPE becomes large, especially at points 1 and 3. Similarly, compared to the 15-minute traffic flow time series, the 5-minute traffic flow is smaller. So, the relative error in the 5-minute prediction is greater, while the absolute error is smaller for RMSE and MAE. Therefore, it can be concluded from the longitudinal comparison of the tables that our experimental results are logical and representative.

Table 7. Performance Comparison of the RMSE for SARIMA, MLP-NN, ERT, Adaboost, and the proposed BO-SVR

		RMSE				
	Detectors	SARIMA	MLP-NN	ERT	Adaboost	BO-SVR
Peak time 5:00AM-10:00 PM interval 5mins	*Point 1*	47.56	49.32	51.95	21.10	43.03
	Point 2	71.29	74.53	80.48	108.74	73.67
	Point 3	70.41	68.07	68.06	92.48	66.16
	Point 4	46.32	49.84	46.66	53.52	47.54
Peak time 5:00AM-10:00 PM interval 15mins	*Point 1*	72.87	104.78	134.85	163.68	101.23
	Point 2	134.63	135.81	160.42	257.92	132.03
	Point 3	116.46	142.03	139.97	170.64	133.53
	Point 4	75.80	100.73	105.11	129.18	100.05

By comparing MAPEs horizontally, we find that the proposed BO-SVR predictions are better than other methods except for individual rows. Especially at point 3, the effect of improvement is obvious. This shows that BO-SVR is more suitable for the prediction of non-stationary sequence. In Table 7 and Table 8, BO-SVR is also significantly better than other algorithms, and the actual error can be reduced by about 3% to 5% than other optimal algorithms. By analyzing the predicted results from different perspectives, it could be concluded that the proposed BO-SVR method is effective for short-term traffic flow prediction.

Table 8. Performance Comparison of the MAE for SARIMA, MLP-NN ERT, Adaboost, and the proposed BO-SVR

		MAE				
	Detectors	SARIMA	MLP-NN	ERT	Adaboost	BO-SVR
	Point 1	31.59	36.58	37.50	38.37	30.95
Peak time 5:00AM-10:00	*Point 2*	62.21	45.54	51.85	87.02	46.19
PM interval 5mins	*Point 3*	47.36	44.69	45.26	70.97	43.01
	Point 4	31.05	31.84	31.59	39.98	30.30
	Point 1	53.47	76.98	100.69	128.14	71.47
Peak time 5:00AM-10:00	*Point 2*	111.86	103.23	111.17	213.98	100.13
PM interval 15mins	*Point 3*	96.94	104.66	97.15	139.85	96.43
	Point 4	60.0	71.81	71.52	102.72	71.63

Table 9. Performance Comparison of 15 Minute Traffic Flow Prediction at Point 1 Using Three Training Sets at Different Time Periods and Different Forecast Methods

SARIMA			MLP-NN			ERT			Adaboost			BO-SVR		
MAPE	RMSE	MAE	MAPE	RMSE	MAE	MAPE	RMSE	MAE	MAPE	RMSE	MAE	MAPE	RMSE	MAE
Training data set duration: 2017.9.25-2017.10.9														
16.84	72.87	53.47	17.33	104.78	76.98	16.38	134.85	100.69	31.04	163.68	128.14	15.79	101.23	71.47
Training data set duration: 2017.6.25-2017.7.9														
89.22	65.41	62.04	46.85	67.71	52.63	60.99	62.64	49.68	121.45	92.27	73.34	33.70	61.46	46.67
Training data set duration: 2016.9.25-2016.10.9														
20.36	88.01	69.26	14.25	81.44	68.57	12.68	87.87	72.87	21.97	112.12	100.18	13.63	81.91	67.71

In order to better verify the effectiveness of the algorithm and explore the traffic flow characteristics in different years and different seasons. We select three different phases of data sets for repeated experiments from 2016-9-25 to 2016-10-9, from 2017-6-25 to 2016-7-9 and from 2017-9-25 to 2017-10-9 respectively. Table 9 shows the comparison results of 15 minutes of traffic flow prediction at the point 1 using three training sets at different time periods and different forecast methods. The experimental results show that the proposed BO-SVR method can still achieve good results and has good generalization ability in different data sets.

UNDERSTAND TRAVEL REGULARITY

Travel regularity is an important aspect of trajectory research, especially the trajectory for private cars. The driving of private cars is based on personal travel needs, which is directly related to personal work, life and social activities. In most cases, it reflects the individual travel demand of people with long-term use of vehicles, there are frequent driving modes, showing the characteristics of regular travels. Their travels are often concentrated to specified areas such as residential areas, workplaces, and hotspots, such regularity reflects individual's different sociodemographic attributes (Goulet-Langlois et al. 2017). Two methods to understand travel regularity are described in detail as follows.

TRAJECTORY AGGREGATION DETECTION ALGORITHM BASED ON TRAJECTORY CLUSTERING

Method Overview

The aggregation characteristics of the trajectory are of great importance for understanding the travel behaviors of private car users. Motivated by the fact that people are likely to visit and stay at a few places frequently, while the parking spaces of private cars might be ever-changing, for example, the private car owners who do not buy a fixed parking space need to find available parking places all the time. It will lead to various size of aggregation areas.

The point set where vehicle stayed has spatial aggregation. To capture this, we design DBSCAN (Ester et al. 1996) based trajectory clustering method to find out the possible area that the vehicles visit in specified time periods.

There are two significant parameters, i.e., the minimum threshold of vehicle's neighbor radius V_{nr} and the minimum number of location points denoted by M_{np}. All these M_{np} points are located within the circle whose center is the vehicle and the radius is V_{nr}. We have two types of points in the cluster, core points (the GPS points which contains more than M_{np} in the radius V_{nr}) and border points (those points are not core point, but they are less than V_{nr}

from other core points). Some definitions associated with our method are as follows (Ester et al. 1996).

Definition 1. (V_{nr}- Neighborhood of a point). Let $N_{V_{nr}}(p)$ be the V_{nr}-Neighborhood of a point p, which is represented by the equation $N_{V_{nr}}(p) = \{q \in D \mid dist(p,q) \leq V_{nr}\}$. $dist(p,q)$ represents the distance from point p to point q, and the set of points is denote by D.

In this definition, the distance between two points needs to be calculated. The trajectory consists of a series of points which is represented by the latitude and longitude. In our study, the Haversine formula (Ghazi et al. 2016; Das et al. 2014) is employed to calculate the distance between two sampling points. Let (*LonA, LatA*) and (*LonB, LatB*) denote the latitude and longitude coordinates of point *A* and point *B*, respectively. Based on the Haversine formula, we obtain.

$$dist(A, B) = r.c, \tag{83}$$

where *dist(A,B)* is the distance between two spherical coordinate points *A* and *B*. *r* is the radius of the earth. Here we use the average radius of the Earth, that is, 6371:004 km.

$$c = 2 * \tan^{-1}(\sqrt{a(1-a)}) \tag{84}$$

$$a = \sin^2(\frac{\Delta lat}{2}) + \cos(\Delta lat) + \sin^2(\frac{\Delta lon}{2}) \tag{85}$$

$$\Delta lat = LatA - LatB \tag{86}$$

$$\Delta lon = LonA - LonB. \tag{87}$$

Definition 2. (directly density-reachable). Given V_{nr} and M_{np}, a point p is directly density-reachable from a point q if $p \in N_{V_{nr}}(q)$ and $\left| N_{V_{nr}}(q) \right| \geq M_{np}$.

Definition 3. (density-reachable). For a sample set D, if there is an object chain $P_1, P_2, ..., P_n$, $P_1 = q, P_n = p$, $P_i \in D \ (1 \leq i \leq n)$, and P_{i+1} is directly density-reachable from P_i, then the object p is density-reachable from the object q with respect to V_{nr} and M_{np}.

Definition 4. (density-connected). If there is an object $O \in D$ such that objects p and q are all accessible to O with respect to V_{nr} and M_{np}, then object p is density-connected with respect to V_{nr} and M_{np}.

By applying the proposed TAD algorithm, we can obtain two or three aggregation areas where people often visit and stay for a certain period of time. To further study the aggregation effect and understand the travel behaviors, we proposed a classification method such as to define the regularity of private cars and divide it into three types, namely A-Regularity, B-Regularity and Irregularity.

Definition 5. (travel regularity). Let $R > 0$ denote the number of areas detected by applying the proposed TAD algorithm to the i-th vehicle's trajectory within a given time period,

$$R = \begin{cases} 2, & \textit{vehicle i is } A - \textit{Regularity} \\ 3, & \textit{vehicle i is } B - \textit{Regularity} \\ \textit{else,} & \textit{vehicle i is irregularity} \end{cases} \tag{88}$$

A-Regularity is for people live in a work or home life. They travel back and forth in residential areas and the working place every day. Perhaps they would like to go to the supermarket shopping occasionally, while this does not affect our experimental results.

By applying the proposed TAD algorithm to the trajectory, if we can find two clustered areas, which represent the two places or areas the driver appears and stays frequently during certain time period, then the vehicle will be defined as A-Regularity. We regard a vehicle as B-Regularity when three areas are detected.

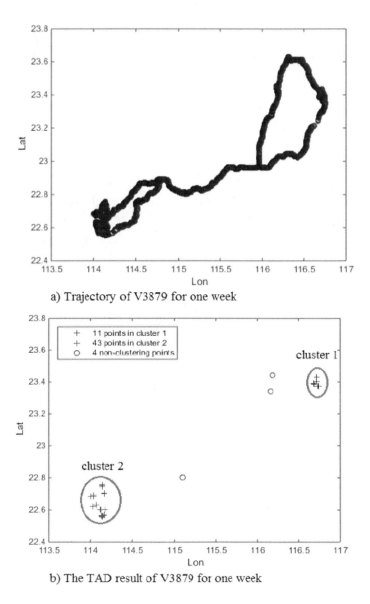

a) Trajectory of V3879 for one week

b) The TAD result of V3879 for one week

Figure 31. Results of V3879 from Jan 4, 2016 to Jan 8, 2016.

For other cases, people are irregular travelers, such as the car owners who have a partnership with the popular software platform Uber. They carry passengers in different areas, and they are likely to stay in different areas at different times. We can presume that only one clustered area can be detected, namely the residential area. In addition, people who have more than three areas to visit are also defined as irregular, since they don't act regular travel in daily life.

Experiments Based on Real-World Trajectory Data

In this section, in order to understand travel regularity, we apply the proposed TAD algorithm to trajectory data which is collected from 1000 vehicles randomly selected in Shenzhen. Each vehicle has trajectory points for six months from February 2015 to January 2016. Taking into account the situation that some people have a weekend holidays, the weekend trajectory data is filtered out. People's travel is mainly occurred in the time of going to or getting off works, and the working time is generally from 9:00 am to 5:00 pm in Shenzhen. Therefore, we further extract the data whose stay time is not between 9:00 am and 5:00 pm from the vehicle trajectory information. In this regard, a vehicle is with either A-Regularity or B-Regularity when each aggregation area has at least 8 points if we investigate the regularity in a week.

Figure 31 presents an example of a vehicle 'V3879', in which the data is collected within a week, from January 4, 2016 to January 8, 2016. Note that the weekends are excluded. Figure 31 (a) gives the trajectory of 'V3879'. Figure 31 (b) shows the experimental result of the stay positions by applying the proposed TAD algorithm. As seen in Figure 31 (b), there are 11 points in cluster 1. By examining the time of these points, which are around 6:00 am to 9:00 am in the morning, we can tell that cluster 1 indicates the residential area. For cluster 2, we obtain 43 points, which can be reasonably inferred as the working area. Hence, this vehicle has a regular trip and can be categorized as A-Regularity according to Definition 5. The other points, such as the black circle points in Figure 31 (b), are not clustered. This indicates that the owner may occasionally leave home to some places, for instance, driving to supermarket for shopping or leisure sites for entertaining with friends after work. In addition, when we observe the point located around ($N22°6'$, $E115°1'$), which is an isolated point while the stay points should appear in pair, hence this demonstrates there must be positioning errors during the data collecting process.

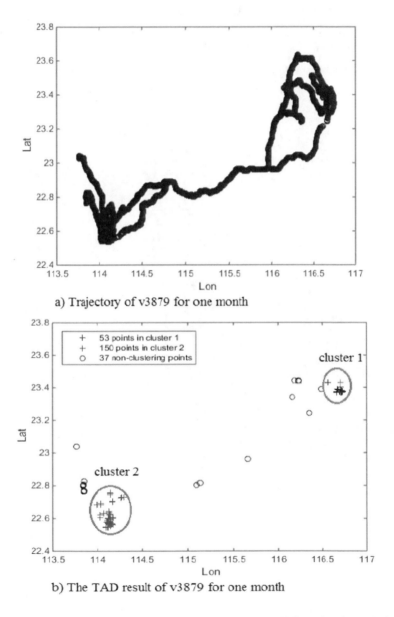

a) Trajectory of v3879 for one month

b) The TAD result of v3879 for one month

Figure 32. Results of V3879 from Jan 4, 2016 to Jan 31, 2016(weekends excluded).

Figure 32 shows the trajectory for a month, the TAD algorithm results of 'V3879', in which the data is collected from January 4, 2016 to January 31, 2016. There are 20 working days in January 2016. If 'V3879' is with A-Regularity in this month, two aggregation areas should be able to detect and each has at least 32 (40*0.8) points, which are verified based on the results in Figure 32. To sum up, according to the results in Figure 31 and Figure 32, consistent results can be obtained that this vehicle has regular driving behavior (namely A-Regularity) not only in a short term, but a week or a month.

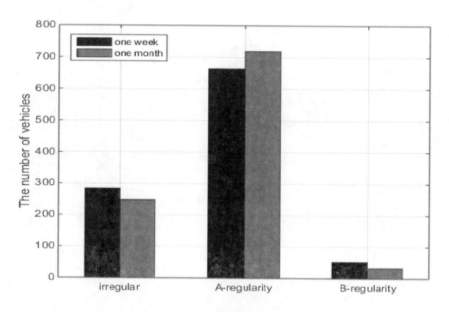

Figure 33. Results of 1000 vehicles.

To further study the private cars' regularity, we randomly select 1000 private cars to evaluate the performance of our proposed method. We use the data in December 2015. The results are shown in Figure 33. We first look into the result in one week which is from December 7 to December 11. There are 716 vehicles with regular traces wherein 664 vehicles are with A-Regularity and 52 vehicles are with B-Regularity, respectively. The remaining 284 vehicles are defined as irregular.

MEASURING THE DISTANCE BETWEEN SPARSE TRAJECTORIES BASED ON TRANSFER LEARNING AND IERP

A novel method which combines transfer learning with IERP (Improved Edit distance with Real Penalty) algorithm, which is a novel algorithm to measure the distance between sparse trajectories is proposed.

Definition 1. (Regular travel behavior). Regular travel behavior is defined as the trajectories of individual private car that are similar in fixed period of time on workdays.

According to Definition 1, the private cars, which have trajectories in a particular period of workdays, can be divided into two types: regular travel and Irregular travel. After having studied the notion of regular travel behavior, we define the relevant concepts to study the regular travel behavior of private cars.

Definition 2. (Vehicle trajectory). A vehicle trajectory is a sequence of positions, $Traj = < p_1, p_2, ..., p_k >$, where $p = (lat_i, lon_i, t_i), 1 \le i \le k$, t_i is a timestamp for a snapshot, $\forall_{1 \le i < k}, t_i < t_{i+1}$, and (lat_i, lon_i) are 2-D locations denoted by latitude and longitude.

Definition 3. (Trajectory similarity). The trajectory similarity between two vehicle trajectories A and B is denoted as

$$simlarity(A, B) = 1 - \frac{Dist(A, B)}{\sqrt{length(A) \cdot lenght(B)}},$$ (89)

where $length(A)$, $lenght(B)$ are the length of A and B, respectively, $Dist(A, B) = \sum_{i,j} Dist(p_i, r_j)$, where $Dist(p_i, r_j) = \sqrt{(lon_{p_i} - lon_{r_j})^2 + (lat_{p_i} - lat_{r_j})^2}$ is the distance between two points p_i (p_i is a point in trajectory A) and r_j (r_j is a point in trajectory *B*). According to Definition 3, the distance between two trajectories is the negative factor of the trajectory similarity, which means that 'the shorter the distance, the greater the similarity'.

In our trajectory dataset, some trajectory points have large deviation, for example, the trajectory points of vehicles on the road is drifted into the sea. We remove these over-deviated points. As shown in Figure 34, our method of regular travel behavior mining for private cars consists of three main steps. In step 1, we construct the trajectory similarity matrix for each individual private car. The trajectory similarity matrix of each vehicle is constructed by calculating the similarity between any two trajectories. In step 2, we reduce the feature matrix dimension of the trajectory similarity matrix to enhance the performance of the model and improve the calculation speed. These two steps are for the expression and extraction of trajectory similarity features. In step 3, we utilize the idea of transfer learning to train a classifier, which is used to mine the private cars with regular travel behavior.

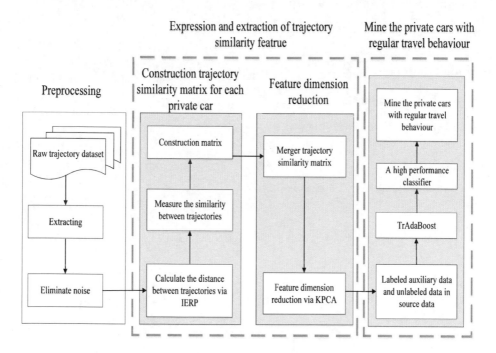

Figure 34. The proposed trajectory processing framework.

Construction of the Trajectory Similarity Matrix

Edit Distance with Real Penalty (ERP)(Chen et al. 2004) provides the cost function of insert, delete and replace operations, but it uses the gap between the operation element and a fixed value as the penalty value for the insert and delete operations, which lacks the rationality of spatial significance. Since our collected trajectories are spatiotemporal, we propose the IERP algorithm, which is an improvement of ERP, to measure the distance of sparse trajectories. We use appropriate cost function to calculate the penalty value of insert, replace, and delete in IERP, and its use on sparse trajectories has a good performance.

In our algorithm, suppose that we have two sparse trajectories, P and R, and all operations are conducted on P. That is, the distance between P and R is the cost of converting P to R. In IERP, the penalty value of editing operations between P and R are defined in (90), and the penalty value of insert, delete, and replace operations are defined in (91), (92), and (93) respectively.

$$IERP(P,R) = \begin{cases} \sum_{j=1}^{n} insert(r_j) & m = 0 \\ \sum_{i=1}^{m} delete(p_i, \varphi) & n = 0 \\ \min\{IERP(\text{Rest}(P), \text{Rest}(R)) + replace(p_m, r_n), & \text{others} \\ \quad IERP(\text{Rest}(P), R) + delete(p_m, r_n), \\ \quad IERP(P, \text{Rest}(R)) + insert(r_n) \} \end{cases} \quad (90)$$

$$insert(r_j) = \begin{cases} Dist(r_j, r_{j-1}), Dist(r_j, r_{j-1}) > \varepsilon, j > 1 \\ Dist(r_2, r_1), \quad Dist(r_2, r_1) > \varepsilon, j = 1 \\ 0, \quad\quad\quad\quad Dist(r_j, r_{j-1}) \le \varepsilon \end{cases} \quad (91)$$

$$replace(p_i, r_j) = \begin{cases} Dist(p_i, r_j), Dist(p_i, r_j) > \varepsilon \\ 0, \quad\quad\quad Dist(p_i, r_j) \le \varepsilon \end{cases} \quad (92)$$

$$delete(p_i,r_j) = \begin{cases} Dist(p_i,r_j), & Dist(p_2,p_1) > \varepsilon, r_j \neq \phi \\ Dist(p_i,p_{i-1}), Dist(p_2,p_1) > \varepsilon, r_j = \phi, i > 1 \\ Dist(p_2,p_1), & Dist(p_2,p_1) > \varepsilon, r_j = \phi, i = 1 \\ 0, & Dist(p_2,p_1) \leq \varepsilon \end{cases} \tag{93}$$

Let ε to be the length of the unit. If the Euclidean distance between two points is less than ε, the cost is considered to be0. We get the trajectory distance between P and R by using the *IERP* algorithm, since there is a small difference between the cost of converting P to R and the cost of converting R to P, we use (94) to obtain the minimum distance of the two trajectories P and R.

$$MinimumIERP(P,R) = \min(IERP(P,R), IERP(R,P)) \tag{94}$$

According to Definition 3, we can get the similarity between the two trajectories, in which we use $MinimumIERP(A,B)$ instead of $Dist(A,B)$ in Definition 3. Therefore, the similarity of sparse trajectory between P and R is represented as

$$similarity(P,R) = 1 - \frac{MinimumIERP(P,R)}{\sqrt{length(P) \cdot lenght(R)}}. \tag{95}$$

Feature Dimension Reduction

In our method, we obtain the trajectory similarity matrix in the first step. For each private car, we obtain a matrix of $D*D$. For the value of each row, which represents the similarity between the trajectories, and redundant features exist. To enhance the performance of the model and improve the calculation speed, we reduce the feature dimension of the trajectory similarity matrix.

The classical Principal Component Analysis (PCA) (Wold et al. 1987) is one of the most commonly used methods for dimension reduction, but it is a linear algorithm that cannot extract non-linear structures. The kernel function mapping method provides a method to solve the problem. Here, we adopt the KPCA method, which is a non-linear method which maps the original input data space into the high-dimensional feature space using non-linear functions, which has been proved in (Goel et al. 2017) that it has good performance in dimension reduction. If we are dealing with the trajectory of N private cars, we combine N matrices together to form $N*D$ matrices, where $N_1 = N*D$. We set the dataset of the input space as follows.

$$S=\{similarity_1, similarity_2, ..., similarity_{N_1}\}, \tag{96}$$

where $similarity_i$ is the dimensional vector, and $N*D$ is the number of samples in the dataset. Then, KPCA using non-linear functions Φ as in (95) maps data to the Hilbert Spaces in high dimensions and performs the PCA transformation in the high-dimensional feature space.

$$\begin{cases} \Phi: \ R^d \to F \\ simy_i \mapsto \Phi(simy_i) \end{cases}, \tag{97}$$

where F is feature space, and the dataset of the feature space can be obtained by the mapping function and as follows.

$$\Phi(simy) = (\Phi(simy_1), \Phi(simy_2), ..., \Phi(simy_{N_1})). \tag{98}$$

According to (Goel et al. 2017), we reduce the feature dimension of the trajectory similarity matrix. We expect to have a composite similarity eigenvalue with other trajectories for each trajectory of the private car, therefore, we obtain a $N_1 \times 1$ matrix. Then, we transform the matrix into a $N*D$ matrix as S_{new}, for each private car with D eigenvalues. S_{new} is the sample data that will be classified and recognized in the third step.

Mining the Private Cars with Regular Travel Behavior

In our study, there are only two cases when private cars have regular travel behavior, the problem can be translated into binary classification problems. TrAdaBoost is evolved from the AdaBoost (Schapire.2003) algorithm. In a training set that contains source training data and auxiliary training data, TrAdaBoost will adjust the weight of the training sample.

Formally, D_s is the source instance space, which is target space, D_d is the auxiliary instance space, l_s and l_d are the sizes of D_s and D_d, respectively. c is a function mapping from D_d to Y, Y is the set of category labels, and $c(x)$ returns the label for the instance x. The test dataset is denoted as $S = \left\{ \left(x_i^t \right) \right\}$, where, the size of the test dataset S is k, $x_i^t \in D_s \left(i = 1,\ldots,k \right)$, which is unlabeled. The training dataset $T \subseteq \{D \times Y\}, D = D_s \cup D_d$. Among them, $D_d = \left\{ \left(x_i^d, c\left(x_i^d \right) \right) \right\}$, where $x_i^d \in D_d \left(i = 1,\ldots,n \right)$. The combined training dataset $T = \left\{ \left(x_i, c\left(x_i \right) \right) \right\}$ is defined as

$$
x_i = \begin{cases} x_i^d, i = 1,\ldots,l_d \\ x_i^s, i = l_d + 1,\ldots,l_d + l_s \end{cases}.
$$
(99)

The learning goal of TrAdaBoost is to train a classifier, which reduce the classification error on the test dataset as much as possible, and then combine with the automatic adjustment weight mechanism to obtain the final hypothesis. Therefore, the classification error and weight adjustment need to satisfy both (100) and (101).

$$
\xi_t = \sum_{i=l_d+1}^{l_d+l_s} \frac{w_i \left| h_t \left(x_i \right) - c\left(x_i \right) \right|}{\sum_{i=l_d+1}^{l_d+l_s} w_i^t}
$$
(100)

$$w_i^{t+1} = \begin{cases} w_i^t \beta^{|h_t(x_i)-c(x_i)|}, i = 1, \dots l_d \\ w_i^t \vartheta^{-|h_t(x_i)-c(x_i)|}, i = l_d+1, \dots l_d+l_s \end{cases}, \tag{101}$$

where h_t is a hypothesis, ξ_t is the error rate of h_t on D_d, w is a weight, t is the number of iterations. The parameter β from $Hedge(\beta)$ (Freund et al. 1997)is used to decrease the weight of harmful instances, and $\beta \in [0,1]$. The parameter ϑ is used to decrease the weight of instances that are misclassified. Their weights are being reduced by a factor of $\vartheta^{-|h_t(x_i)-c(x_i)|}$ in each iteration if a source domain instance is mistakenly predicted. Thus, in the next round, the misclassified source domain training instances will have less effect on the learning process. After several iterations, the auxiliary training instances that fit the source domain better will have larger training weights, while the auxiliary training instances that are not similar to the source domain will have lower weights. The instances with large training weights will help the learning algorithm to train better classifiers.

Experimental Results

In this section, we evaluate the performance of the proposed method based on private cars trajectory collected from real urban environment. By designing a low-cost trajectory collection device (Xiao et al. 2018), our team has collected a trajectory dataset of more than 40,000 private cars from the Pearl River Delta region in China, worked with Shenzhen Maigu Technology Co., Ltd. Among them, 10,637 private cars are from Shenzhen.

In our work, trajectory data of 500 private cars in Shenzhen were selected, which have travel trajectories during the period (January 11 - 15, 2016) between 7:00 am and 10:00 am. For our experiments, each data point contains a timestamp, it records the latitude and longitude during the recording time. In our experiment, we marked label for 100 private cars that constitutes the auxiliary data in our method. The source data comes from 100 unlabeled data, which is our target data, and 300 samples are used as test samples. We manually mark 100 private cars and carry out sampling confidence calculation (Proschan. 1953). In our 100 samples, 34 are regular travel samples, marked as $Y=1$. And the remaining 66 are irregular travel samples, marked as $Y=0$. We calculate the sample mean from this sample, $\bar{x}=\dfrac{1\times34+0\times66}{n}=0.34$, and

sample variance $s^2=\dfrac{34\times(1-0.34)^2+66\times(0-0.34)^2}{n-1}=0.2267$, $s=0.4761$, where n

is the number of samples selected. With n removal, the biased estimates of the population variance are obtained. After extensive simulation, it can be concluded that using $n-1$ as the divisor is the smallest deviation estimate. We use the calculated s as an estimate of the overall variance, $\sigma\approx s$. Thus, we can use the values calculated by the sample we have chosen to estimate the value in the sampling distribution of the sample mean, $\mu_{\bar{x}}=\bar{x}$, and standard

deviation, $\sigma_{\bar{x}}=\dfrac{\sigma}{\sqrt{n}}$. Of course, such estimates are biased, with a margin error

$=2\sigma_{\bar{x}}$. The larger the number of samples selected, the smaller the margin error. We find that $\mu_{\bar{x}}=0.34$, $\sigma_{\bar{x}}=0.04761$, and margin error = 0.09522. To sum up, we have 95% confidence that the overall average is between 0.24478 and 0.43522, and the margin error = 0.09522. In our method, we study the regular travel behavior of private cars within two weeks of working days, we choose two weeks of trajectories on working days to verify the efficiency of the proposed method, that is to say, we set the value of $D=10$.

In order to evaluate the performance and effectiveness of the proposed method, the well-performed learning method including Support Vector Machine (SVM)(Burges 1998), Multilayer Perception Classifier (MLPC) (Zanaty 2012), Label Propagation (LP) (Chapelle Oet al. 2006) and Transductive Support Vector Machines (TSVM) (Thorsten Joachims. 1999)are applied in the experiments. In this experiment, each method is modeled and predicted under the same conditions. We use SVM as the basic learner in our method, and we use the Gaussian radial basis function as the kernel function, and Bayesian optimization to select parameters for each classification model to optimize the classification performance. To compare the performance of different methods, classification accuracy (*Acc*), precision (P), recall ratio (R) and $F1$ are used as the evaluation metric in this chapter, where $F1$ is the comprehensive indicator of P and R . The four metrics are described in (102), (103), (104) and (105), respectively.

$$Acc = \frac{TP + TN'}{N'} \tag{102}$$

$$P = \frac{TP}{TP + FP} \tag{103}$$

$$R = \frac{TP}{TP + FN'} \tag{104}$$

$$F1 = \frac{2 \cdot (P \cdot R)}{(P + R)}, \tag{105}$$

where N' represents the total number of private cars, which are to be tested. *TP* denotes the number of private cars with regular travel behavior and correctly judged. *TN'* indicates the number of private cars without regular travel behavior and correctly judged. *FP* is the number of private cars without regular travel behavior but mis-judged, and *FN'* is the number of private cars with regular travel behavior but mis-judged. After conducting six randomized sample experiments, the results of our proposed method, SVM, MLPC, LP, and TSVM are as follows.

Table 10 shows the results of the classification accuracy using SVM, MLPC, LP, TSVM, and the proposed method on real private cars' trajectory dataset. According to the results of our method, it achieves the highest classification accuracy (96.7%) among all methods considered. The lowest classification accuracy (70%) is obtained by MLPC. Figure 35 shows the minimum, maximum, and average classification accuracy using SVM, MLPC, LP, TSVM, and the proposed method. It is obvious that the proposed method is 15.5%, 12.2%, 17.8%, and 10% better than SVM, MLPC, LP, and TSVM on average, respectively. The reason is that these supervised learning methods only use labeled training samples, however, the amount of training data is not enough to train a high-precision classifier. The classifiers trained by label propagation is unstable, and randomness is the fatal flaw of the algorithm. Thus, the proposed method can obtain better classification accuracy.

Table 10. The classification accuracy of different methods

	SVM	MLPC	LP	TSVM	Proposed
Group 1	83.3%	86.7%	76.7%	83.3%	**96.7%**
Group 2	73.3%	93.3%	80%	90%	**96.7%**
Group 3	86.7%	80%	86.7%	93.3%	**96.7%**
Group 4	76.7%	86.7%	80%	83.3%	**93.3%**
Group 5	86.7%	86.7%	73.3%	90%	**96.7%**
Group 6	76.7%	70%	73.3%	76.7%	**96.7%**

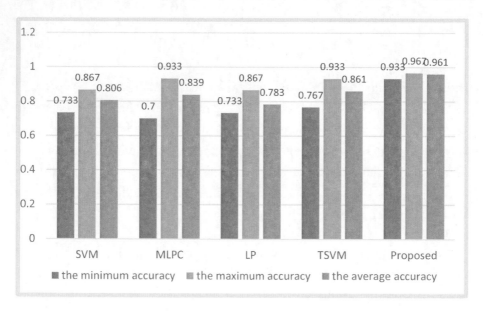

Figure 35. The minimum, maximum, and average classification accuracy of different methods.

TRAJECTORY DATA MINING OF URBAN PRIVATE CARS

During daily driving, people stop their car when they reach certain locations (L. Xiang et al. 2016), which are normally preset destinations such as locations of offices, shopping areas, residential areas, and frequented public areas. In addition, cars stay and wait for certain periods of time since people will spend time at these places with their own purposes before they come back to their cars and drive away. This travel behavior can be referred to as stop-and-wait (SAW) and can be observed when studying the SAW points originating from the trajectory data. Therefore, people driving in the city exhibit a specific SAW behavior and hence generate aggregation effects (Alfeo et al. 2018), which in turn lead to a form of hot zones in urban environments. Furthermore, the SAW data offer valuable information for understanding the development of urban traffic, thereby being capable of benefiting trajectory data mining and urban computing (Feng et al. 2017; Zheng et al. 2014).

To investigate the aggregation effect, Let S_u^d denote the SAW data for the d-th day on the u-th week, where $S = \{(x_i, y_i, t_i)\}_{i=1,\cdots,n}$, with n being the number of SAW points; x_i and y_i denote the latitude and longitude of the i-th SAW point, respectively; and t_i is the timestamp for (x_i, y_i). The goal is to obtain the predicted density distribution for S_u^{d+1}, namely, $\hat{P}_u^{d+1}$, by learning from the historical SAW data. To achieve this, we construct a three-dimensional kernel density estimation model (3D-KDE) wherein the historical SAW data sequence S, i.e., $\{S_u^d, S_u^{d-1}, \cdots, S_u^{d-(T-2)}, S_{u-1}^{d+1}\}$, is taken as the first input. Then, we obtain the corresponding output of the 3D-KDE model, namely, the density distributions P, which can be expressed as $\{P_u^d, P_u^{d-1}, \cdots, P_u^{d-(T-2)}, P_{u-1}^{d+1}\}$. Apart from the historical SAW data, the predicted $\hat{P}_u^{d+1}$ is highly related to the weight coefficients $E = \{e_0, \cdots, e_{T-1}\}$, which are used to evaluate the impact of each day's SAW data in the training sequence. To achieve the optimal E, we use the SAW data of the previous week to conduct the parameter selection. In detail, the second input is denoted as $\{S_{u-1}^{d+1}, S_{u-1}^d, \cdots, S_{u-1}^{d-(T-2)}, S_{u-2}^{d+1}\}$, where $S_{u-1}^{d+1}, S_{u-1}^d, \cdots, S_{u-1}^{d-(T-2)}, S_{u-2}^{d+1}$ can be used to obtain the predicted SAW density distribution $\hat{P}_{u-1}^{d+1}$ with the weight parameter, and the true SAW data S_{u-1}^{d+1} can be used to generate the true density distribution P_{u-1}^{d+1}. During the parameter training process, we use the MIW-PSO method to select the optimal E, which is used to guarantee that $\hat{P}_{u-1}^{d+1}$ is sufficiently close to the true P_{u-1}^{d+1} based on the output $\{P_{u-1}^{d}, P_{u-1}^{d-1}, \cdots, P_{u-1}^{d-(T-2)}, P_{u-2}^{d+1}\}$ of the 3D-KDE model. The details of the proposed approach are presented below.

3D KERNEL DENSITY ESTIMATION

The proposed approach based on three-dimensional kernel density estimation (3D-KDE) is designed to identify the spatio-temporal correlation in the SAW data, which can be used to generate a density surface from a set of SAW points located in a geographic space at any time. The approach can be implemented by bandwidth selection and kernel functions. Generalized SAW data in S contain three basic elements (x, y, t), namely, the latitude and longitude of the SAW points, and the timestamp. For each voxel given the coordinates (v_x, v_y, v_t) in the considered 3D region, its density is estimated based on the surrounding points (x_j, y_j, t_j) in S, the transform formula can be expressed as

$$f(v_x, v_y, v_t) = \frac{1}{nh_s^2 h_t}\Sigma_{j|d_j<h_s,t_j<h_t} k_s(\frac{v_x-x_j}{h_s}, \frac{v_y-y_j}{h_s}) \times k_t\left(\frac{v_t-t_j}{h_t}\right), \quad (106)$$

where f is the SAW density estimate function at the location (v_x, v_y, v_t), n is the number of SAW points, and h_s denotes the spatial bandwidth that forms a circle, whereby the temporal bandwidth h_t extends the circle to a cylinder based on the spatio-temporal orthogonal relationship, as shown in Figure 36. The spatial and temporal distances between the voxel and the SAW points are given by d_j and t_j respectively. More importantly, the Gaussian kernel is used in defining the functions k_s and k_t. Based on the Silvermans' rule of thumb, the computational formula of the bandwidth selection for the Gaussian kernel can be written as follows (B. W. Silverman. 1998):

$$\begin{cases} h_s = (\frac{4\widehat{\sigma_1}^5}{3n})^{\frac{1}{5}} \\ h_t = (\frac{4\widehat{\sigma_2}^5}{3n})^{\frac{1}{5}} \end{cases} \tag{107}$$

where $\widehat{\sigma_1}$ and $\widehat{\sigma_2}$ are the standard deviation of the SAW data in the space and time dimension, respectively.

To improve the comparability, we extract some fixed sampling voxels using an appropriate set of d_x, d_y, d_t to divide the considered 3D region into $n_a \times n_b \times n_c$ space-time cubes, as shown in Figure 36. Therefore, the value of the center point in the cube (see the red voxel in Figure 36) can be computed by (108) based on (106) and (107):

$$P_{a,b,c}(x_{ma}, y_{mb}, t_{mc}) = f(x_0 + \frac{2a-1}{2} \times dx, y_0 + \frac{2b-1}{2} \times dy, t_0 + \frac{2c-1}{2} \times dt), \tag{108}$$

where $P_{a,b,c}$ represents the SAW density estimation for the space-time cube in (a, b, c) from the 3D region, $(x_{ma}, y_{mb}, t_{mc})|_{a=1,\cdots,n_a, b=1,\cdots,n_b, c=1,\cdots,n_c}$ denotes the coordinates of the space-time cube center, and (x_0, y_0, t_0) represents the starting point.

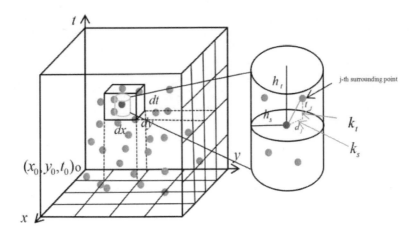

Figure 36. The computation of 3D-KDE in a space-time cube.

OPTIMIZATION OF PARAMETER SELECTION IN SAW DENSITY PREDICTION

To achieve the optimal E, we use the SAW density distributions of the previous week to forecast the known density distribution through the weight parameter training. In detail, let $E = \{e_0, \cdots, e_{T-1}\} \in [0,1]$ denote the vector of weight coefficients; e_0 represents the weight value of P_{u-2}^{d+1}; and the remaining $e_1, e_2, \cdots, e_{T-1}$ are the corresponding weights of $P_{u-1}^k|_{k=d,d-1,\cdots,d-(T-2)}$. Then, the predicted distribution can be denoted as

$$\hat{P}_{u-1}^{d+1} = e_0 \times P_{u-2}^{d+1} + \sum_{i=1}^{T-1} e_i \times P_{u-1}^{d-i-1}. \tag{109}$$

Selecting the optimal E requires a huge amount of computing work, especially for multi-dimensional and multi-modal data. To obtain the weights with high precision and fast convergence, we design the MIW-PSO method to achieve the appropriate E to minimize the differences between the true and predicted SAW density distributions. The proposed MIW-PSO method prevents the algorithm from falling into a local optimum and achieves fast convergence. The search space is shaped by all possible values from the T-dimensional vector within the range $[0,1]$. The m-th particle of the swarm can be denoted as $E_m = \left(e_{m_0}, e_{m_1}, \cdots, e_{m_{T-1}}\right)$ to represent its position change. $lbp_m = (lbp_{m_0}, lbp_{m_1}, \cdots, lbp_{m_{T-1}})$ is used to record the best position of the m-th particle; the best position of all particles is $gbp_g = (gbp_{g_0}, gbp_{g_1}, \cdots, gbp_{g_{T-1}})$. Similarly, the velocity can be described by another T-dimensional vector $V_m = (v_{m_0}, v_{m_1}, \cdots, v_{m_{T-1}})$. According to (J. Kennedy et al. 1995), the update formula of the velocity and position at the k-th iteration of each particle can be written as

$$V_{m_t}^{k+1} = w_m^k V_{m_t}^k + C^1 R^1 \left(lbp_{m_t}^k - E_{m_t}^k\right) + C^2 R^2 \left(gbp_{g_t} - E_{m_t}^k\right) \tag{110}$$

$$E_{m_t}^{k+1} = E_{m_t}^k + V_{m_t}^{k+1}, \tag{111}$$

where m denotes the m-th particle of the swarm and $m = 1, \cdots, N_{size}$ and N_{size} is the total number of particles. The w_m^k in MIW-PSO is not a fixed constant and changes continuously to balance the global and local search ability for the purpose of speeding up the convergence and avoiding local optima. Using the KL divergence (Do et al. 2002), we define a fitness function to measure the distribution difference between the true SAW density distribution and the predicted SAW density distribution. Combining (108) and (109), the fitness function can be written as

$$F(E_m^k) = \sum_{a,b,c} P_{u-1}^{d+1}(a, b, c) \log \frac{P_{u-1}^{d+1}(a,b,c)}{\hat{P}_{u-1}^{d+1}(a,b,c)|_m^k}. \qquad (112)$$

Based on the aforementioned definitions and formulas, the weight for the m-th particle at the k-th iteration can be deduced as

$$w_m^k = \frac{1}{(1+e^{-\Delta F})} \qquad (113)$$

$$\Delta F = F(E_m^{k-1}) - F(E_m^{k-2}), \qquad (114)$$

where the value of w is limited to the range of $[0,1]$, and it is randomly generated when k is less than 2. Meanwhile, ΔF denotes the change in the fitness value. When ΔF is relatively large, it increases the global search ability. When the value of ΔF is relatively small, this leads to an enhancement in the local search capability.

Experimental Results and Analysis

In order to evaluate the performance of the SAW prediction of the proposed 3D-KDE method, we conduct experiments based on the real world trajectory data. We adopt the device in(J. Kennedy et al. 1995) to obtain the positions of vehicles and read the driving status information through the on-board diagnostics (OBD) interface. Moreover, this device can record the position and time when the vehicle starts and shuts off the engine. We have thus generated a large-scale trajectory dataset, for which the trajectory data of more than 50,000 private cars were collected from two cities in China: Shenzhen and Shanghai. We perform the experiments using the SAW data for five weeks (excluding weekends and public holidays) from Shenzhen and Shanghai. Specifically, as shown in Table 11, we select the SAW data collected from the Luohu District, Shenzhen, from January 4, 2016 to February 5, 2016 and the SAW data from the Pudong District in Shanghai from June 25, 2018 to July 27, 2018 to perform the experiments.

Table 11. The selected SAW data from Shenzhen and Shanghai

City	Time(five weeks excluding weekends	Latitude	Longitude
Luohu District, Shenzhen	Jan.4,2016 ~Feb.5,2016	22.50 ~22.65	114.0 ~114.2
Pudong District, Shanghai	Jun.25,2018 ~Jul.27,2018	31.10 ~31.26	121.54~121.68

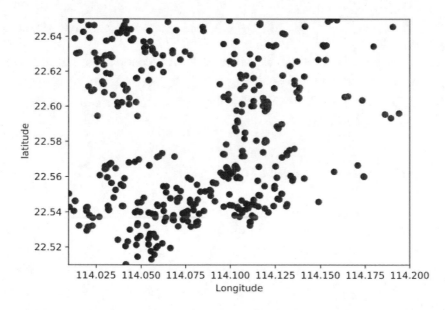

Figure 37. Original SAW data from the Luohu District, Shenzhen, 8:00 January 27, 2016.

Figure 37 presents the original SAW points at 8:00 on January 27, 2016 for the Luohu District, Shenzhen. Figure 38 presents the results of the density distribution of the SAW behaviors, in which we normalize the density value to within [0,1] to avoid stretching effects. The bar graph on the right in Figure 38 is used to describe the varying of the SAW density. The deep green denotes an area with a high SAW density, which indicates the aggregation effect and the forming of a hot zone. The deep red represents a low SAW density for the corresponding areas. Comparing Figure 37 with Figure 38, we determine that the proposed 3D-KDE performs well in showing the SAW density of private cars and captures the aggregation effect in selected areas.

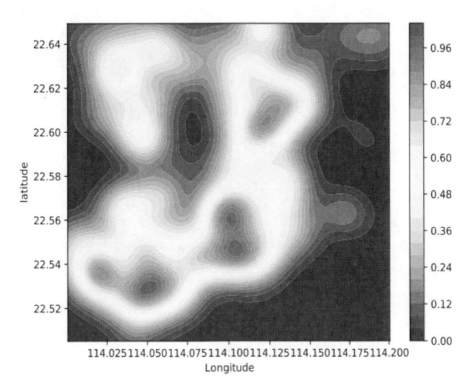

Figure 38. Density estimation of SAW data from Luohu District, Shenzhen, 8:00 January 27, 2016.

APPENDIX

Estimation of the Noise Sequences α$_t$ and β$_t$ Using MLE

In this chapter, the method of maximum likelihood estimation (MLE) is adopted since for a given set of data and underlying statistical model, the MLE picks out the set of values of the model parameters that maximizes the likelihood function. This method is the most attractive; thanks to its large sample or asymptotic properties comparing to other statistical estimation techniques (Boccato et al. 2012; Mazucheli, Louzada, and Ghitany 2012). Moreover, MLE is a good estimator for the unknown but fixed parameters. For each sample D, consider $\theta(b)$, a parameter value at which $L(\theta \mid b)$ attains its maximum as a function of θ. A maximum likelihood estimator of the parameter θ based on D is $\hat{\theta}(b)$. Then, if the likelihood function is C^2, the MLE of θ_i are the θ_m's which maximize the likelihood function and the necessary conditions for an optimum are given by:

$$\frac{\partial}{\partial \theta_i} L(\theta_1, \theta_2, \ldots, \theta_m \mid b_1, b_2, \ldots, b_N) = 0 , \qquad \text{(A-1)}$$

where $b = [b_1, b_2, \ldots, b_N]^T$ and $\theta = [\theta_1, \theta_2, \ldots, \theta_m]^T$ and such that

$$L(\theta_1, \theta_2, \ldots, \theta_l \mid b_1, b_2, \ldots, b_N) = \prod_{i=1}^{n} f(b_i \mid \theta_1, \theta_2, \ldots, \theta_m) \qquad \text{(A-2)}$$

is the joint PDF (or likelihood) of $D_1, \ldots, D_N$. Moreover, MLE is equivalent to the maximum log-likelihood estimation which is provided by:

$$l(\theta_1, \theta_2, \ldots, \theta_l \mid b_1, b_2, \ldots, b_N) = \sum_{i=1}^{n} log(f(b_i \mid \theta_1, \theta_2, \ldots, \theta_m)) . \qquad \text{(A-3)}$$

Let now determine the MLE of the mean μ_t under the assumption that g and σ_t are known. According to (5), (6), (A-1), (A-2), and (A-3), the estimated mean $\hat{\mu}_\alpha$ of μ_α and $\hat{\mu}_\beta$ of μ_β are given by:

$$\hat{\mu}_\alpha = \sum_{i=1}^{N} \left| \alpha_t^i - \mu_t \right|^{\frac{1-g}{1+g}}, \text{ for } g \neq \{-1,1\} \tag{A-4}$$

$$\hat{\mu}_\beta = \sum_{i=1}^{N} \left| \beta_t^i - \mu_t \right|^{\frac{1-g}{1+g}}, \text{ for } g \neq \{-1,1\}. \tag{A-5}$$

Proof of (A-4) and (A-5). By applying (A-2), the likelihood function is then computed as follows:

$$L = \prod_{i=1}^{N} p\left(\alpha_t^i, g, \sigma_t, \mu_t\right) = p\left(\alpha_t^1, \alpha_t^2, ..., \alpha_t^N\right)$$
$$= \left(M(g)\sigma_t^{-1}\right)^N \exp\left[-J(g)\left|\frac{\alpha_t^1 - \mu_t}{\sigma_t}\right|^{\frac{2}{1+g}}\right] \exp\left[-J(g)\left|\frac{\alpha_t^2 - \mu_t}{\sigma_t}\right|^{\frac{2}{1+g}}\right] ... \exp\left[-J(g)\left|\frac{\alpha_t^N - \mu_t}{\sigma_t}\right|^{\frac{2}{1+g}}\right]$$
$$= \left(M(g)\sigma_t^{-1}\right)^N \exp\left[\sum_{i=1}^{N}\left(-J(g)\left|\frac{\alpha_t^i - \mu_t}{\sigma_t}\right|^{\frac{2}{1+g}}\right)\right] \tag{A-6}$$

The maximum log-likelihood estimation is defined as:

$$\log L = l = N\log\left(M(g)\sigma_t^{-1}\right) - \sum_{i=1}^{N}\left(J(g)\left|\frac{\alpha_t^i - \mu_t}{\sigma_t}\right|^{\frac{2}{1+g}}\right). \tag{A-7}$$

The MLE of the means μ_α and μ_β related to the process and measurement noises are obtained by using (A-1):

$$\frac{\partial}{\partial\mu}(log\,L) = \frac{\partial}{\partial\mu}\left[N\,log\big(M(g)\sigma_t^{-1}\big) - \sum_{i=1}^{N}\left(J(g)\left|\frac{\alpha_t^i - \mu_t}{\sigma_t}\right|^{\frac{2}{1+g}}\right)\right] = 0 \qquad \text{(A-8)}$$

$$\Leftrightarrow \frac{\partial}{\partial\mu}\left[\sum_{i=1}^{N}\left(\left|\frac{\alpha_t^i - \mu_t}{\sigma_t}\right|^{\frac{2}{1+g}}\right)\right] = \sum_{i=1}^{N}\left(|\alpha_t^i - \mu_t|^{\frac{1-g}{1+g}}\right) = 0$$

Then, the estimated means $\hat{\mu}_\alpha$ and $\hat{\mu}_\beta$ of μ_α and μ_β are provided by $\hat{\mu}_\alpha = \sum_{i=1}^{N}|\alpha_t^i - \mu_t|^{\frac{1-g}{1+g}}$, and $\hat{\mu}_\beta = \sum_{i=1}^{N}|\beta_t^i - \mu_t|^{\frac{1-g}{1+g}}$, for $g \neq \{-1,1\}$ respectively as stated in (A-4) and (A-5) **Q.E.D.**

Moreover, the estimated variances $\hat{\sigma}_\alpha^2$ and $\hat{\sigma}_\beta^2$ of σ^2, under the assumption that g and μ_t are known are given by:

$$\hat{\sigma}_\alpha^2 = \frac{2J(g)\sum_{i=1}^{N}|\alpha_t^i - \hat{\mu}_\alpha|^{\frac{2}{1+g}}}{N(1+g)}, \text{ for } g \neq -1 \qquad \text{(A-9)}$$

$$\hat{\sigma}_\beta^2 = \frac{2J(g)\sum_{i=1}^{N}|\beta_t^i - \hat{\mu}_\beta|^{\frac{2}{1+g}}}{N(1+g)}, \text{ for } g \neq -1 \qquad \text{(A-10)}$$

Proof of (A-9) and (A-10). By using (A-1), the MLE of the variances σ_α^2 and σ_β^2 of σ^2 related to the process and measurement noises is as follows:

$$\frac{\partial}{\partial\sigma_t^2}(log\,L) = \frac{\partial}{\partial\sigma_t^2}\left[N\,log\left(M(g)(\sigma_t^2)^{-\frac{1}{2}}\right) - \sum_{i=1}^{N}\left(\frac{J(g_t)}{(\sigma_t^2)^{\frac{1}{1+g}}}|\alpha_t^i - \mu_t|^{\frac{2}{1+g}}\right)\right] = 0$$

$$\Leftrightarrow \frac{\partial}{\partial\sigma_t^2}\left[N\,log\,M(g) - \frac{N}{2}log\,\sigma_t^2 - \frac{J(g)}{(\sigma_t^2)^{\frac{1}{1+g}}}\sum_{i=1}^{N}\left(|\alpha_t^i - \mu_t|^{\frac{2}{1+g}}\right)\right] = 0$$

$$\text{s.t. } B = \begin{bmatrix} G_t & \Delta(\hat{X}_{t-1}) \\ \Delta(\hat{X}_{t-1})^T & \Sigma_\xi \end{bmatrix} \geq 0, \quad \text{(A-17)}$$

where $\Sigma_\xi = diag\left(1 - \xi_1 - \xi_2, 0, \xi_1 \breve{R}_{t-1}^{-1}, \xi_2 \breve{Q}_{t-1}^{-1}\right)$ and

$$\Delta(\hat{X}_{t-1}) = \Phi_t E_{t-1} - L_t \left(\Psi_{t-1} X_{t-1} - \Psi_{t-1} \hat{X}_{t-1}\right) + I_{n\times 1} - L_t I_{p\times 1}.$$

Proof. Consider that the estimation error is given by $E_{t-1} = X_{t-1} - \hat{X}_{t-1}$. Then, from (2) and (4) one can get the following formulation:

$$\begin{aligned} E_t &= \Phi_t X_{t-1} + \breve{\alpha}_{t-1} - \Phi_t \hat{X}_{t-1} - L_t \left(\Psi_{t-1} X_{t-1} + \breve{\beta}_{t-1} - \Psi_{t-1} \hat{X}_{t-1}\right) \\ &= \Phi_t \left(\hat{X}_{t-1} + E_{t-1}\right) + \breve{\alpha}_{t-1} - \Phi_t \hat{X}_{t-1} - L_t \left(\Psi_{t-1} X_{t-1} + \breve{\beta}_{t-1} - \Psi_{t-1} \hat{X}_{t-1}\right). \\ &= \Phi_t E_{t-1} - L_t \left(\Psi_{t-1} X_{t-1} - \Psi_{t-1} \hat{X}_{t-1}\right) + \breve{\alpha}_{t-1} - L_t \breve{\beta}_{t-1} \end{aligned}$$

Let us set the vectors $\vartheta = \left[1, -1, -\breve{\alpha}^T, \breve{\beta}^T\right]^T$ and $\Delta(\hat{X}_{t-1}) = \Phi_t E_{t-1} - L_t \left(\Psi_{t-1} X_{t-1} - \Psi_{t-1} \hat{X}_{t-1}\right) + I_{n\times 1} - L_t I_{p\times 1}$ then,

$$E_t = \Delta(\hat{X}_{t-1})\vartheta. \quad \text{(A-18)}$$

Inequality (20) is therefore equivalent to:

$$\begin{aligned} & E_t E_t^T \leq G_t \\ \Leftrightarrow\ & \Delta(\hat{X}_{t-1})\vartheta \vartheta^T \Delta(\hat{X}_{t-1})^T \leq G_t \quad \text{(A-19)} \\ \Leftrightarrow\ & 1 - \Delta(\hat{X}_{t-1})^T \vartheta^T G_t^{-1} \Delta(\hat{X}_{t-1})\vartheta \geq 0 \\ \Leftrightarrow\ & \vartheta^T diag(1,0,0,0)\vartheta - \Delta(\hat{X}_{t-1})^T \vartheta^T G_t^{-1} \Delta(\hat{X}_{t-1})\vartheta \geq 0. \end{aligned}$$

By assuming that $\lambda = 1$, the additional constraints (21) and (22) can be approximated as follows:

$$\left.\begin{array}{l}\breve{a}_{t-1}-a_{t-1}\leq1\\\breve{b}_{t-1}-b_{t-1}\leq1\end{array}\right\}\approx\left\{\begin{array}{l}\breve{\alpha}^{T}_{t-1}\breve{R}^{-1}_{t-1}\breve{\alpha}_{t-1}\leq1\\\breve{\beta}^{T}_{t-1}\breve{Q}^{-1}_{t-1}\breve{\beta}_{t-1}\leq1\end{array}\right.,\qquad(\text{A-20})$$

where $\breve{R}$ and $\breve{Q}$ are the optimized covariance matrices from the previous objective Θ_{1} and Θ_{2} functions. In terms of the vector ϑ, these inequalities become:

$$\begin{cases}\vartheta diag(1,0,-\breve{R}^{-1}_{t-1},0)\vartheta^{T}\geq0\\\vartheta diag(1,0,0,-\breve{Q}^{-1}_{t-1})\vartheta^{T}\geq0\end{cases}.\qquad(\text{A-21})$$

Based on (A-21) and the non-negative scalars ξ_{1} and ξ_{2}, one can get the equivalence of (A-19) as follows:

$$diag(1-\xi_{1}-\xi_{2},0,\xi_{1}\breve{R}^{-1}_{t-1},\xi_{2}\breve{Q}^{-1}_{t-1})-\Delta(\hat{X}_{t-1})^{T}G^{-1}_{t}\Delta(\hat{X}_{t-1})\geq0.\qquad(\text{A-22})$$

Equation (A-22) is equivalent to:

$$\Sigma_{\xi}-\Delta(\hat{X}_{t-1})^{T}G^{-1}_{t}\Delta(\hat{X}_{t-1})\geq0.\qquad(\text{A-23})$$

Moreover, by multiplying G_{t} on both sides of (A-23) yields

$$G_{t}\Sigma_{\xi}-\Delta(\hat{X}_{t-1})\Delta(\hat{X}_{t-1})^{T}\geq0.\qquad(\text{A-24})$$

Finally, by applying the Schur complements method (Yu 2013) on (A-24); we get the LMI provided in (A-17):

$$\begin{bmatrix}G_{t}&\Delta(\hat{X}_{t-1})\\\Delta(\hat{X}_{t-1})^{T}&\Sigma_{\xi}\end{bmatrix}\geq0\ \text{Q.E.D.}\qquad(\text{A-25})$$

This proof follows a similar approach to (Yang, Li, and Liu 2008) except that the considered system in our case does not contain the uncertainty model.

Depending on the specific objective function, several different optimization criteria, including the determinant, trace, and maximum eigenvalues of the covariance matrix; have been developed in the literature (Yang, Kaplan, and Blasch 2012). There are some attractive relations between geometric properties of the ellipsoid and algebraic properties of the covariance matrix. Indeed, the lengths of the axes for the ellipsoid are proportional to the eigenvalues of the covariance matrix whereas the trace of the covariance matrix is the sum of the length of the axes, and the determinant represents the volume of the ellipsoid. Since the constraint (20) that defines the upper bound for the state estimation error is considered as positive definite, the determinant or trace can be chosen as optimization criteria for the matrices measure (Benavoli, Chisci L, and Alfonso 2007). Let us assume that the ellipsoid $\varepsilon\left(\hat{X}_t, G_t\right)$ parameterized by $\hat{X}_t$ and G_t contains the polytope with K vertices; then the optimization problem (A-16) subject to (A-17) can be reformulated as follows:

$$\breve{\Theta}_3 - \min_{G_t > 0, L_t, \xi_1 \geq 0, \xi_2 \geq 0} det(G_t) \tag{A-26}$$

$$\text{s.t. } B^{(k)} = \begin{bmatrix} G_t & \Delta^{(k)}\left(\hat{X}_{t-1}\right) \\ \Delta^{(k)}\left(\hat{X}_{t-1}\right)^T & \Sigma_{\xi} \end{bmatrix} \geq 0, \, k = 1, \ldots, K, \tag{A-27}$$

where $\Delta^{(k)}\left(\hat{X}_{t-1}\right) = \Phi_t^{(k)} E_{t-1} - L_t\left(\Psi_{t-1} X_{t-1} - \Psi_{t-1}\hat{X}_{t-1}\right) + I_{n \times 1} - L_t I_{p \times 1}$ and *det* stands for determinant. The proof of this assumption is similar to the one provided previously for (A-17). Specifically, from this assumption, we deduce that (A-17) can be interpreted as the linear combination of (A-27) and is provided by:

$$B = \sum_{k=1}^{K} \phi_k B^{(k)} \geq 0, \tag{A-28}$$

where $\phi_k \geq 0$ and $\sum_{k=1}^{K} \phi_k = 1$.

Given that the inequalities (A-27) are linear to the parameters G_t, L_t, ξ_1 and ξ_2, problem (A-26) can be solved by interior-point methods for semidefinite programming (SDP) (Koochakzadeh et al. 2015). Finally, with the intention of getting the smallest error for the state estimate, the determinant of the covariance matrix G_t is minimized at each time step.

CONCLUSION

In this chapter, we have explored three important aspects of intelligent transportation system: vehicle location awareness, traffic flow prediction, and private car trajectory data mining.

In the study of vehicle location awareness, we have proposed a distributed filtering scheme for cooperative positioning in VANETs. Our proposed CP algorithm is able to guarantee good accuracy because of the particle weights that embedded finite difference approach during the particle update. Additionally, the measurement optimization approach improves the state and covariance estimation. We also presented a two-task hierarchical method named hierarchical constrained tri-objective optimization (HCTO) to improve the vehicle state accuracy. In this approach, processing and measurement noises are first optimized separately and then, based on the obtained optimal solutions, the upper bound for the state estimation error is addressed.

In the research of traffic flow prediction, several approaches to predict short-term traffic volume are introduced. Firstly, a novel short-term traffic flow prediction method called Ensemble Real-time Sequential Extreme Learning Machine (ERS-ELM) with simplified single layer feed-forward networks (SLFN) structure under freeway peak traffic condition and non-stationary condition is proposed. Secondly, a novel incremental regression framework under the concept drifting environment is proposed, with ensemble learning as the major solution for updating the distribution representation. A regression to classification (R2C) procedure is incorporated to construct a more accurate classification-type loss function to be utilized in ensemble learning. Lastly, a novel regression framework for short-term traffic flow prediction with automatic parameter tuning is proposed, with the SVR being the primary regression model for traffic flow prediction and the Bayesian optimization being the major method for parameters selection. Through comparing with classical SARIMA, MLP-NN, ERT, and Adaboost methods in typical sections of real road. The results indicate the superior advantage and generalization of BO-SVR in different conditions.

In the research of traffic flow prediction, we have proposed a TAD algorithm with a purpose of capturing spatial-temporal aggregation characteristic of private cars' trajectory. The extensive experiments based on trajectory data from real urban environment demonstrate that the proposed method is able to effectively identify the travel regularity of private cars. Moreover, we also presented a novel method to understand regular travel behavior of private cars and discover private cars with regular travel behavior, which is beneficial to analyze the contribution of private cars on road congestion during certain period of time, and help us optimize transportation facilities and traffic management strategies. Finally, a 3D-KDE based prediction model to characterize the dynamic spatio-temporal aggregation effect is proposed, which stems from the inherent relationship between the present SAW density and the future SAW aggregation. We conduct experiments based on real-world large-scale private car SAW data. The experimental results demonstrate that our proposed method outperforms other current methods.

Overall, our work provides a new insight for vehicle trajectory processing and our method can identify the private cars with regular travel behavior effectively. In the future, firstly, we will study the impact of private cars with regular travel behavior on traffic congestion and will integrate our approach with urban models to further explore individual travel activities and the evolution of traffic flow. Secondly, we may consider to use larger traffic flow data to construct a deep architecture of traffic flow forecasting and to acquire more accurate prediction results. What's more, combining the proposed framework with TrAdaBoost to solve the regression problem in transfer learning is worth investigating. Lastly, we will focus on how to deal with the case of large-scale missing traffic flow data in order to improve the accuracy.

REFERENCES

Alfeo, A. L., Mario G. C. A. Cimino, S. Egidi, B. Lepri and G. Vaglini. 2018. "A stigmergy-based analysis of city hotspots to discover trends and anomalies in urban transportation usage." *IEEE Transactions on Intelligent Transportation Systems* 19(7); 2258–2267.

Almazan J. Full. 2013. "auto-calibration of a smartphone on board a vehicle using IMU and GPS embedded sensors." *IEEE Intelligent Vehicles Symposium*: 1374 -1381.

Arioli M., Gratton S. 2012. "Linear regression models, least-squares problems, normal equations, and stopping criteria for the conjugate gradient method."*Computer Physics Communications* 183(11): 2322–2336.

Barolli A., Spaho E., Barolli L. 2011. "QoS Routing in Ad-Hoc Networks Using GA and Multi-Objective Optimization." *Mobile Information Systems* 7(3):169-188.

Bauer C.2013.*On the (In-) Accuracy of GPS Measures of Smartphones: A Study of Running Tracking Applications, Proceedings of MoMM* 2013:335-341.

Benavoli A., Chisci L. and Alfonso F. 2007. "Estimation of Constrained Parameters with Guaranteed MSE Improvement." *IEEE Transactions on Signal Processing* 55(4): 1264 -1275.

Bhatt D., Aggarwal P., Devabhaktuni V. 2014. "A novel hybrid fusion algorithm to bridge the period of GPS outages using low-cost INS." *Expert Systems with Applications*40: 2166– 2173.

Bishop C. M. *Pattern Recognition and Machine Learning*. 2006. New York: Springer.

Boccato L., Krummenauer R., Attux R. and Lopes, A. 2012. "Application of natural computing algorithms to maximum likelihood estimation of direction of arrival." *Signal Processing* 92(5): 1338–1352.

Boucher C., Lahrech A. and Noyer J. C. 2004. "Non-linear filtering for land vehicle navigation with GPS outage." *IEEE International Conference on Systems, Man and Cybernetics*: 1321-1326.

Bourgain J., Dilworth S. J., Ford K. 2010. "Explicit constructions of rip matrices and related problems", *Duke Math. Journal* 159(1): 145-185.

Burges C. J. C. 1998. *"A Tutorial on Support Vector Machines for Pattern Recognition."* Kluwer Academic Publishers.

C. N. S. Bureau. 2011-2017. "Beijing: China Statistical Publishing House." *China Statistical Yearbook.*

Cai, H., X. Zhan, J. Zhu, X. Jia, A. S. Chiu and M. Xu. 2016. "Understanding taxi travel patterns." *Physica A: Statistical Mechanics and its Applications* 457:590–97.

Candes E J. 2008. *The restricted isometry property and its implications for compresses sensing.* C. R. Math. Acad. Sci. Paris 346: 589–592.

Caramia M., Dell'Olmo P. 2008. *Multi-objective Management in Freight Logistics: Increasing Capacity, Service Level and Safety with Optimization Algorithms.* New York: Springer.

Chapelle O., Schölkopf B., Zien A. 2006. "Label Propagation and Quadratic Criterion." *Semisupervised Learning* 41(3):538.

Chen J, Cheng L and Gan M. 2013. "Extension of SGMF Using Gaussian Sum Approximation for Nonlinear/NonGaussian Model and its Application in Multipath Estimation." *Acta Automatica Sinica* 39(1):1 - 10.

Chen Jie, Zhu Xiao, Dong Wang, Daiwu Chen, Vincent Havyarimana, Jing Bai, and Hongyang Chen. Dec. 5,2018. "Towards Opportunistic Compression and Transmission for Private Car Trajectory Data Collection." *IEEE Sensors Journal.* Accessed Dec. 5, 2018.DOI:10.1109/JSEN.2018.2885121.

Chen L, Ng R. 2004. "On the marriage of Lp-norms and edit distance." *Thirtieth International Conference on Very Large Data Bases.* ELSEVIER: 792-803.

Chen S, Hong X and Harri CJ. 2008. "An orthogonal forward regression technique for sparse kernel density estimation." *Neurocomputing* 71: 931–943.

Das, Rajib Chandra and T. Alam.2014. "Location based emergency medical assistance system using Openstreet Map." *International Conference on Informatics, Electronics & Vision:*1-5.

Do M. N. and M. Vetterli.2002. "Wavelet-based texture retrieval using generalized gaussian density and kullback-leibler distance." *IEEE Transactions on Image Processing*, 11(2): 146–158.

Ester Martin.1996. *A Density-Based Algorithm for Discovering Clusters in Large Spatial Databases with Noise.*

Feng. Z. and Y. Zhu.2017. "A survey on trajectory data mining: Techniques and applications." *IEEE Access* 4: 2056–2067.

Feng Z., Wen-fang X, Xi L. 2011. "Overview of Nonlinear Bayesian Filtering Algorithm." *Advanced in Control Engineering and Information Science, Procedia Engineering* 15: 489 – 495.

Fisher R. A. 1912. "On an absolute criterion for fitting frequency curves." *Messenger of Mathematics* 41(1): 155–160.

Fonseca R. M., Leeuwenburgh O., VandenHof P. M. J. 2014. "Ensemble-based hierarchical multi-objective production optimization of smart wells." In *Computation Geosciences,* edited by Fonseca R M, Leeuwenburgh O, VandenHof P M J:449–461. New York: Springer.

Foucart S., Rauhut H.2013. *A Mathematical Introduction to Compressive Sensing, Applied and Numerical Harmonic Analysis.* ISBN:978-0-8176-4947-0.

Freund, Y., R.E.Schapire.1997. "A decision-theoretic generalization of on-line learning and application to boosting." *J. Comput. Syst. Sci.* 55(1): 119-139.

Geurts P, D. Ernst and L. Wehenkel. 2016. *Extremely randomized trees.* Kluwer Academic Publishers.

Ghazi, Irtsam, Haq, I. U., Maqbool, M. R. and Saud, S. 2016."GPS based autonomous vehicle navigation and control system." *International Bhurban Conference on Applied Sciences and Technology.*

Giannotti F., Nanni M., and Pedreschi D. 2011. "Unveiling the complexity of human mobility by querying and mining massive trajectory data." *Vldb Journal* 20(5):695.

Gao L., P. Kou, F. Gao and X. Guan. 2010. "Adaboost regression algorithm based on classification-type loss." *2010 8th World Congress on Intelligent Control and Automation,* 682–687.

Goel and V. P. Vishwakarma. 2017. "Gender classification using KPCA and SVM." *IEEE International Conference on Recent Trends in Electronics, Information and Communication Technology*: 291–295.

Goulet-Langlois, G., H. N. Koutsopoulos, Z. Zhao and J. Zhao.2017. "Measuring Regularity of Individual Travel Patterns." *IEEE Transactions on Intelligent Transportation Systems:* pp(99): 1–10.

Guangdong Province Bureau. 2011-2017. "Beijing: China Statistics Press."*Statistical Yearbook of Guangdong Province*.

Guo L., Wang H. 2006. "Minimum entropy filtering for multivariate stochastic systems with non-Gaussian noises." *IEEE Trans. Autom Control* 51(4): 695–700.

Hamid M. R., Baker A., Aziz T. Z. 2014. "Non-Gaussian probabilistic MEG source localisation based on kernel density estimation." *NeuroImage* 87: 444–464.

Han M., Liang Z. and Li D. 2011. "Sparse kernel density estimations and its application in variable selection based on quadratic Renyi entropy." *Neurocomputing* 74(10): 1664–1672.

Hassana Maigary Georges, Zhu Xiao and Dong Wang.2016. "Hybrid Cooperative Vehicle Positioning using Distributed Randomized Sigma Point Belief Propagation on Non-Gaussian Noise Distribution." *IEEE Sensors Journal* 16(21): 7803-13.DOI: 10.1109/JSEN.2016. 2602847.

Haupt J., Applebaum L., Nowak R. 2010. "On the restricted isometry of deterministically subsampled Fourier matrices." *IEEE Proc. 44th Annual Conf. on Information Sciences and Systems,* Princeton: 1-6.

Hong X., Chen S. and Harris C. J. 2004."Sparse kernel density construction using orthogonal forward regression with leave-one-out test score and local regularization." *IEEE Trans. Systems, Man and Cybernetics, Part B* 34(4): 1708-17.

Hong X., Chen S. and Harris C. J. 2010."Sparse Kernel Density Estimation Technique Based on Zero-Norm Constraint." *International Joint Conference on Neural Networks:* 1-6.

Hong X., Chen S., Qatawneh A. 2013. "Sparse probability density function estimation using the minimum integrated square error." *Neurocomputing* 115: 22–129.

Huang, G., Q. Zhu and C. Siew. 2006. "Extreme learning machine: theory and applications." *Journal of Neurocomputing* 70(1):489–501.

Iturbide E., Cerda J. and Graff M.2013. "A Comparison between LARS and LASSO for Initialising the Time-Series Forecasting Auto-Regressive Equations." *Procedia Technology* 7: 282–288.

Jeong Y. S., Castro-Neto M M, Jeong, Y. S, Byon, Y. J, Castro-Neto, M. M and Easa, S. M. 2013. "Supervised Weighting-Online Learning Algorithm for Short-Term Traffic Flow Prediction." *IEEE Transactions on Intelligent Transportation Systems* 14(4):1700-1707.

Jiang S., Ferreira J., Gonzalez M. C.2017. "Activity-Based Human Mobility Patterns Inferred from Mobile Phone Data: A Case Study of Singapore." *IEEE Transactions on Big Data* 3(2): 208-219.

Jin R., Chen W., Simpson Tw. 2001. "Comparative studies of metamodelling techniques under multiple modelling criteria." *Structural and Multidisciplinary Optimization* 23(1):1-13.

Kaplan E., Hegarty D. 2005. *Understanding GPS: Principles and Applications, Artech House,* Norwood, Mass, USA. London: artech house.

Kayri M. 2010. "The Analysis of Internet Addiction Scale Using Multivariate Adaptive Regression Splines." *Iranian Journal of Public Health* 39(4):51-63.

Kennedy J. and R. Eberhart. 1995. Particle swarm optimization." *IEEE International Conference on Neural Networks, Proceedings 4*: 1942–1948.

Koochakzadeh, A., Malek-Mohammadi, M., Babaie-Zadeh, M., and Skoglund, M. 2015. "Multi-antenna assisted spectrum sensing in spatially correlated noise environments." *Signal Processing* 108: 69-76.

Kumar S. V., L. Vanajakshi. 2015. "Short-term traffic flow prediction using seasonal ARIMA model with limited input data." *European Transport Research Review* 7 (3): 21.

Kung-Chung L., Oka A., Pollakis E. and Lampe, L. 2010. "A comparison between Unscented Kalman Filtering and particle filtering for RSSI Based tracking." *Positioning Navigation and Communication (WPNC)*: 157 – 163.

Kushner, and Harold J. 1964. "A new method of locating the maximum point of an arbitrary multipeak curve in the presence of noise." *Journal of Fluids Engineering* 86(1).

Lan Y., Soh Y.C. and Huang G.-B. 2009. "Ensemble of online sequential extreme learning machine."*Neurocomputing* 72: 3391–3395.

Lee S., Chon Y. and Cha H. 2013. "Smartphone-Based Indoor Pedestrian Tracking Using Geo-Magnetic Observations."*Mobile Information Systems* 9(2): 123-137.

Li, D., T. Miwa and T. Morikawa.2016. "Modeling time-of-day car use behavior: A Bayesian network approach." *Transportation Research Part D Transport and Environment* 47: 54–66.

Li G., Yang H.2010. "Iterated square root unscented Kalman Particlefilter." *IEEE Information Computing and Telecommunications*: 222 – 225.

Li Z., Ding B., Han J., Kays, R. and Nye, P. 2010. "Mining periodic behaviors for moving objects." *ACM SIGKDD International Conference on Knowledge Discovery and Data Mining ACM*: 1099-1108.

Linzhouting C. and Jiancheng F. 2014. "A Hybrid Prediction Method for Bridging GPS Outages in High-Precision POS Application." *IEEE Transactions on Instrumentation and Measurement* 63(6):1656-1666.

Loo K. K., Tong I. and Kao B. 2005."Online algorithms for mining inter-stream associations from large sensor networks." *Advances in knowledge discovery and data mining* 3518:143-149.

Louie H. and Strunz K. 2006. "Hierarchical Multiobjective Optimization for Independent System Operators (ISOs) in Electricity Markets." *IEEE Transactions on Power Systems* 21(4): 1583-1592.

Magdon-Ismail M., Jonathan Purnell T. 2010. "Approximating the Covariance Matrix of GMMs with Low-Rank Perturbations." *Intelligent Data Engineering and Automated Learning* 6283:300-307.

Martinez D. L., Chen V. C. P., Kim S. B. 2015. "A convex version of multivariate adaptive regression splines." *Computational statistics & data analysis* 81: 89-106.

Mazimpaka J. D. and Timpf S. 2016. "Trajectory data mining - A review of methods and applications." *Journal of Spatial Information Science*: 61-99.

Mazucheli J., Louzada F. and Ghitany M. E. 2013. "Comparison of estimation methods for the parameters of the weighted Lindley distribution." *Applied Mathematics and Computation* 220: 463–471.

Mok E., Retscher G. and Chen. 2012. "Initial test on the use of GPS and sensor data of modern Smartphone for vehicle tracking in dense high rise environments." *Proceedings of the Ubiquitous Positioning, Indoor Navigation, and Location Based Service*: 1 -7.

Morelande M. R., Challa S. 2005. "Manoeuvring target tracking in clutter using particle filters." *IEEE Transactions on Aerospace and Electronic Systems* 41(1):252-270.

Noureldin A, El A. 2011. "GPS/INS integration utilizing dynamic neural networks for vehicular navigation." *Information Fusion* 12(1):48–57.

Prakash J., Sachin C. P.and Sirish Shah L. 2008. "Constrained State Estimation Using Particle Filters." *Proceedings of the 17th World Congress, International Federation of Automatic Control*: 6472 -6478.

Proschan F. 1953. "Confidence and Tolerance Intervals for the Normal Distribution". *Publications of the American Statistical Association* 48(263):550-564.

Rasmussen, C. E. and Williams, C. K. I. 2005. *"Gaussian Processes for Machine Learning."* MIT Press.

RE Schapire. 2003. *The Boosting Approach to Machine Learning: An Overview.* Springer New York 171:149-171.

Read J., Achutegui K., Míguez J. 2014. "A distributed particle filter for nonlinear tracking in wireless sensor networks." *Signal Processing* 98: 121–134.

Richard Baraniuk, Mark Davenport, Ronald DeVore, and Michael Wakin. 2008. "A Simple Proof of the Restricted Isometry Property for Random Matrices." *Constructive Approximation*: 253–263.

Salas Arnold, S. J. Roberts and M. A. Osborne. 2015. "A variational Bayesian State-Space Approach to Online Passive-Aggressive regression." *Journal of Physics Conference Series.*

Shao-Wen Yu. 2013. "Ranks of a Constrained Hermitian Matrix Expression with Applications." *Journal of Applied Mathematics*2013:1-9.

Shukuan Lin, Shaomin Zhang, Jianzhong Qiao, Hualei Liu and Ge Yu.2008. "A parameter choosing method of svr for time series prediction." *Young Computer Scientists, Icycs 2008, the International Conference for*: 130–135.

Silverman W. 1998. "Density Estimation for Statistics and Data Analysis." *Chapman & Hall/CRC*.

Srilatha Indira Dutt V. B. S., Sasi Bhushana R. G., Swapna R. S. 2009. "Investigation of GDOP for Precise user Position Computation with all Satellites in view and Optimum four Satellite Configurations." *J. Ind. Geophys. Union* 13(3): 139-148.

Thorsten Joachims. 1999. *Transductive inference for text classification using support vector machines.*

Tillmann M. A., Pfetsch E. M. 2014. "The Computational Complexity of the Restricted. Isometry Property, the Nullspace Property, and Related Concepts in Compressed Sensing." *IEEE Transactions on Information Theory* 60(2): 1248-1261.

Tinu Theckel Joy, Santu Rana, Sunil Gupta, and Svetha Venkatesh. 2017. "Hyperparameter tuning for big data using bayesian optimisation." *International Conference on Pattern Recognition*: 2574–2579.

Vincent Havyarimana, Damien Hanyurwimfura, Philibert Nsengiyumva and Zhu Xiao. 2018. "A novel hybrid approach based-SRG model for vehicle position prediction in multi-GPS outage conditions". *Information Fusion* 41: 1-8. Accessed May,2018.http://dx.doi.org/10.1016/j.inffus.2017.07.002.

Walter O., Schmalenstroeer J., Engler A. and Haeb-Umbach, R. 2013. "Smartphone-based sensor fusion for improved vehicular navigation."*10th Workshop on Positioning Navigation and Communication:* 1-6.

Wang Dong, Jiaojiao Fan, Zhu Xiao, Hongbo Jiang, Hongyang Chen, Fanzi Zengand Keqin Li. 2018. "Stop-and-Wait: Discover Aggregation Effect Based on Private Car Trajectory Data." *IEEE Transactions on Intelligent Transportation Systems*. DOI: 10.1109/TITS.2018.2878253.

Wang W., Wainwright M. J. and Ramchandran K. 2010. "Information-theoretic limits on sparse signal recovery: Dense versus sparse measurement matrices." *IEEE Transactions on Information Theory* 56(6):2967 – 2979.

Wei Yuan, Deng P, Taleb T., Wan, J. and Bi, C. 2016. "An Unlicensed Taxi Identification Model Based on Big Data Analysis." *IEEE Transactions on Intelligent Transportation Systems* 17(6): 1703-1713.

Williams, B. M., L. A. Hoel. 2003. "Modeling and Forecasting Vehicular Traffic Flow as a Seasonal ARIMA." *Theoretical Basis and Empirical Results, Journal of Transportation Engineering* 129 (6): 664–672.

William W. H., Yong L. and Tan F. W. 2006. "Optimization of generalized mean square error in signal processing and communication." *Linear Algebra and its Applications* 416: 815–834.

Wold S., Esbensen K. and Geladi P. 1987. "Principal component analysis." *Chemom. intell. Lab* 2(1):37-52.

Woo A. K., Chan K. 2014. "Approximate conditional least squares estimation of a nonlinear state-space model via an unscented Kalman filter." *Computational Statistics and Data Analysis* 69: 243–254.

Xiang, L., M. Gao and T. Wu. 2016. "Extracting stops from noisy trajectories: A sequence oriented clustering approach." *ISPRS International Journal of Geo-Information* 5(3): 29.

Xiao Jianhua, Zhu Xiao, Dong Wang, Jing Bai, Vincent Havyarimana and Fanzi Zeng. 2018. *Short-term traffic volume prediction by ensemble learning in concept drifting environments, Knowledge-Based Systems.* Accessed November 7, 2018. https://doi.org/10.1016/j.knosys.2018.10.037.

Xiao Zhu, Pingting Li, Vincent Havyarimana, Hassana Maigary Georges, Dong Wang and Keqin Li. 2018. "GOI: A Novel Design for Vehicle Positioning and Trajectory Prediction under Urban Environments." *IEEE Sensors Journal* 18: 5586-94. Accessed July, 2018.DOI: 10.1109/JSEN.2018.2826000.

Xiao Zhu, Vincent Havyarimana, Tong Li and Dong Wang. 2016. "A Nonlinear Framework of Delayed Particle Smoothing Method for Vehicle Localization under Non-Gaussian Environment." *Sensors* 16(5):692-708. DOI:10.3390/s16050692.

Xiao Zhu, Xiangyu Shen, Fanzi Zeng, Vincent Havyarimana, Dong Wang, Weiwei Chen, and Keqin Li. 2018. "Spectrum Resource Sharing in Heterogeneous Vehicular Networks: A Non-Cooperative Game-Theoretic

Approach with Correlated Equilibrium." *IEEE Transactions on Vehicular Technology* 67(10):9449-58. DOI 10.1109/TVT.2018.2855683.

Xinying Wang, MinHan. 2014. "Online sequential extreme learning machine with kernels for non-stationary time series prediction." *Journal of Neurocomputing* 145:90–97.

Xu Yanyan, Qing Jie Kong and Yuncai Liu. 2013. *Short-term traffic volume prediction using classification and regression trees* 36(1):493–498.

Yang C., Kaplan L. and Blasch E. 2012. "Performance Measures of Covariance and Information Matrices in Resource Management for Target State Estimation." *IEEE Transactions on Aerospace and Electronic Systems* 48(3):2594- 2614.

Yang F., Li Y., Liu X. 2008. "Robust error square constrained filter design for systems with non-Gaussian Noises." *IEEE Signal Processing Letters* 15(12): 930-933.

Yee Whye Teh, Matthias Seeger, and Michael Jordan. 2005. "Semiparametric latent fact or models." *Artificial Intelligence and Statistics*: 565-568.

Yibin Ye, Stefano Squartini nand Francesco Piazza.2013. "Online sequential extreme learning machine in non-stationary environments." *Journal of Neurocomputing* 116:94–101.

Yibin Ye, Stefano Squartini n and Francesco Piazza. 2013. "Online sequential extreme learning machine in non-stationary environments." *Journal of Neurocomputing* 116:94–101.

Yukihiro K, Jinling W.2008. "INS/GPS Integration Using Gaussian Sum Particle Filter." *Proceedings of the 21st International Technical Meeting of the Satellite Division of the Institute of Navigation, Savannah:* 1345-1352.

Zanaty E. A. 2012. "Support Vector Machines (SVMs) versus Multilayer Perception (MLP) in data classification." *Egyptian Informatics Journal* 13(3):177-183.

Zhang F., Jin B., Wang Z., Hu, J. and Zhang, L. 2016. "On Geocasting over Urban Bus-Based Networks by Mining Trajectories." *IEEE Transactions on Intelligent Transportation Systems* 17(6): 1734-1747.

Zhang H., Dai G., Sun J and Zhao, Y. 2013. "Unscented Kalman filter and its nonlinear application for tracking a moving target." *Optik* 124: 4468–4471.

Zhang Z. 2013. "Bayesian growth curve models with the generalized error distribution." *Journal of Applied Statistics* 40(8): 1779-1795.

Zheng Yu, L. Capra, O. Wolfson and H. Yang. 2014. "Urban computing: concepts, methodologies, and applications." *Acm Transactions on Intelligent Systems & Technology* 5(3): 1–55.

Zheng Yu, Wu W, Chen Y, Qu, H and Ni, L. 2016. "Visual Analytics in Urban Computing: An Overview." *IEEE Transactions on Big Data* 2(3): 276-296.

Zheng Yu. 2015. "Trajectory Data Mining: An Overview." *Acm Transactions on Intelligent Systems and Technology* 6(3): 29.

In: Vehicular Networks   ISBN: 978-1-53615-978-3
Editors: P. H. J. Chong and I. W-H. Ho © 2019 Nova Science Publishers, Inc.

Chapter 4

SOFTWARE-DEFINED VEHICULAR AD-HOC NETWORKS

Ling Fu Xie[1,], Ivan Wang-Hei Ho[2]*
and Peter Han Joo Chong[3]
[1]Faculty of Electrical Engineering and Computer Science,
Ningbo University, Ningbo, China
[2]Department of Electronic and Information Engineering,
The Hong Kong Polytechnic University, Hong Kong
[3]Department of Electrical and Electronic Engineering,
Auckland University of Technology, Auckland, New Zealand

ABSTRACT

This chapter introduces the application of software-defined networking (SDN) to vehicular ad-hoc networks (VANET). SDN, rendering a new networking paradigm by featuring software implemented controllers to manage network devices, can greatly ease the implementation of new network control schemes. VANET, due to the need to support multiple applications given the limited network resources (e.g., bandwidth), generally involves a number of design issues and challenges that call for various solutions on resource management.

---
*Corresponding Author's E-mail: xiel0002@ntu.edu.sg.

Therefore, SDN can benefit the development of VANET. This chapter presents both flat and hierarchical architectures to apply SDN to VANET, and explains in detail 1) how most existing design issues in current VANET applications can be better addressed, 2) how new features can be incorporated, and 3) how a transition from traditional VANET can be accomplished.

INTRODUCTION

Vehicular ad-hoc networks (VANET) enable wireless communications among vehicles with high mobility and between vehicles and road-side infrastructure nodes. It provides the following three major services or applications to vehicles (or drivers) (Hartenstein and Laberteaux 2010). The first is the traffic safety application, with which the road safety can be enhanced or even guaranteed. Specifically, this application provides a vehicle with the knowledge of its surroundings (e.g., the speed, the position, the emergency brake light status of the vehicles in the vicinity, etc.) and alerts the vehicle of any potential accidents. The second is the efficiency application, which allows path planning for the driver.

This application generally collects and disseminates information of a larger area, e.g., the congestion status of each road in the city. The third is the infotainment application, which refers to all applications (e.g., Internet access or multimedia streaming) other than the first two mentioned above. Especially, the Internet access for vehicles is normally supported by road-side units (RSU) deployed in VANET.

The communication modes in VANET for the three applications above differ from each other in general. For safety applications, each vehicle only needs to periodically broadcast current information regarding its position, speed, etc. (Hafeez et al. 2013). For efficiency applications, the information about a certain location or area needs to be disseminated over multiple hops to distant vehicles or RSUs (Lochert et al. 2008). The information in both applications above is generally collected by the on-board units (OBU) installed on vehicles. To support Internet access in infotainment applications, a multi-hop connection between a vehicle and a RSU (or a gateway) needs to be setup via certain routing protocols (Li and Wang 2007). Figure 1 shows the brief protocol stack for the three applications in VANET.

However, the design for each of the three applications involves a number of issues or challenges. For example, for safety applications, how to properly set the broadcasting rate, transmission power (Khorakhun, Busche and Rohling 2008), and various IEEE 802.11p MAC parameters are challenging. Furthermore, the IEEE 802.11p standard defines six service channels for efficiency and infotainment applications, and thus, how to effectively assign these channels poses a big challenge for the design of these applications (Omar, Zhuang and Li 2012). For VANET to succeed, efficient solutions and network innovations that are easy to implement are critical.

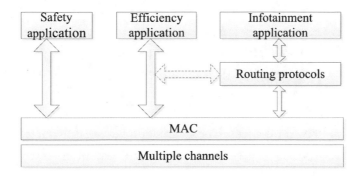

Figure 1. A brief protocol stack for different applications in VANET.

In recent years, software defined networking (SDN) becomes appealing for network innovations (Open Networking Foundation2012). The defining feature of SDN is that it introduces centralized controllers that exert network control with centralized network intelligence. This dispenses with programming on traditional network devices such as switches and routers for network innovations, and thus makes a network more programmable. As a new networking paradigm capable of significantly easing network management hassles, SDN has wide practical applications and nowadays has been drawing enormous attention from research communities. For VANET, not surprisingly, SDN is a valuable technique to reform its architecture(s) and enable a rapid development. This chapter presents two architectures for the application of SDN in VANET, and explains in detail 1) how most existing design issues in current VANET applications can be better addressed, 2) how new features can be incorporated, and 3) how a transition from traditional VANET can be accomplished.

SOFTWARE-DEFINED NETWORKING

SDN provides a dramatically different networking approach than the traditional ones. In traditional networks such as the Internet, network devices like switches and routers comprise two planes: the data plane and the control plane, as shown in Figure 2(a). The former deals with packet processing in the hardware layer, e.g., packet forwarding and buffering; the latter incorporates all distributed algorithms to implement various network control functions, e.g., routing and firewall, and controls how packets are processed in the data plane. Implementing various control functions on network devices usually makes them cumbersome for network innovations. By contrast, SDN moves the control plane to the SDN controller(s), which is responsible for controlling all the physical network devices. The interaction between the network devices and the controller can be supported by the OpenFlow protocol (McKeown et al. 2008), as shown in Figure 2(b). Specifically, the data plane in OpenFlow comprises a *flow table* containing the rules and actions for handling all the incoming and outgoing packets of *each flow*, and thus it abstracts the hardware of various types of network devices. The controller in OpenFlow specifies and installs the rules and actions in the flow table via a secure channel. It generally has a global view of the network and is thus capable of making more intelligent decisions on packet processing. Any new applications (e.g., load balancing, access control, etc.) could be executed by the controller to exert control on the network devices. Hence, SDN renders the flexibility for network programming and facilitates network design.

SDN has wide applications to either wired or wireless networks to address various design issues (Rawat and Reddy 2017). Typical examples include dynamic resource allocation problems, load balancing, mobility management like the handover issue, route selection, radio resource management for base stations, and so on. Here, we present the study in (Dely, Kassler and Bayer 2011) to illustrate how SDN is implemented in wireless mesh networks (WMN) to tackle the handover issue.

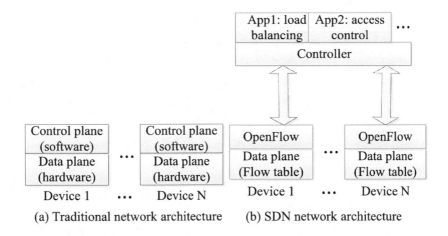

Figure 2. Traditional network architecture and the SDN architecture.

First, Figure 3(a) shows the architecture of a mesh node (i.e., a client, a router, an access point, or a gateway) in SDN-enabled WMN. The node can be equipped with multiple radios. The data plane of each radio is connected to the OpenFlow data path (responsible for rule installation), and the data path uses local sockets to connect to the control path and further to the controller or the network operating system (NOS) that is run on a control sever. The connection between the control path and the controller is realized via a new WMN that is formed using a different Service Set IDentifiers (SSIDs) for the mesh nodes. In addition, each node is required to monitor information like link quality and channel utilization and install a monitoring and control agent to report information to the control server. The connection between the agent and the server can be established via the newly formed WMN.

Second, the architecture of the control server is shown in Figure 3(b). It is composed of multiple databases, NOS, and various applications. The databases maintain the up-to-date information about the network status (e.g., network topology and association between a client and access points).The NOS not only makes use of these databases to execute applications for optimizing network operations, but also installs optimized rules on the mesh nodes.

With the architectures in Figure 3, the handover issue can be resolved as follows. Once the control server detects from the databases that the service from an associated access point (AP) deteriorates for a client (e.g., due to heavy load on the AP), it triggers the execution of the mobility management application to look for a new AP to associate with that client. The server first sets temporary rules for the three nodes (i.e., the client and the two APs) to let the client forward traffic to both APs, and then mandates the client to associate with the new AP and the current AP to remove forwarding rules for the flows of this client.

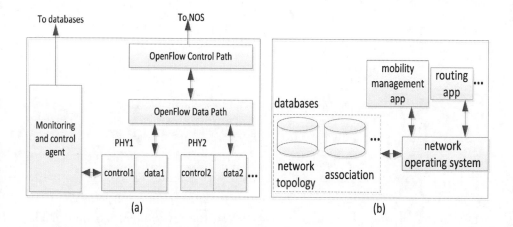

Figure 3. Node architectures in SDN-enabled WMN.

VANET is also a field where SDN can find great success. On one hand, most design issues in different layers in VANET, such as power control in the PHY layer, channel assignment in the MAC layer, and routing in the network layer, are about the control and the use of network resources for different levels of quality of service (QoS) guarantee or network performance improvement. On the other hand, SDN programs the controller to implement various network control functions, which can avoid many network management hassles, e.g., the programming and replacement of individual network devices, and enable a rapid network development. This chapter presents two architectures, a flat one and a hierarchical one, to exploit SDN in VANET.

SOFTWARE-DEFINED VEHICULAR NETWORKS

We first illustrate the hierarchical architecture of software-defined vehicular networks (SDVN) and explain how it works by comparing to traditional VANET. Then, we turn to the flat SDVN, a simplified network structure of the hierarchical one. After that, the benefits and design challenges follow.

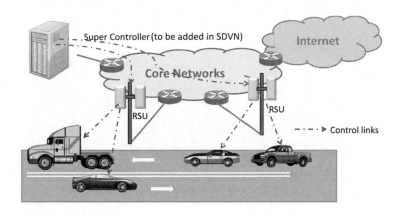

Figure 4. A typical scenario of VANET with interconnected RSUs.

Hierarchical SDVN

In VANET, vehicles are equipped with transceivers to wirelessly communicate with one another. If two vehicles are within the radio transmission range of each other, they can directly communicate; otherwise, the communication needs to be relayed in a multi-hop manner (i.e., in ad-hoc mode). In particular, to increase the connectivity and the capacity of the communication network, RSUs are deployed along road side in VANET, which act as message repositories or gateways to other networks such as the Internet. Each RSU can directly communicate with the vehicles passing by, as shown in Figure 4. The RSUs can be either standalone or interconnected (Banerjee et al. 2008). By 'interconnected (standalone) RSUs', we mean all RSUs are (not) connected by the core network. The core network comprises switches and routers as shown in Figure 4, and it can facilitate the communications among RSUs. In general, the interconnected case can benefit the performance of VANET more. However, we emphasize that the hierarchical SDVN (or H-SDVN for short) can work in both cases, and the benefits to be presented below also apply to both cases.

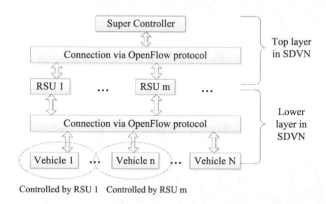

Figure 5. The hierarchical architecture of H-SDVN.

Towards the information exchange and dissemination in VANET, it is usually implicitly assumed that each vehicle or RSU has a control plane as depicted in Figure 2 to install various distributed algorithms to control packet transmissions (e.g., regarding how to adjust the transmission power and rate). In contrast, H-SDVN, by adopting the concept of software-defined networking, moves most functionalities of those distributed algorithms to the control planes of RSUs, and treats them as distributed controllers in VANET. In other words, a RSU in H-SDVN is responsible for controlling the packet transmission of vehicles within its vicinity as shown in Figure 4. A RSU, for instance, can instruct a vehicle to adjust its transmit power. In addition, H-SDVN further assumes a remote super controller to oversee the RSUs as depicted in Figure 4. With such a super controller and its broader view of the network, the RSUs can be coordinated to serve vehicles better, and the network can be further optimized. For example, the super controller can dynamically assign distinct radio channels to RSUs within a region to enhance the overall network throughput. The interaction between the RSUs and vehicles will be further discussed later in this section. As a summary, H-SDVN is a two-layer hierarchical architecture as illustrated in Figure 5, with the RSUs in the lower layer controlling vehicles passing by and the super controller in the top layer controlling all the RSUs.

In particular, Figure 6 illustrates the internals of vehicles and RSUs in H-SDVN. First, as shown in Figure 6(a), the software of vehicles mainly consists of an OpenFlow client and a local control plane, both running on the operating system of the devices (McKeown et al. 2008). The former interacts with RSUs to operate the flow table, and the latter executes local distributed algorithms. This local control plane is critical for the transition from traditional VANET to H-SDVN, which will be discussed later in this section. Second, compared to vehicles, which act only as source and relay nodes in VANET, RSUs in H-SDVN additionally act as the controllers to exert control on vehicles. Thus, RSUs incorporate an extra set of components (within the dashed line in Figure 6(b)) to execute various control applications (which are developed in the network operating system in SDN). Note that the internals of the super controller is similar to that depicted in Figure 3(b).

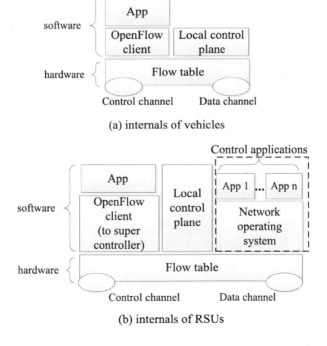

(a) internals of vehicles

(b) internals of RSUs

Figure 6. The internals of vehicles and RSUs in H-SDVN.

For the case of interconnected RSUs by the core network, H-SDVN can additionally exert control on the top-layer network. This is because the switches or routers connecting these RSUs in the core network can be controlled by the super controller. For example, the load-balancing application can be developed at the super controller to properly distribute Internet traffic to vehicles.

Flat SDVN

If we disable the control functions of the RSUs on the vehicles passing by and let them act as relay nodes or routers only, the SDVN in Figure 5 then becomes a flat SDVN (F-SDVN for short). In this F-SDVN, there is only one controller, i.e., the remote super controller, and all vehicles and RSUs are peer nodes, with the internals given in Figure 6(a). In general, F-SDVN fits small-scale VANET or VANET with sparse or no RSUs, whereas the hierarchical counterpart, H-SDVN, is more scalable. In particular, the benefits from F-SDVN also apply to H-SDVN. Hence, we focus on elaborating the benefits of H-SDVN below.

Benefits of Hierarchical SDVN

Here we elaborate the benefits of H-SDVN. Our major objectives here are to show how the existing key design issues in VANET can be better resolved within the H-SDVN architecture, and how new features can be incorporated into H-SDVN readily. In particular, we present the benefits from the following five aspects:

(1) Better serving a demand: Here, a demand can be (i) a broadcast in safety applications; (ii) a spread of collected information in efficiency applications; or (iii) a multi-hop flow in infotainment applications.

For (i), the key issues in VANET traditionally involve how to configure the proper period, transmit power, and transmission rate of a broadcast. In general, the optimal values of these parameters for a vehicle largely depend on the channel load and the vehicular density nearby (Jiang, Chen and Delgrossi

2007). For example, if the vehicular density is high, the transmit power should be lowered for reducing the interference or collision level. With a RSU as the controller to monitor the traffic density in a particular road segment, vehicles entering the road can be instructed to adjust these parameters, thus avoiding the need and time for detecting the surrounding traffic condition. Note that the RSU can acquire knowledge regarding the traffic distribution at any given time along the road from periodic beacon broadcasts generated by nearby vehicles (Hafeez et al. 2013).

For (ii), information like the road congestion status is normally needed by many distant vehicles, and thus flooding is usually used to disseminate the message (Hartenstein and Laberteaux 2010). The key issue here is how to limit the number of packets in the flooding. Various criteria can be designed to select only appropriate vehicles for rebroadcasting the message (Ducourthial, Khaled and Shawky 2007; Korkmaz et al. 2004). Basically, these criteria are related to the relative positions between the sender and receivers. For example, we can choose to let the farthest neighbors within the transmission range rebroadcast the message (Korkmaz et al. 2004). With RSUs monitoring the vehicles passing by in H-SDVN, proper or even the optimal candidates for the message rebroadcasts can be readily identified, while it is generally more difficult in traditional VANET to select the optimal candidates due to the distributed partial information at each node.

For (iii), a multi-hop flow can be established between two vehicles or between a vehicle and a RSU. Due to vehicle mobility, a route being used may suffer from low link quality and frequent route disruption, and thus the key issue is how to look for a relatively stable and robust path. The following two examples show how the mobility is better addressed in H-SDVN. First, within H-SDVN, a flow could avoid choosing a link with low quality. For example, if the red car in Figure 4 intends to transmit data to the truck, the latter will be prevented to be the immediate next hop for the former by the road-side controller. It is because the two vehicles move in opposite directions and the signal transmitted will suffer from drastic Doppler shift in addition to the short contact time. Instead, the RSU on the left can be chosen as the relay for the red car. Second, within H-SDVN, the route disruption for a flow can be mitigated. A variety of traditional distributed routing protocols, such as DSR and GPSR, might be inefficient in some situations. For example, GPSR will suffer from a local maximum when there is no next hop neighbor that is closer to the destination (Li and Wang 2007). However, a RSU with a broader view in its vicinity can effectively identify the local maximum in advance and help prevent it from happening.

In addition, other issues in (iii) such as the handover of a vehicle between two RSUs can also be better solved with the broader view of the RSUs or super controller. For example, if the super controller detects that a RSU, say RSU A, is congested, it can inform neighboring RSUs of RSU A to raise its transmit power to defer the handover of vehicles approaching the defected RSU.

(2) Better QoS guarantee: In IEEE 802.11p, each channel implements four types of queues, which correspond to four access categories (AC). Each AC defines its own contention window size, and thus packets in these four queues are prioritized in the MAC layer into four data types. H-SDVN, using OpenFlow, can define more different types of applications via SDN controllers. This allows further differentiation of packets from the application point of view, and provides more QoS control methods within a relay at upper layers. For example, it is likely that the connectivity for certain VANET scenarios could be poor due to high vehicle mobility, and thus packets may need to be carried in the vehicles' buffers for a certain period of time before reaching the receivers. In H-SDVN, packets can be prioritized not only according to the data type, but also the application type, hence, in case of buffer overflow, packets labeled with crucial importance are more likely to be retained in the buffer for better QoS guarantee.

(3) Facilitating Network optimization: Traditionally, given a number of demands, how to optimize the network performance is a challenging issue in distributed networks. By contrast, the broader view of the controllers in H-SDVN, especially the super controller, can ease the performance optimization. See two typical examples as follows.

First, H-SDVN can facilitate the implementation of load balancing, which is generally needed for achieving high network performance. By collecting each RSU's workload statistics on the Internet traffic, the super controller can balance the workload on all RSUs to better serve the demands. In Figure 4, for example, if the super controller detects that the RSU on the left is much more congested than the one on the right, the RSU on the right can be instructed to serve more vehicles, especially those on the border of the two RSUs, possibly by increasing its transmit power.

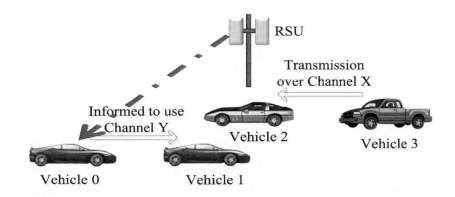

Figure 7. Channel selection and collision avoidance within H-SDVN.

Second, H-SDVN can facilitate the channel resource management process via dynamic channel allocation to reduce the interference among users (Omar, Zhuang and Li 2012). Such channel assignment can be performed by one or multiple RSUs. Considering a RSU assigning channels to its users (vehicles), the interference within the local area of the RSU can be minimized. Specifically, a RSU can monitor the channel usage within its region, and then announce the free channels to a portion of vehicles in the vicinity. Figure 7 shows a scenario where vehicle 3 is transmitting data to vehicle 2 using channel X, and vehicle 0 intends to transmit data to vehicle 1 which is close to vehicle 2. With the guidance of the RSU, vehicle 0 will not select channel X and the collision at both vehicles 1 and 2 can be avoided. For the case of multiple RSUs, the set of RSUs is generally coordinated by the super controller for the use of appropriate channels to communicate with vehicles within their respective regions, which is very similar to radio resource management among base stations in a cellular network (Li, Mao and Rexford 2012).

(4) Offloading network functionalities from RSUs: It can be seen that the first three benefits above are attained at the expense of much heavier workload on the RSUs. To reduce the burden on the RSUs in H-SDVN, some of its functionalities can be offloaded to some typical vehicles. Here, we present an

example related to security in VANET. It is known that a vehicle with a certificate signed by the certificate authority (CA) is trustable to others, and there is generally a need of certificate revocation and renewal (Hartenstein and Laberteaux 2010). First, if misbehaving vehicles are identified, their certificates need to be reported to the CA, which then instructs RSUs to disseminate the revoked certificates to other vehicles. Obviously, this dissemination task can be performed by some special vehicles such as buses. The CA can let the buses carry and continuously broadcast the revoked certificates along their trajectories. For the renewal of certificates, the CA can employ the RSUs to authorize the buses to perform the task by the same token. Therefore, we can see that H-SDVN is flexible, considering its ability to offload the network functionalities from one network device to another.

(5) Introducing new network functionalities: Besides the ability to resolve the key issues in VANET shown above, H-SDVN can help incorporate new features into VANET. Here, we consider two examples emerging in recent years, i.e., physical-layer network coding (PNC) (Liew, Zhang and Lu 2013) and vehicular cloud (VC) (Lee, Lee and Gerla 2014).

PNC can be used as performance boosters in wireless communication networks. Its implementation in VANET can be facilitated by H-SDVN. In Figure 8, assuming vehicles 1 and 2 intend to send packets P1 and P2 to each other respectively, both via the RSU, then, with PNC, the three nodes perform the transmissions as follows. First, vehicles 1 and 2 send their packets to the RSU simultaneously. Second, after receiving the mixed signal, the RSU deduces the packet P1 $\oplus$ P2 and broadcasts it to vehicles 1 and 2. Finally, upon receiving P1 $\oplus$ P2, both vehicles can decode the desired packets. For example, vehicle 1 can obtain P2 by performing P1 $\oplus$ (P1 $\oplus$ P2). In H-SDVN, when a vehicle generates a new flow, it usually requests its controller or RSU for a route (McKeown, Anderson, Balakrishnan, Parulkar, Peterson, Rexford, Shenker and Turner 2008). Thus, if a RSU receives requests from two vehicles (such as the two in Figure 8) for the routes to each other, it can readily identify the opportunity of performing PNC among them, and then command the two vehicles to transmit simultaneously at some synchronized time. Therefore, the opportunity identification and the transmission synchrony

(Liew, Zhang and Lu 2013), which are crucial in realizing PNC in VANET, can be eased by H-SDVN through the road-side controllers.

A VC consists of a group of vehicles and/or RSUs who share their resources (e.g., the sensors and storages) with each other, and it is useful for information/content-centric networking (Lee, Lee and Gerla 2014). The formation of a VC and its operations can be greatly eased in H-SDVN. Consider Figure 7 for example. The RSU can act as the cloud leader and invite all the vehicles passing by to join the cloud. Then, in case that vehicle 0 wants to start the autonomous driving, it could request the vehicles ahead (e.g., vehicle 3), via the RSU, to report the sensed data about their surroundings.

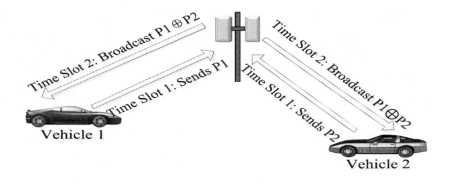

Figure 8. Physical-layer network coding in H-SDVN.

Challenges and Potential Solutions

This subsection discusses major foreseeable challenges in H-SDVN and presents potential solutions.

First of all, the number of RSUs might not be sufficient to cover the entire road networks, especially in the initial phase of VANET deployment. Therefore, some basic functionalities might need to be maintained in the control plane of vehicles (which is shown in Figure 6 as the local control plane). For example, the routing module for flow route discovery should remain. Similarly, RSUs in H-SDVN should also retain the local control plane to keep working in case of disconnection to the super controller. This indicates that a hybrid architecture for the vehicles and RSUs in H-SDVN should be exploited during the transition period from the traditional network architecture to the software-defined one in VANET.

In addition, how to ensure the timely interaction between the RSUs and the vehicles is another critical issue for H-SDVN to succeed. Traditionally, each vehicle only needs to collect the information about the network state and execute the distributed algorithms to make its own decision. By contrast, in H-SDVN, the collected information may need to be passed to the RSUs for decision making. Furthermore, the decisions (e.g., the rules and actions to be taken in the data plane of the vehicle) made by the RSUs need to be sent back to the vehicle. Obviously, it might be too late for a vehicle to receive decisions from the RSUs due to its high speed and the busy or loss of communication channels. In this case, the decisions made by the RSUs will become ineffective, and the network performance will be degraded.

Another direct consequence of this RSU-based control process is the extra bandwidth consumption due to the overhead incurred in the interactions between the RSUs and the vehicles, which increases the burden on the radio channels in VANET. As a result, we can see that ensuring timely interactions between the RSUs and the vehicles at a controlled cost is vital in H-SDVN.

To mitigate the above problems in H-SDVN, we might need to adopt advanced communication protocols and technologies within the framework. Few possible attempts can be as follows:

(1) Multiple wireless technologies, e.g., 5G LTE and millimeter wave communications, can be utilized at vehicles and RSUs to reduce the delay of communications between the control plane and the data plane. However, diversifying the radio technologies may incur higher cost. Consequently, optimization problems have to be formulated to minimize the cost given the delay constraints, just as done in (Li, Dong and Ota 2016; He, Zhang and Liang 2016).

(2) The WAVE Short Message Protocol (WSMP) (Hartenstein and Laberteaux 2010) was proposed in IEEE 1609.3 for safety-related applications. With WSMP, the length of control packets in safety-related applications can be greatly reduced, and transmissions can be expedited by skipping some

processing steps involved in forming a Basic Service Set (BSS) (Hartenstein and Laberteaux 2010). Apparently, similar lightweight protocols could be designed for the interactions between RSUs and vehicles in H-SDVN as well.

(3) Consider the case that some decisions from a RSU are common to a group of nearby vehicles. The RSU can adopt random linear network coding to serve those vehicles (He, Zhang and Liang 2016). It can encode those decisions (each represented by one or multiple packets) into a set of linearly independent coded packet blocks and distribute them among vehicles. Later, vehicles in the group exchange the received coded blocks among themselves, and each vehicle attempts to collect a certain number of linearly independent coded blocks to recover the encoded messages or decisions. Obviously, in this way the RSU can be offloaded from serving a group of vehicles, and especially the problem of missing a specific piece/packet in a decision for a vehicle due to unstable communication channel can be avoided.

CONCLUSION

This chapter presented both flat and hierarchical architectures for software-defined vehicular networks (SVDN) to enable a rapid development of vehicular ad-hoc networks (VANET). The hierarchical SDVN (H-SDVN) is a two-layer network structure, wherein the lower layer, the road-side units (RSUs) serve as distributed SDN controllers to manage the vehicles passing by, while in the top layer, the super controller oversees all RSUs. The flat one eliminates the control functions of the RSUs on the vehicles in the vicinity. These two network structures, especially the two-layer SDVN, renders the ability to better address most existing design issues in VANET and facilitate the incorporation of new features. We enumerated a number of practical examples, such as the network parameter control for certain network scenarios and the implementation of advanced communication technologies, to illustrate the benefits of H-SDVN. In addition, the major challenges in H-SDVN, e.g., the transition from traditional VANET to H-SDVN and the overhead/delay issue incurred in the communications between the data and control planes, and potential approaches to address them were discussed in detail. We believe that more research efforts into the study of these challenges areneeded for H-SDVN to come true.

REFERENCES

Banerjee, N., Corner, M. D., Towsley, D. and Levine, B. N. (2008). 'Relays, base stations, and meshes: enhancing mobile networks with infrastructure'. In *IEEE MobiCom*.

Dely, P., Kassler, A. and Bayer, N. (2011). 'OpenFlow for wireless mesh networks'. In *IEEE ICCCN*.

Ducourthial, B., Khaled, Y. and Shawky, M. (2007). Conditional transmissions: performance study of a new communication strategy in VANET. *IEEE Transactions on Vehicular Technology*, 56, 3348-3357.

Hafeez, K. A., Zhao, L., Ma, B. and Mark, J. W. (2013). Performance analysis and enhancement of the DSRC for VANET's safety applications. *IEEE Transactions on Vehicular Technology*, 62, 3069-3083.

Hartenstein, H. and Laberteaux, K. P. (2010). *VANET: vehicular applications and inter-networking technologies*. New York: John Wiley & Sons Ltd.

He, Z., Zhang, D. and Liang, J. (2016). Cost-efficient sensory data transmission in heterogeneous software-defined vehicular networks. *IEEE Sensors Journal*, 16, 7342-7354.

Jiang, D., Chen, Q. and Delgrossi, L. (2007). 'Communication density: a channel load metric for vehicular communications research'. In *IEEE MASS*.

Khorakhun, C., Busche, H. and Rohling, H. (2008). 'Congestion control for VANETs based on power or rate adaptation'.In *5th International Workshop on Intelligent Transportation*.

Korkmaz, G., Ekici, E., Ozguner, F. and Ozguner, U. (2004). 'Urban multi-hop broadcast protocol for inter-vehicle communication systems'. In *1st ACM International Workshop on Vehicular Ad Hoc Networks*.

Lee, E., Lee, E-K. and Gerla, M. (2014). Vehicular cloud networking: architecture and design principles. *IEEE Communications Magazine*, 52, 148-155.

Li, F. and Wang, Y. (2007). Routing in vehicular ad hoc networks: a survey. *IEEE Vehicular Technology Magazine*, 12-22.

Li, H., Dong, M. and Ota, K. (2016). Control plane optimization in software-defined vehicular ad hoc networks. *IEEE Transactions on Vehicular Technology*, 65, 7895-7904.

Li, L. E., Mao, Z. M. and Rexford, J. (2012). 'Toward software-defined cellular networks'. In *European Workshop on Software-Defined Networking*.

Liew, S. C., Zhang, S. and Lu, L. (2013). Physical-layer network coding: Tutorial, survey, and beyond. *Physical Communication*, 6, 4-42.

Lochert, C., Scheuermann, B., Wewetzer, C., Luebke, A. and Mauve, M. (2008). 'Data aggregation and roadside unit placement for a VANET traffic information system'. In *5th ACM International Workshop on Vehicular Inter-Networking*, 58-65.

McKeown, N., Anderson, T., Balakrishnan, H., Parulkar, G., Peterson, L., Rexford, J., Shenker, S. and Turner, J. (2008). 'OpenFlow: enabling innovation in campus networks'. In *ACM SIGCOMM*.

Omar, H. A., Zhuang, W. and Li, L. (2012). 'VeMAC: a novel multichannel MAC protocol for vehicular ad hoc networks'. In *IEEE INFOCOM*, 413–418.

Open Networking Foundation (2012). *Software-defined networking: the new norm for networks*. White Paper.

Rawat, D. B. and Reddy, S. R. (2017). Software defined networking architecture, security and energy efficiency: a survey. *IEEE Communication Surveys & Tutorials*, 19, 325-346.

In: Vehicular Networks   ISBN: 978-1-53615-978-3
Editors: P. H. J. Chong and I. W-H. Ho © 2019 Nova Science Publishers, Inc.

Chapter 5

MOBILE EDGE COMPUTING: ARCHITECTURE, TECHNOLOGY AND DIRECTION

Arslan Rasheed, Xuejun Li and Peter Han Joo Chong[*]
Department of Electrical and Electronic Engineering,
Auckland University of Technology, Auckland, New Zealand

ABSTRACT

The increasing trend of handheld devices containing wireless interfaces has posed number of challenges such as; increased burden on the core network, efficient bandwidth utilization and network management. Furthermore, the futuristic applications such as live streaming, online gaming, augmented virtual reality and connected vehicles are not only resource hungry but also delay sensitive. One of the proposed solutions for such applications is cloud computing that involves the offloading of computation at the core of the network. However, it remains challenging to solve the issues of delay and bandwidth. Fortunately, these issues can be mitigated if the computing resources are placed near the users. Recently, a new paradigm called Mobile Edge Computing (MEC) emerged, which combines the cloud computing capabilities with cellular infrastructure. With the help of MEC, users can access the rich computing resources with high bandwidth and ultra-low latency. The key idea of MEC lies in placing servers in closed proximity to users that results in higher bandwidth, efficient resource utilization, improved quality of experience (QoE), reduced

---

[*]Corresponding Author's E-mail: peter.chong@aut.ac.nz.

burden on the backbone network, higher computation resources and ultra-low latency. Due to its peculiar architecture, MEC has lot to offer meeting the requirements of futuristic applications. MEC sees its scope in many fields such as Internet of Things (IoT), Wireless Sensor and Actuator Networks (WSAN), computing offloading, gaming and vehicular networks. This chapter enlightens different aspects of MEC, such as architecture, security and privacy, economic traits, potential challenges, applications, mobility management, computation offloading and future directions.

INTRODUCTION

The last decade witnessed the increasing trend of using handheld devices such as smart phones, tablets, smart watches and smart glasses. It is estimated that users of handheld devices will reach 11.6 billion by 2020 (Cisco 2016b). It is also anticipated that data generated by these devices may reach up to 49 Exabyte monthly by 2021 (Cisco 2016a). The projected data is about 4,000 times more than last decade. Furthermore, the nature of existing communication systems is passive as they function as communication gateway between user entities (UEs) and internet servers residing away from the UE (Wong et al. 2017). Moreover, the need of extensive computation for futuristic applications to meet good quality of experience (QoE) would cause quick depletion of UE batteries. Besides above-mentioned challenges, increasing demand in Internet of Things (IoT) could also be the potential stagger for wireless networks (Borgia et al. 2016). All aforementioned factors pose challenges for both wireless and backbone networks. These challenges include but not limited to unwanted delay, higher bandwidth demand, energy consumption and high storage capacity (Edmonds and Bohnert 2016). These challenges led to an idea of combining cloud computing capabilities with wireless network resulting in Mobile Cloud Computing (MCC) (Mtibaa et al. 2013). According to the concept of MCC, a UE can access the powerful resources via mobile network. MCC offers high capacity storage for UEs, promoting numerous sophisticated applications with higher battery utilization efficiency.

Although MCC brings multiple benefits to wireless networks, it involves excessive processing delay due to the distant placement of servers and creates burden on the backhaul network. As estimated by the Cisco, data generated by handheld devices will reach up to 500 zettabytes by 2019 (Sardellitti, Scutari, and Barbarossa 2015). This explosion of data generation could lead to serious challenges on backbone causing high latency and degraded QoE. Furthermore, increasing demand in applications such as augmented reality, video streaming and other similar applications would require interactivity and high computation. Hence, a unified interactive communication solution is necessary to address the communication latency issue while providing high computation capabilities at the edge of the network. Hence, cloud computing in closed proximity to the UE may reduce the latency which is called Edge Computing (EC) (Wong et al. 2017). The edge computing has been foreseen as a saviour that has ability to address above mentioned problems.

For clarity, a comparison between edge computing and MCC is provided in Table 1.

Initially a concept of combining the resources of UEs to form an ad-hoc cloud was conceived by (Mtibaa et al. 2013). The ad-hoc cloud works in a way that it combines the resources of UEs in the vicinity and performs different computational tasks. The main advantage of ad-hoc cloud is cost effective and involves less complexities. However, the ad-hoc cloud has following serious challenges:

- Coordination among UEs
- Realization to ensure a secure and reliable communication
- Find UE with appropriate computing capabilities and persuade the eligible UE to share its resources.

Table 1. Comparison between MCC and Edge Computing

MCC	Edge Computing
High Computational Power	Limited Computational Power
High Storage Capability	Limited Storage Capability
High Latency	Low Latency
Distant from UE	Closed Proximity to UE
High Jitter	Low Jitter
Centralized	Distributed

To overcome these problems, a new concept of computation offloading is introduced, in which the processing of tasks i.e., computation could be handled mutually by the UE and network as shown in Figure 1. It is estimated that 63% of the computation will be offloaded to the network. The computational offloading phenomenon poses great challenge for network operators, as handling such big amount of data requires high bandwidth and involves extensive computation, which may result in unnecessary delay. Therefore, it is better to exploit the edge computing as discussed by (Shi et al. 2016). The concept of edge computing is implemented in three different ways: fog computing, cloudlet computing and mobile edge computing. According to the theory of edge computing, the computing resources are distributed in between the UE and core network from where users can access them easily yielding significantly reduced latency (Sardellitti, Scutari, and Barbarossa 2015).

Figure 1. Mobile Cloud Computing.

According to cloudlet, special purpose devices called micro data centres are placed closer to the edge of the network at strategic places leveraging high computation power and low latency (Verbelen et al. 2012). These micro data centres are called cloudlets that provide efficient offloading capabilities with ultra-low latency to provide computation and communication resources using Wi-Fi interface. The cloudlet can be viewed analogous to Wi-Fi hotspots, where cloudlet devices are providing computation resources to the UE instead of the core network. The cloudlet offers efficient offloading capabilities and meets the requirements of higher bandwidth and low latency.

It works efficiently by providing high computation environment. However, due to small coverage area Wi-Fi access is inadequate for mobile devices (Jararweh et al. 2016). While considering the limitations of cloudlet computing, Cisco introduced the concept of fog computing in 2012 (Bonomi et al. 2012). A layer of distributed resources is formed between the end users and core cloud. Nowadays, fog computing is a generalized name of cloud computing in the context of IoT (Zhu et al. 2013). The fog computing offers variety of services as compared with cloudlet, such as extended coverage area, lower latency, high computational capabilities and heterogeneity.

Ultimately, bringing the cloud capabilities closer to the edge network has many advantages, however, there are still many challenges associated with fog and cloudlet computing. The futuristic applications have many restrictions on latency, computation resources, context awareness, geographical coverage and bandwidth that need to be addressed yet. For example, the cloudlet is accessed with the Wi-Fi covering very small geographical area and fog computing gives variable delay and degraded services as the resources are scattered. Furthermore, the fog computing must support multiple access technologies. The coordination among the resources, if any, is also subject of exploration yet.

To mitigate aforementioned issues, European Telecommunications Standards Institute (ETSI) introduced a new solution called Mobile Edge Computing (MEC) combining IT infrastructure with wireless communications. The essence of MEC is to place a powerful server at the base station (BS) which is capable enough to fulfil the computing requirements of the users. The placement of server at the BS results in quick response, higher computation resources at the edge, larger coverage area, context-awareness and higher bandwidth. MEC is being considered as one of the strongest candidates among 5G technologies as it is envisioned a key enabler. The Network Function Virtualization (NFV) is a strong aspect of MEC as it supports the virtualization of physical resources leveraging efficient network management. From the operator's perspective, MEC provides efficient resource management. That is why many operators such as Vodafone,

Telecom Italia, DOCOMO Japan and ISG of ETSI are putting efforts to materialize the concept of MEC. They are keen in developing the use case scenarios where MEC may play its role such as connected vehicles, feature recognition, edge video orchestration, video editing, augmented virtual reality, online gaming, and interactive communication. Similarly, the vendors such as Huawei, Intel, IBM and Ericsson are also showing interest in the standardization of MEC (Hu et al. 2015). From a user's perspective, MEC has potential to meet the stringent requirements of latency, computation offloading and bandwidth. MEC overcomes all the shortcomings of fog and cloudlet implementation of edge computing as it provides higher context-awareness, larger coverage area, ultra-low latency, closer proximity to the users and efficient utilization of resources. Such marvellous features make the MEC most promising technology for the future.

The research community is also committed to play its role as contributor towards the realization of MEC. In this regard, Abbas and Zhang have overviewed the security aspects as well as the future trend in MEC (Abbas et al. 2018). Similarly, a tremendous survey is written by (Mach and Becvar 2017), in which they have done a great discussion on the computation offloading techniques, use cases and architecture. However, none of them covered all traits of MEC in detail. Another survey on potential security challenges in MEC is presented by (Roman, Lopez, and Mambo 2018). Both the academia and industry are striving hard to establish the MEC standard as soon as possible.

This book chapter aims at enlightening different traits of MEC including computation offloading, architecture, applications, security, economic perspectives, mobility management and potential future directions.

EDGE COMPUTING TECHNIQUES

Traditionally, data generation occurs at the edge of the network while data processing is done at the core. For example, a self-driving car produces data at the rate of 1 Gbps and processing at the distant cloud would cause too much delay (Chiang and Zhang 2016). Keeping in view the capacity of the network, the computation time and delay involved in fulfilling the request will cause trouble towards realization of self-driving car. Similarly, smart home concept with thousands of sensors produce data at much higher rate. Hence, it is a good idea to bring computation down to the edge of the network. Edge computing is a promising solution for providing computation and communication at closed proximity to the users in mobile networks (Shi et al. 2016). According to (Yi et al. 2015), edge computation has reduced the computing time by 4 folds in case of face recognition. Similarly, energy efficiency is also increased by offloading computation at the edge of the network (Chun et al. 2011).

Types of Edge Computing

There are three different proposals introduced for the realization of edge computing, namely the cloudlet computing, fog computing and mobile edge computing illustrated in Figure 2. In this section, we present a comprehensive comparison of different EC implementations.

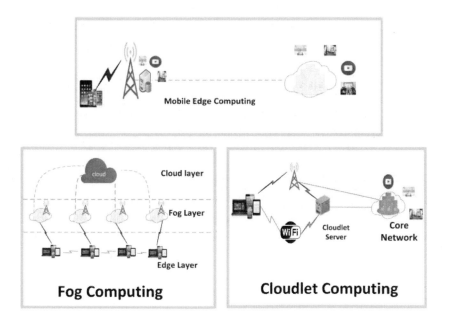

Figure 2. Edge Computing Paradigms.

Cloudlet Computing

In 2009, Satyanarayanan et al. proposed a new architecture for EC named cloudlet computing, also termed as "datacentre in the box" (Satyanarayanan et al. 2014). The proposed architecture consists of a device with capabilities of mini datacentre that provides extensive computation near to the UE as depicted in Figure 3. A cloudlet can be viewed as a virtual machine that provisions the computation and communication resources to the edge users exploiting Wi-Fi interface. The cloudlet is one hop communication paradigm thus providing low latency and high bandwidth. According to Verbelen et al. (2012), the proposed architecture consists of three layers; component layer, node layer and cloudlet layer. The component layer provides interface to higher layers for different services, node layer is responsible for execution of the services running on operating system (OS) and cloudlet layer manages the layer formed by set of nodes with the help of a cloudlet manager.

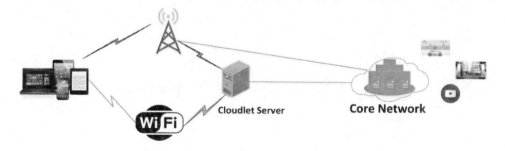

Figure 3. Cloudlet Computing.

Similarly, the architecture proposed by Satyanarayanan et al. (2014) explored the potential of cloudlet in context of cognitive assistance applications. A backbone virtual machine leveraging cognitive functionalities gathers the resources from different virtual machines nearby to serve a request. The request handling in cloudlet is hierarchical; the cloudlet layer has a cloudlet agent that manages all the nodes. The agent passes information to the underlying nodes via execution environment. The hierarchical flow of information from the agent to the nodes and back helps in handling the requests at different levels while considering the complexity of the request. In this way, nodes with high computation capacity handle more complex queries resulting in optimized utilization of resources.

Cloudlet offers many advantages such as high capacity for data storage and pre-processing of tasks on the cloud. Interestingly, cloudlet designates a new VM for each task and updates once the task is completed. The cloudlet technique backs up the data on to the cloud and supports limited node-node communication. The main drawback of cloudlet is its access mechanism, which allows only WLAN that limits the context-awareness and coverage, making it inadequate for many applications.

Fog Computing

As described in Section 1, fog computing is a new edge computing paradigm introduced by Cisco in 2012 (Bonomi et al. 2012). So far, the most studied paradigm of edge computing is fog computing. Fog computing is an extension to the cloud computing with an intermediate layer providing interface between mobile user and cloud. The intermediate layer consists of high capacity devices such as switches, routers, firewalls and servers (Luan et al. 2015). The intermediate layer of resources is called fog layer and nodes involved are termed as fog computing nodes (FCN). Fog computing is a platform that facilitates multiple access technologies such as WiFi, cellular networks (like 3G, LTE, 5G), dedicated short distance communication (DSRC), Bluetooth, Zigbee and WiMAX. Cisco introduced a fog device called IOx that hosts the applications in a Guest Operating System (GOS). A hypervisor is required to interface different operating systems (Velte and Velte 2013). This platform provides programmability and flexibility due to open-sources Linux platform, where programmers can run scripts of their own choice. A conceptual distributed architecture of fog computing as shown in Figure 4 consists of multiple nodes in which each fog node is connected to the core cloud. The fog computing fully supports the node to node communication as shown in Figure 4.

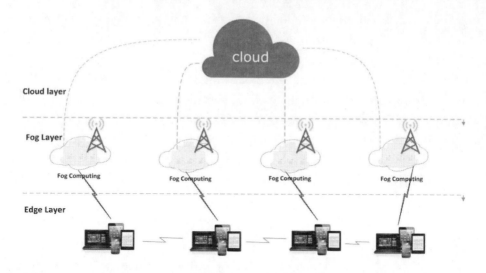

Figure 4. Fog Computing.

Many researchers have made remarkable achievements in improving fog computing by presenting different models. A geo-spatially distributed fog computing model is proposed in (Hong et al. 2013). The proposed model involves high-level programming that divides the applications into two categories: delay-sensitive and delay-tolerant applications. The latency-sensitive applications are served at the edge of the network, while the remaining applications are dealt by the cloud. In this way, the mobile model deals with the latency for specific applications leaving all other applications for core cloud. Moreover, applications requiring complex computation are also sent to the core cloud. However, the proposed model cannot be considered as a general model. It can be used for specific applications, hence more generic architecture is required. Another architecture proposed by (Nishio et al. 2013) formulates a mathematical model based on convex optimization for resource sharing by considering the service-oriented utility function. The main objective is to maximize the sum and product of utility functions. An application-awareness model is proposed by (Ottenwälder et al. 2013), which proves that if application is already known, it can save the bandwidth and lessen the burden on the virtual machines during migration. However, the prediction of application in advance is not an easy task, which requires further investigation. A reasonable analysis on the reliability requirements for Wireless Sensor and Actuator Network (WSAN), smart grid and cloud computing combined is presented by (Madsen et al. 2013) that leads to an unswerving fog computing network. They have combined together the concept of WSAN and cloud computing in context of Smart Grid, however, the proposed study did not push forward fog computing architecture.

Concept of fog computing is traditionally used in the context of IoT. The beauty of fog computing lies in its fog abstraction layer that keeps end user unaware of heterogeneity. Another aspect of fog computing is its support for non-IP based traffic. The decentralized architecture involves a service orchestration layer that is responsible for resources allocation. The requests from users in the form of policies specifying the requirements of bandwidth, QoS, load balancing and latency arrive at the orchestrator. The orchestrator selects the most suitable node that meets the requirements of tasks subject to availability of the node. This is the main issue with fog computing because delay-critical applications may be served by a distant node. It works well with wired networks, however challenges still exist for mobile networks. Because of its distant proximity, the requirements of context-awareness is not fully justified.

MEC

Modern applications such as augmented reality and connected vehicles impose very strict conditions of latency and context-awareness on fog computing in context of mobile users particularly. These are serious challenges that need to be addressed. For this, ETSI introduced the concept of MEC by placing a resource-rich server within radio access network (RAN). MEC brings resources and computation closer to the proximity of UE to fulfil the requirements of context-awareness and ultra-low latency in context of cellular networks. All the computation, data storage, application and communication resources are enclosed in RAN (Neal 2016). Analogous to fog computing abstraction layer, MEC has an orchestrator that is responsible for resource allocation and application management. A server located within RAN performs virtualization, radio resource management, scheduling and computational offloading (Wong et al. 2017). A UE initiates a request by describing all requirements is handled by orchestrator, which maintains a list of all running applications. Based on the nature of request, there are three possible ways to handle:

- If the requested application is already running, the request is redirected to the application;
- If the application is not running but supported by MEC server, it is instantiated at once depending upon available resources;
- If the application is not supported, it is redirected to the core network.

From the above discussion, it is clear that information handling is almost same for all kinds of edge computation, i.e., in hierarchical manners. However, fog computing is different due to its heterogeneous nature necessitating an abstraction layer. The cloudlet and MEC paradigms have advantage over fog because it does not need abstraction layer. A brief comparison among different edge computing paradigms is given in Table 2.

Table 2. Edge Computing Techniques Comparison

Characteristic	Cloudlet	Fog	MEC
Latency	Low	Medium	Ultra-low
Access Technologies	Wi-Fi	Heterogeneous	Cellular Network
Proximity	One hop	Vary from one to multiple hops	One hop
Nodes	Specialized micro data-centre	Routers, Switches, Firewalls, IoT Gateways, Aps and etc.	MEC Server
Software Architecture	Cloudlet Agent	Fog Abstraction Layer	Orchestrator layer
Inter-node Communication Support	Limited	Yes	Limited
Context-Awareness	Low	Partial	Full

MEC USE CASES

MEC enjoys its close proximity to the end user, thus resulting in ultra-low latency, high bandwidth, interactive communications, as well as context-aware computation. MEC has the potential to offer efficient services to all the stakeholders (Hu et al. 2015). In this section, we divide the use cases of MEC from the user's and the operator's points of view as viewed in Figure 5.

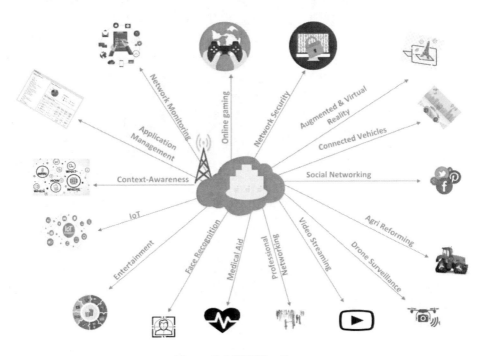

Figure 5. MEC Use Cases.

Operator-Oriented Applications

Local caching can relieve the stress on the core, bringing context-awareness for applications highly dependent on geographical location and help utilizing the network resources more efficiently. The web contents popular in a particular geographical area are cached on MEC server and provided to the subscriber on-demand meeting the latency requirements (Wong et al. 2017). MEC uses advanced location tracking techniques to provide strong context-aware services. MEC takes application requirements into account to decide the appropriate technique, such as analytical modelling, trajectory based calculation or even machine learning techniques.

MEC provides optimum resource utilization because of its strong coordination with the core network.

MEC is foreseen as an aggregation point for IoT nodes as they are mostly abundant and generate large amount of data. As IoT nodes face capacity limitations, MEC can provide them a platform to aggregate their data for processing and act as a gateway for IoT. Furthermore, MEC server forwards only important data to the core instead of raw data produced by nodes, thus saving backhaul capacity (Hu et al. 2015).

User-Oriented Applications

ETSI describes following attractive use cases of MEC from the perspective of users:

Connected Vehicles

One of the major envisioned application of MEC is connected vehicles as MEC can provide ultra-low latency, larger coverage area, high bandwidth and context-awareness. Thousands of sensors are installed on autonomousvehicles, which generate large amount of data, causing lot of stress on the vehicular networks (Gerla 2012). Due to enormous data generation, safety requirements and tight delay constraints, the connected vehicles have created challenge for computation and communication technologies. The researchers have investigated this area intensively and proposed multiple solutions. MEC provides ultra-low latency, which fulfils the requirements of connected vehicles as discussed by (Xie, Ho, and Magsino 2018), (Qiu et al. 2015) and (Ho, Leung, and Polak 2011).

Augmented Reality

Recently augmented reality (AR) has emerged as a new application in which real and virtual environments coexist (Azuma et al. 2001). Many gadgets such as Google glass, Sony watch, Oculus Rift and Layar are becoming increasingly popular because of their wide variety of applications. Augmented reality gadgets involve real-time intensive computation that is highly sensitive to delay, require high bandwidth and good quality of service (QoS) (Yuen, Yaoyuneyong, and Johnson 2011). Augmented reality enriches the user experience by providing extra details about real world. For example, a user is moving in a street, the camera captures the location. With the help of precise location awareness, an application supplements with additional information about that location. As the user moves, the environment changes and hence requires real-time information and computation with ultra-low latency. MEC has potential to meet the requirements of AR as it carries out computation at the edge of the network with very low latency and offers high bandwidth (Hu et al. 2015).

Accelerated Video Streaming

The main objective of MEC is to perform computation locally so as to reduce burden on the core network and avoid unnecessary delay. Currently, transport control protocol (TCP) is used for video streaming that involves hand-shaking and acknowledgement between end points, making it inappropriate for wireless communication. Furthermore, the coverage of a local event or viral video has local significance. Therefore, it is more lucrative to perform processing at MEC server instead of sending back to the cloud and then downloading from the Internet. In case of heavy traffic, multiple streams might cause excessive delay and consume extra bandwidth, which could be saved if caching of such videos is achieved at server level and all processing is carried out locally. This not only enhances the QoE of customers, but also lessens the burden on core network (Hu et al. 2015).

Feature Recognition, Interactive Communication and Gaming

The feature recognition is becoming very popular such as facial, retinal and expression, which involves not only complex computation but also imposes latency requirements. Moreover, with the popularity of wireless interface, mobile and other handheld devices are becoming more ubiquitous. These devices have limited computing power and batteries in order to carry out operations. On the contrary, applications like online gaming, interactive communication and video streaming require heavy computation that results in draining the battery of handheld devices quickly. To address this issue, a computational offloading technique is adopted in MEC that allows the UE to offload computationally-intensive applications to the server. In this way, a UE can partially or completely offload the computation tasks to the server to save its battery. Thus, the computational offloading techniques can affect the server capacity adversely in case all the computation is executed on the server. MEC maintains balance between UE and MEC server load.

From the above discussion, it is clear that MEC is key enabler for contemporary applications.

MEC ARCHITECTURE

MEC is a relatively young technology. Hence, a lot of research is being carried out in this field and people are putting their efforts to improve its implementation, architecture and standardization. Along with the efforts of researchers, ETSI attempts to standardize the MEC paradigm. In this section, we present architecture of MEC from the perspective of latency and integration with IT infrastructure.

Mobile Micro Cell (MMC)

MMC is a new concept revealed by (Wang et al. 2013), offers very low latency in accessing the resources. An MEC server is placed at each BS that fulfils thecomputational needs of the users. The BS is connected to the core cloud through a backhaul link. As there is only single node involved in operation, intermediate manager or entity is not required. However, the MMCs are connected to each other to provide mobility management. It is a simple architecture with closed proximity to the end user, bringing computation at the edge of the network. The proposed architecture is depicted in Figure 6.

The main advantage of MCC is ultra-low latency that can satisfy the requirements of delay-sensitive applications. However, limited resources placed at the edge of the network bring other challenges, such as load balancing, low capacity and single point of failure (Mach and Becvar 2017).

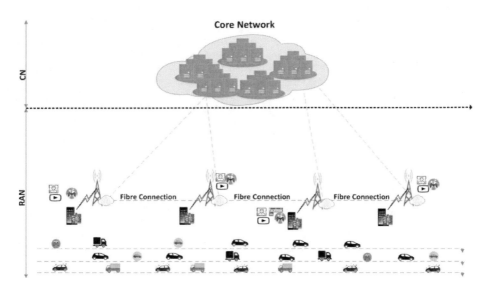

Figure 6. MMC Architecture.

Small Cell Cloud

To enhance the computation and storage capacity of small cells, a European project TROPIC introduced the concept of Small Cell Cloud (SCC) (Pirinen 2014). The idea is to form a pool of resources by combining femto, pico and micro cells resources together. SCC exploits the concept of NFV for pool formation and resource sharing. Contrary to MMC, this architecture involves number of cells, hence a controller called small cell manager (SCM) is required for coordination. SCM is responsible for resource management, coordination among SCeNBs and virtualization (Lobillo et al. 2014). SCM can be centralized and placed near to the SCeNBs cloud or hierarchical divided into local SCM and remote SCM. The local SCM is placed near the edge of the network, while remote SCM is more close to the core network distant from UE (Becvar et al. 2017). The advantage associated with SCC includes high computation capabilities. However, coordination among the nodes and strategic placement of SMC still requires extensive research. Another problem with femto cell is the availability of resources due to its peculiar nature of turning ON and OFF. A pictorial representation of the concept is shown in Figure 7.

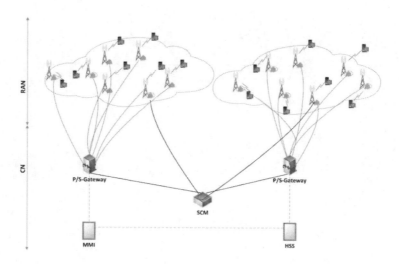

Figure 7. Small Cell Cloud Architecture.

MobiScud

Software defined networking (SDN) offers programmability, flexibility and scalability by separating the data plane from control plane (Alqallaf 2016). By considering the rich features of SDN, Wang et al. proposed MobiScud, which employs SDN along with NFV functionality into the edge computing (Wang et al. 2015), as shown in Figure 8. Contrary to the SCC and MCC, MEC server is not co-located with the BS, but computation resources aredistributed throughout the RAN. As the network resources are scattered, coordination and management of resources is necessary. This is achieved by an entity called MobiScud manager. MobiScud manager not only manages the resources, but also interacts with the SDN network. The main advantages of MobiScud include programmability, scalability, flexibility and high computation resource. However, it is inevitable to select another node for offloading due to its distributed nature. Strong coordination among SDN and cellular network is compulsory so that selection of optimum node could be beneficial for UE.

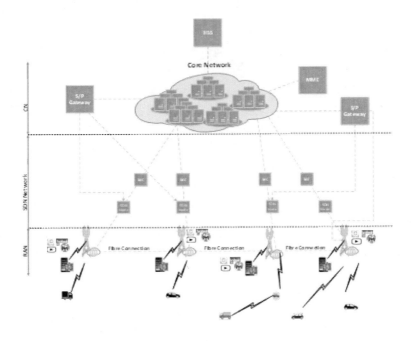

Figure 8. MobiScud Architecture.

Follow Me Cloud (FMC)

A very classical mobile cloud is proposed by (Taleb and Ksentini 2013b), in which the cloud of resources follow the trajectory of the UE. FMC is fully distributed architecture with resources distributed throughout the network. A cloud of resources follow the movement of user as it roams in the network.

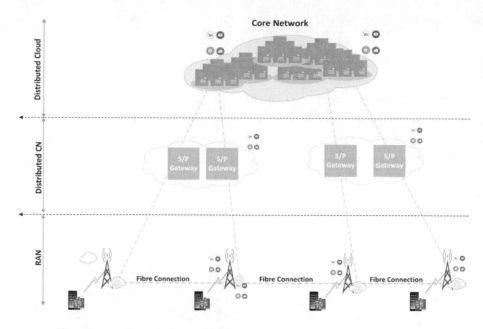

Figure 9. Follow Me Cloud (FMC) Architecture.

Similarly, the core network is also distributed. The concept is equivalent to MobiScud without SDN functionality. The distribution of resources makes them instantly available everywhere in the network. However, due to its distributed nature, the issue of coordination is yet to be investigated. The concept of following the trajectory of UE efficiently addresses the issue of increasing number of customers. Due to distributed nature like SCC and MobiScud, an entititycalled FMC controller (FMCC) is required. The FMCC is responsible for managing resources, determining which datacentre (DC) should be selected for computation offloading. There are two options to deploy FMCC: centrally or hierarchically, which are termed as global and local controller, respectively (Taleb and Ksentini 2013b). In addition to FMC controller, FMC has a Data Centre/Gateway (DC/GW) mapping entity due to distributed data centres. The DC/GW mapping entity is responsible for mapping DCs to service provider's gateways taking into account various factors not limited to no.of hops between DC and CN, location and etc. A pictorial concept is shown in Figure 9.

CONCERT

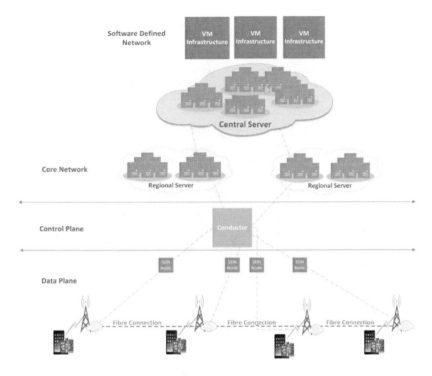

Figure 10. CONCERT Architecture.

Convergence of Cloud and Cellular Systems (CONCERT) is a new concept for implementation of MEC proposed in (Liu et al. 2014). It takes into account the functionalities of SDN and NFV just like MobiScud. The controller in CONCERT is termed as "conductor" that is responsible for resources management, virtualization and coordination between SDN nodes and cellular network. The difference between MobiScud and CONCERT is the distribution of resources in a way that resources are distributed in hierarchical manners while MobiScud has distributed resources. The hierarchical distribution of resources makes it easy to manage them. The requests from the UE are treated in a hierarchical manner, which makes it easy to find the right node for offloading. CONCERT is the most promising solution proposed so far. The architecture of CONCERT is shown in Figure 10.

ETSI Standardization

ETSI has put tremendous efforts in the standardization of MEC. In this section, we overview the recent efforts and progress to integrate MEC concept into mobile network by ETSI. The industry specification group (ISG) is an ETSI group dedicated to specify the architecture, specifications, requirements and terminologies related to MEC. With the help of NFV functions, resources in the MEC are virtualized but readily available for users and operators via standardized APIs (Wong et al. 2017). This is the reason for ultra-low latency of MEC as virtual machine (VM) is accessible at the edge with high speed computation. Besides computation, MEC server also provides with other cloud services, such as traffic monitoring, content caching, video analytic, data compression, local information service and information aggregation.

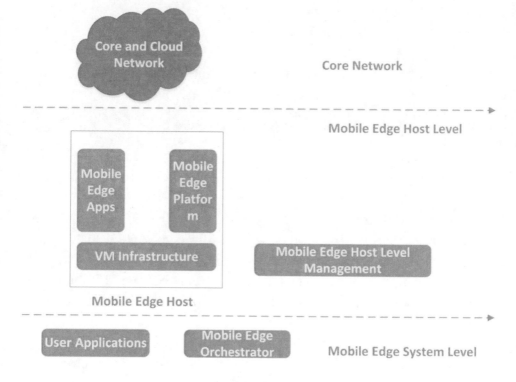

Figure 11. ETSI Reference Architecture.

According to ETSI architecture, there are three layers in MEC as shown in Figure 11. The first layer is called "mobile edge system level" and it makes the UE part. The second layer is called "mobile edge host level," which is MEC, while "networks" layer is core layer. The MEC server layer consists of a functional and a management block. The functional block has three main parts: the virtualization infrastructure, the mobile edge platform and mobile edge applications. The mobile edge platform provides DNS services, life-cycle of applications, operational rules, security and service requirements. Other services, such as resource allocation, resource management, computational offloading management, virtualization, UE location information, radio network optimization, radio link information and bandwidth management are performed by mobile edge host level. The mobile edge applications are applications supported by virtualization box (ETSI 2016).

On the other hand, the "mobile edge system level" layer consists of mobile edge orchestrator and UE applications. The orchestrator in this layer is the main player at UE end. It is the part of the UE that interacts with network and provides coordination among MEC server, UEs and core networks (Wong et al. 2017).

COMPUTATION OFFLOADING

The computationally demanding applications such as 3D gaming, video editing, augmented reality, video streaming and etc. are putting more stress on both the network and the UE battery due to limited computation capacity and battery power. Considering the increasing trend of computation rich applications, limited battery life of UE and delay constraints, an idea of handing over such applications to the cloud could be beneficial. Hence, a new concept of computation offloading emerged, as illustrated in Figure 12. Computation offloading refers to handing over computation tasks to the core network for delay-sensitive applications (Ahmed and Rehmani 2017), (Hu et al. 2015). In this way, not only the capacity of the UE increases but also the computation needs of UE are met. Many researchers have proposed different strategies for offloading as discussed below.

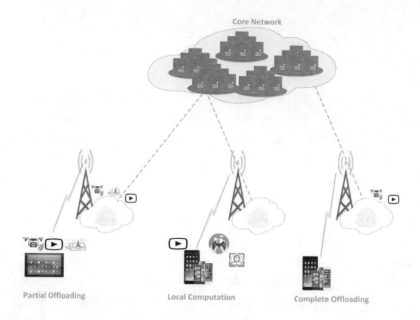

Figure 12. Computation Offloading.

According to (Zhang et al. 2012), the concept of offloading looks very fascinating, but it actually casts serious challenges. It is very important to know how much to offload and what to offload. Based on this, there are three types of computation offloading:

- **Full Offloading:** the whole computational task is offloaded to the cloud. The complete task is handled by MEC server.
- **No Offloading:** If it is not profitable to offload application at core cloud, no offloading is done at all and computation is performed by UE completely.
- **Partial Offloading:** The partial offloading is quite challenging in a sense that computation is to be done partially at the MEC server and partially at the UE. The amount of application to be offloaded is very challenging to decide.

For partial offloading, successive convex approximation (SCA) technique is proposed by (Sardellitti, Scutari, and Barbarossa 2015). SCA-based algorithm is proposed for applications requiring high computation under limited battery constraints. They presented the computation offloading as an optimization problem for a highly dense network. Initially, a single user scenario was considered, which resulted into non-convex optimization problem. Then, it was extended to multiuser scenario, in which several UEs offload on to the MEC server. In the case of multiuser, local optimal solution is achieved and results show that SCA is more efficient as compared to disjoint optimization techniques.

In (Habak et al. 2015), the authors proposed a technique for femto cloud, in which a femto cloud system is developed in order to form a cloud of mobile users. The mobile users are made self-configurable with the help of a service installed on mobiles that calculate energy of mobile, the capacity and resources available for sharing. This information is shared over the cloudlet. Computation tasks to be offloaded are sent to the cloudlet in the form of codes so that all other mobile users could share the resources. The main drawback of femto cloud system is its access via Wi-Fi. However, it could be extended to MEC.

Currently, browsing is a key parameter to measure the QoE. To address the issue of slow browsing, an Edge Accelerated Browsing (EAB) offloading is proposed by (Takahashi, Tanaka, and Kawamura 2015). The EAB proposes to bring the contents down to the edge server placed within RAN. It separates the web traffic from other traffic by creating two different streams, i.e., web and non-web traffic stream. The web requests are handled at EAB server, while remaining traffic is served at EAB-backend.

Another challenge is to minimize the energy consumption with minimum delay. To achieve an optimal solution, (Cao et al. 2015) proposed to use combinatorial optimization. The application is divided into offloadable and non-offloadable parts, and then combinatorial optimization is applied. However, combinatorial optimization introduces complexity into the system, which is normalized by optimal adaptive algorithm. The results show that proposed algorithm is very efficient in saving energy up to 48%. It could yield better results if signal to interference and noise ratio (SINR) gets better. However, the research considers only a single user, which is unrealistic. A realistic model for multiple users is proposed by (Zhao et al. 2015), but it does not divide the application into offloadable and non-offloadable parts. The computation offloading is presented as non-linear constraint problem involving high complexity, which is solved by linear programming. The results show that energy could be saved up to 40% when compared with no offloading, if exhaustive search is implemented. It is assumed that all the users are being served by the same quality channels with homogeneous computing capabilities, which also results in the main drawback of proposed study.

Traditional technique time division multiple access (TDMA) is suggested for multiuser offloading case by (You and Huang 2016). Every user is allotted a timeslot of T duration in which part of the task is offloaded onto MEC server. The amount of offloaded task depends on energy consumption, capacity and link quality. For fairness, higher priority is given to latency-sensitive applications and UEs with limited computation capabilities. The authors extended their work using orthogonal frequency division multiple access (OFDMA) technique by (You et al. 2017), which shows that OFDMA performs ten times more efficient than TDMA.

The connected vehicles is one of the potential applications of MEC as proposed by ETSI. For connected vehicles specifically, a contract-based resource allocation scheme is proposed by (Zhang et al. 2016). The vehicles pay for renting the resources based on pay-as-you-go concept. The concept considers the following factors to make a decision: price, latency-sensitivity and computational power of vehicles.

MOBILITY MANAGEMENT

Handover is an important feature of cellular networks in which the resources are handed over to the next BS to support mobility. Computational offloading is entirely different from simple handover in which resources areonly traffic channels and controlled via transmission power. To maintain the service throughout the network, applications offloaded to one MEC server must be handed over to the next server for mobile users. It involves high complexity due to multiple factors, such as availability of resources on hosting MEC server, amount of resources required and VM migration. There are two cases for handling mobility in case of MEC: one way is VM migration involving selection of new eNB while the other is traditional power control in case of low mobility.

NFV is a key enabler for MEC implementation that turns the generic hardware into network-specific device such as switch, router or IP gateway. The main objective of NFV is to separate the software from hardware leveraging flexible deployment and provisioning of services (Wong et al. 2017). However, main issue is the degradation in performance due to the lack of dedicated hardware. The situation becomes even worse in case of small cells where the coverage is limited and the challenge of virtualized services performance still exists.

VM migration comes into play when a serving BS is unable to accommodate the computation task in order to satisfy the QoS. As described earlier the challenging task is to find out whether VM migration is profitable or not. It is addressed by (Ksentini, Taleb, and Chen 2014), where the authors proposed a model for FMC exploiting the Continuous Time Markov Chain. An optimal decision is formulated to calculate threshold of VM migration if CostM < GainM. In contrast, traditional handover involves the distance and power control only. Simulation results show that proposed model outperforms the traditional handover techniques. The research considers simple ID mobility model and involves high complexity.

It should be noted that VM migration is a trade-off in which low latency is achieved at the expense of time and resources acquired to offload the applications. Hence, it is worth investigating how VM migration influences the performance of UE. The issue is addressed by (Taleb and Ksentini 2013a) in which authors proposed a Markov chain based model. It is found that VM migration can increase the cost, however reduce the latency. It is concluded that VM migration should be done after handover. It results in improved performance with ultra-low latency, improved QoE and optimum MEC server selection.

To decrease the cost of VM migration and latency, a new study using Mixed-Integer quadratic programming is presented by (Sun and Ansari 2016). The technique is called Profit Maximization Avatar Placement (PRIMAL), in which VM migration is formulated as NP hard problem achieving 90% less migration cost. Another technique proposed by (Wang et al. 2017) aims at minimizing the migration cost based on future prediction. The anticipated technique predicts the future VM migration cost with an upper limit on prediction error. For this purpose, an offline algorithm is developed first. It defines a window size for a specific task in which arrival as well as departure of a task is known. This assumption is unrealistic with complexity of $O(M^2T)$, where T is the window size and M is the number of tasks at MEC server. The window size T plays a vital role in VM migration as it can affect the offloading. In other words, too short window size can result into incomplete execution of the task and too long window size can take the predicted values too far away from real values. For a second step, calculation of an optimum value for window size T is done with the help of binary search algorithm. The results show that proposed PRIMAL technique reduces the cost up to 32%. The main drawback of PRIMAL is complexity involved in system and consideration of single user scenario only. To make a realistic model for VM migration, work extended in (Wang et al. 2017) from (Wang et al. 2013) proposing an online algorithm which is simple and more realistic. Simulation results show that it outperforms PRIMAL and saves up to 50% of computation cost.

When the mobility of UE is limited to a small vicinity, power control mechanism is employed for mobility management. A lot of research addressing this issue is available in context of wireless communication.

SECURITY

The three major building blocks of security enlisting confidentiality, availability and integrity evaluate the level of security. This section discusses the security aspects of MEC. There are mainly four traits in terms of security, namely edge network security, backbone network security, MEC server security and VM infrastructure security.

Edge Network Security

Traditionally, the security measures are taken at the core network by the network administrator. However, due to closed proximity and integration of multiple access technologies, MEC faces many security threats. The most common threats include denial of service (DOS), eavesdropping, hijacking and etc to hack the server placed at eNB (Patel et al. 2014). This may cause excess utilization of resources and may jam the network. Another threat of security is man-in-the-middle attack which may cause intercepting of the data. To combat these issues, Han et al. introduced the concept of round-trip time based algorithm that detects the false gateway and prevents the users to get connected with them (Han et al. 2011). The proposed technique exploits the time taken between the domain name system (DNS) server and the UE for identification.

Backbone Network Security

Due to cloud services, the data is managed by the vendors such as Google, Amazon, Microsoft and etc. MEC operator cannot rely solely on the vendors for security. Therefore, measures must be taken as MEC supports device-to-device communication and this can cause a serious threat to the core network. Although, impact of such attacks does not stretch to a big level still users sensitive information may be compromised. These kind of attacks may result into DOS and access problems.

Figure 13. Network Security.

MEC Server Security

MEC servers not only face internal but also physical external threats as they are placed at eNBs. The attackers can physically harm the server if security is compromised somehow. Once the physical access is gained by the attackers, they can harm the server in many ways; execution of malicious code or software, DOS execution or redirect the traffic to a rogue gateway. On the other hand, data floating between the MEC server and data centre can be compromised with malicious attacks.

VM Infrastructure Security

VM infrastructure is more vulnerable because a compromised or hacked VM server can affect the whole infrastructure. For this purpose, special care is needed in order to carry out the operations. This may lead to excessive delay, DOS attacks, inadequate resources, underutilization of resources and stolen personal data in the worst case. The impact of such attacks may lead to poor network operations. To address such issues and make the infrastructure secure, G. Pek et al. proposed an algorithm that defines different policies regarding hypervisor hardening, network isolation and network abstractions (Pék, Buttyán, and Bencsáth 2013).

ECONOMIC PERSPECTIVE

For a technology to be successful, revenue plays a vital role and hence economic perspective must be analysed critically. The main challenge, as for many technologies, is reduction in cost and increased revenue. For good QoE, it involves multiple factors, such as integrity, security, innovative applications, Value Added Services (VAS) and low latency. With the rapid growth in data generation from mobile devices, in particular, has not only strained the backhaul capacity but also casts challenges for QoE. Furthermore, IoT and smart home concepts have been emerged as new challenges for operators to cater in context of data production that could be potential threat to QoE.

The operators are in competition to provide new applications and services to regular customers, industries and institutions. Furthermore, technology integration, flexible architecture, context-awareness, virtualization and latency are the key enablers for MEC deployment. Keeping in view the above mentioned factors, it is foreseen that MEC has many use cases, such as software defined vehicular networks, augmented reality, health care, IoT, web caching, gaming and WSAN. The major lucrative benefit of MEC lies in its closed proximity to the UE that brings cloud into the RAN. Furthermore, knowledge about real-time radio networks can increase the context-awareness, leading to optimized resource utilization and improved QoE (ETSI 2016). Another characteristic of MEC is efficient web caching and accelerated interactivity having huge impact on user experience. MEC provides flexibility and agility by offering the application developers to develop new applications and services. In this way, a new opportunity on the business horizon will appear.

MEC can play key role in the implementation of 5G due to its peculiar characteristics providing new business opportunities in many fields. MEC is being envisioned as s new paradigm with variety of business opportunities on a single platform. So far, there is a large room available for investigating the economic perspective of MEC implementation in 5G. To the best of our knowledge, there is no significant literature available to discuss the potential economic aspects of MEC in 5G. There is a need of concrete business model across the board.

POTENTIAL RESEARCH DIRECTIONS

This section describes the potential challenges faced by MEC and enlists the possible research directions. As MEC is comparatively young technology, there exists lot of issues to be addressed. We explain those potential research areas and directions for researchers in this section.

Software Defined Networking Integration

Software Defined Networking (SDN) is a new paradigm that separates data plane from control plane leveraging flexibility, programmability and scalability into the network (Liu et al. 2017). SDN has been witnessed as a promising solution for a wide range of networks such as data centres, vehicular networks, wireless communication and etc. Very little work has been done so far to integrate MEC with SDN. Authors of (Jain and Paul 2013) discussed the scope of integrating the SDN with MEC. Similarly, an application of MEC along with SDN for intelligent VANET is proposed in (Deng et al. 2017). The results show that SDN can play a vital role with MEC to mitigate the latency, provide higher data rate and high bandwidth. SDN has opened new horizons for research and it is worth investigating how can MEC exploit it to combat the challenges. Hence, it is very beneficial investigating the scope of integration.

Mobility Management

Mobility management in traditional wireless networks is normally performed by Mobile Switching Centre (MSC). However, in case of MEC special techniques are needed as discussed in Section 3. MEC involves not only handover of communication resources but also computation resources. When a user enters a new cell, both communication channels and VM resources need to be carried forward. Furthermore, the heterogeneity of mobile devices and services involved in MEC makes mobility and handover process more complex. The researchers have contributed remarkably towards mobility management and VM migration. However, most of the research considers single node scenario, in which single BS/eNB is responsible for mobility management. An extensive research is needed to investigate the impact of handover if multiple nodes are involved and determine how frequent VM migration could be avoided. Another challenge associated with VM migration is complexity, which can lead to migration delay as techniques proposed so far involve complex computation.

Computation Offloading

One of the most promising feature of edge computing is computation offloading, which allows power-limited handheld devices to offload their computation to the servers. Researchers so far assume unlimited MEC resources, which is certainly unrealistic. In practice, an MEC server is associated with multiple UEs, who need to offload their tasks. This should be taken into account while considering offloading. Another aspect is the appropriate slicing size of application as network resources keep on changing with time. While performing computational offloading, the researchers have not considered UE mobility, which is not practical particularly for mobile networks. A possible direction is to investigate the scenario of mobile UE while offloading is being done. In context of green networking, it is very important to consider the energy consumption by core devices. This is not addressed as all the work done so far focus on the issue of UE battery consumption. The processing time and cost associated with a computation job must be known so that resources can be efficiently allocated. For this purpose, multiple prediction-based techniques are proposed, which make the real-time computation more complicated.

Resources Management and Scheduling

Edge computing is very different from traditional communication paradigms as it consists of heterogeneous resources. As MEC incorporates a variety of resources, there must be a well-defined mechanism to elegantly manage all those resources. In this regard, a signalling system could be deployed to develop coordination among different entities. Besides coordination mechanism, another research challenge is dynamic resources sharing. According to the literature discussed so far, a UE can access the available resources and allotted resources can't be changed during handover process. This results in inefficient resource utilization. Furthermore, fairness among UEs in terms of resource sharing is a key parameter for MEC performance, which should be dealt with great care. In this context, current research considers only a single server performing scheduling among different jobs. However, MEC requires more complex scheduling technique. This is particularly due to its unique nature of heterogeneity that encompasses multiple servers, access techniques and mobile edge hosts. It is possible via effective scheduling technique and optimal distribution of resources throughout the network.

Security and Privacy

Data integrity and security is one of the basic requirements for a communication platform. Being more exposed to multiple technologies, MEC faces intensive security threats as many UEs offload their applications to common server using wireless interface. This requires a strong security mechanism (Sookhak et al. 2014). Another potential threat of malicious attacks to MEC is due to its distributed nature with resources widespread throughout the radio access network (RAN). MEC is unique in its nature due to stringent requirements imposed, which makes it more vulnerable to security and privacy issues. For example, it is challenging to select a technology for global system that makes it secure in spite of its ubiquitous nature, distributed VM architecture and heterogeneous connection. Hence, new security parameters are needed, from physical to application layer and from integrating different technologies (i.e., communication, computation, NFV and servers) to single edge host level.

CONCLUSION

Mobile edge computing is a key player for 5G due to its peculiar characteristics, which fully meet the requirements of modern application. MEC offers ultra-low latency, intensive computation and communication as a unified package. MEC concept has potential to attract the communication market in the future and is capable to support contemporary applications such as augmented reality, e-health, VANET, video streaming, gaming and interactive communication. MEC offers computational offloading at one hop for UE, thus saving battery consumption of UEs. However, MEC is comparatively a young technology and requires a standard architecture in order to become fully functional. In this regard, works done so far make simple and unreal assumptions. Therefore, it requires rigorous validation through real-time scenarios. In this way, an extensive performance analysis under stringent latency requirements would be validated.

REFERENCES

Abbas, Nasir, Yan Zhang, Amir Taherkordi and Tor Skeie. 2018. "Mobile edge computing: A survey." *IEEE Internet of Things Journal* 5 (1):450-465.

Ahmed, Ejaz and Mubashir Husain Rehmani. 2017. "Mobile Edge Computing: Opportunities, solutions, and challenges." *Future Generation Computer Systems* 70:59-63. doi: https://doi.org/10.1016/j.future.2016.09.015.

Alqallaf, Maha. 2016. *Software Defined Secure Ad Hoc Wireless Networks.*

Azuma, Ronald, Yohan Baillot, Reinhold Behringer, Steven Feiner, Simon Julier, and Blair MacIntyre. 2001. *Recent advances in augmented reality.* Naval Research Lab Washington DC.

Becvar, Zdenek, Matej Rohlik, Pavel Mach, Michal Vondra, Tomas Vanek, Miguel A Puente and Felicia Lobillo. 2017. "Distributed architecture of 5G mobile networks for efficient computation management in mobile edge computing." *5G Radio Access Networks: Centralized RAN, Cloud-RAN and Virtualization of Small Cells* 29.

Bonomi, Flavio, Rodolfo Milito, Jiang Zhu and Sateesh Addepalli. 2012. "Fog computing and its role in the internet of things." *Proceedings of the first edition of the MCC workshop on Mobile cloud computing.*

Borgia, Eleonora, Raffaele Bruno, Marco Conti, Davide Mascitti and Andrea Passarella. 2016. "Mobile edge clouds for Information-Centric IoT services." 2016 *IEEE Symposium on Computers and Communication* (ISCC).

Cao, Shiwei, Xiaofeng Tao, Yanzhao Hou and Qimei Cui. 2015. "An energy-optimal offloading algorithm of mobile computing based on HetNets." *2015 International Conference on Connected Vehicles and Expo (ICCVE).*

Chiang, Mung and Tao Zhang. 2016. "Fog and IoT: An overview of research opportunities." *IEEE Internet of Things Journal* 3 (6):854-864.

Chun, Byung-Gon, Sunghwan Ihm, Petros Maniatis, Mayur Naik and Ashwin Patti. 2011. "Clonecloud: elastic execution between mobile device and cloud." *Proceedings of the sixth conference on Computer systems.*

Cisco. 2016a. *Cisco Visual Networking Index: Glocal Mobile Data Traffic Forecast Update,* 2016-2021 White Paper. Cisco, accessed October

Cisco, Visual Networking Index. 2016b. *Global Mobile Data Traffic Forecast Update, 2015–2020* White Paper. Document ID 958959758.

Deng, Der-Jiunn, Shao-Yu Lien, Chun-Cheng Lin, Shao-Chou Hung and Wei-Bo Chen. 2017. "Latency control in software-defined mobile-edge vehicular networking." *IEEE Communications Magazine* 55 (8):87-93.

Edmonds, Andrew, and Thomas Michael Bohnert. 2016. "Efficient exploitation of mobile edge computing for virtualized 5G in EPC architectures." *4th IEEE International Conference on Mobile Cloud Computing, Services, and Engineering (MobileCloud),* Oxford, 29 Mar-01 Apr, 2016.

ETSI, GSMEC. 2016. "002: Mobile Edge Computing (MEC)." *Technical Requirements* 1.

Gerla, Mario. 2012. *"Vehicular cloud computing."* Ad Hoc Networking Workshop (Med-Hoc-Net), 2012 The 11th Annual Mediterranean.

Habak, Karim, Mostafa Ammar, Khaled A Harras and Ellen Zegura. 2015. "Fem to clouds: Leveraging mobile devices to provide cloud service at the edge." *2015 IEEE 8th International Conference on Cloud Computing (CLOUD).*

Han, Hao, Bo Sheng, Chiu Chiang Tan, Qun Li and Sanglu Lu. 2011. "A timing-based scheme for rogue AP detection." *IEEE Transactions on parallel and distributed Systems* 22 (11):1912-1925.

Ho, Ivan Wang-Hei, Kin K Leung and John W Polak. 2011. "Stochastic model and connectivity dynamics for VANETs in signalized road systems." *IEEE/ACM Transactions on Networking (TON)* 19 (1):195-208.

Hong, Kirak, David Lillethun, Umakishore Ramachandran, Beate Ottenwälder and Boris Koldehofe. 2013. "Mobile fog: A programming model for large-scale applications on the internet of things." *Proceedings of the second ACM SIGCOMM workshop on Mobile cloud computing.*

Hu, Yun Chao, Milan Patel, Dario Sabella, Nurit Sprecher and Valerie Young. 2015. *"Mobile edge computing—A key technology towards 5G."* ETSI white paper 11 (11):1-16.

Jain, Raj and Subharthi Paul. 2013. "Network virtualization and software defined networking for cloud computing: a survey." *IEEE Communications Magazine* 51 (11):24-31.

Jararweh, Yaser, Ahmad Doulat, Ala Darabseh, Mohammad Alsmirat, Mahmoud Al-Ayyoub and Elhadj Benkhelifa. 2016. "SDMEC: Software defined system for mobile edge computing." *2016 IEEE International Conference on Cloud Engineering Workshop (IC2EW).*

Ksentini, Adlen, Tarik Taleb and Min Chen. 2014. "A Markov decision process-based service migration procedure for follow me cloud." *2014 IEEE International Conference on Communications (ICC).*

Liu, Jianqi, Jiafu Wan, Bi Zeng, Qinruo Wang, Houbing Song and Meikang Qiu. 2017. "A scalable and quick-response software defined vehicular network assisted by mobile edge computing." *IEEE Communications Magazine* 55 (7):94-100.

Liu, Jingchu, Tao Zhao, Sheng Zhou, Yu Cheng and Zhisheng Niu. 2014. "CONCERT: a cloud-based architecture for next-generation cellular systems." *IEEE Wireless Communications* 21 (6):14-22.

Lobillo, Felicia, Zdenek Becvar, Miguel Angel Puente, Pavel Mach, Francesco Lo Presti, Fabrizio Gambetti, Mariana Goldhamer, Josep Vidal, Anggoro K Widiawan and Emilio Calvanesse. 2014. "An architecture for mobile computation offloading on cloud-enabled LTE small cells." *Wireless Communications and Networking Conference Workshops (WCNCW), 2014 IEEE.*

Luan, Tom H, Longxiang Gao, Zhi Li, Yang Xiang, Guiyi Wei and Limin Sun. 2015. "Fog computing: Focusing on mobile users at the edge." *arXiv preprint arXiv:1502.01815.*

Mach, Pavel and Zdenek Becvar. 2017. *"Mobile edge computing: A survey on architecture and computation offloading."* arXiv preprint arXiv:1702.05309.

Madsen, Henrik, Bernard Burtschy, G Albeanu and FL Popentiu-Vladicescu. 2013. "Reliability in the utility computing era: Towards reliable fog computing." *International Conference on Systems, Signals and Image Processing (IWSSIP)*, 2013 20th.

Mtibaa, Abderrahmen, Afnan Fahim, Khaled A Harras and Mostafa H Ammar. 2013. "Towards resource sharing in mobile device clouds: Power balancing across mobile devices." *ACM SIGCOMM Computer Communication Review*.

Neal, A. 2016. *"Mobile edge computing (MEC); technical requirements."* ETSI, Sophia Antipolis, France, White Paper no. DGS/MEC-002.

Nishio, Takayuki, Ryoichi Shinkuma, Tatsuro Takahashi and Narayan B Mandayam. 2013. "Service-oriented heterogeneous resource sharing for optimizing service latency in mobile cloud." *Proceedings of the first international workshop on Mobile cloud computing & networking*.

Ottenwälder, Beate, Boris Koldehofe, Kurt Rothermel and Umakishore Ramachandran. 2013. "MigCEP: operator migration for mobility driven distributed complex event processing." *Proceedings of the 7th ACM international conference on Distributed event-based systems*.

Patel, Milan, B Naughton, C Chan, N Sprecher, S Abeta and A Neal. 2014. "Mobile-edge computing introductory technical white paper." *White Paper, Mobile-edge Computing (MEC) industry initiative*.

Pék, Gábor, Levente Buttyán and Boldizsár Bencsáth. 2013. "A survey of security issues in hardware virtualization." *ACM Computing Surveys (CSUR)* 45 (3):40.

Pirinen, Pekka. 2014. "A brief overview of 5G research activities." *2014 1st International Conference on 5G for Ubiquitous Connectivity (5GU)*.

Qiu, Harry JF, Ivan Wang-Hei Ho, K Tse Chi and Yu Xie. 2015. "A methodology for studying 802.11 p VANET broadcasting performance with practical vehicle distribution." *IEEE transactions on vehicular technology* 64 (10):4756-4769.

Roman, Rodrigo, Javier Lopez and Masahiro Mambo. 2018. "Mobile edge computing, fog et al.: A survey and analysis of security threats and challenges." *Future Generation Computer Systems* 78:680-698.

Sardellitti, Stefania, Gesualdo Scutari and Sergio Barbarossa. 2015. "Joint optimization of radio and computational resources for multicell mobile-edge computing." *IEEE Transactions on Signal and Information Processing over Networks* 1 (2):89-103.

Satyanarayanan, Mahadev, Zhuo Chen, Kiryong Ha, Wenlu Hu, Wolfgang Richter and Padmanabhan Pillai. 2014. "Cloudlets: at the leading edge of mobile-cloud convergence." *2014 6ᵗʰ International Conference on Mobile Computing, Applications and Services (MobiCASE).*

Shi, Weisong, Jie Cao, Quan Zhang, Youhuizi Li and Lanyu Xu. 2016. "Edge computing: Vision and challenges." *IEEE Internet of Things Journal* 3 (5):637-646.

Sookhak, Mehdi, Hamid Talebian, Ejaz Ahmed, Abdullah Gani and Muhammad Khurram Khan. 2014. "A review on remote data auditing in single cloud server: Taxonomy and open issues." *Journal of Network and Computer Applications* 43:121-141.

Sun, Xiang and Nirwan Ansari. 2016. "PRIMAL: Profit maximization avatar placement for mobile edge computing." *IEEE International Conference on Communications (ICC), 2016.*

Takahashi, Noriyuki, Hiroyuki Tanaka and Ryutaro Kawamura. 2015. "Analysis of process assignment in multi-tier mobile cloud computing and application to edge accelerated web browsing." *2015 3ʳᵈ IEEE International Conference on Mobile Cloud Computing, Services, and Engineering (MobileCloud).*

Taleb, Tarik and Adlen Ksentini. 2013a. "An analytical model for follow me cloud." *Global Communications Conference (GLOBECOM), 2013 IEEE.*

Taleb, Tarik and Adlen Ksentini. 2013b. "Follow me cloud: interworking federated clouds and distributed mobile networks." *IEEE Network* 27 (5):12-19.

Velte, Toby and Anthony Velte. 2013. *Cisco A Beginner's Guide*: McGraw-Hill Education Group.

Verbelen, Tim, Pieter Simoens, Filip De Turck and Bart Dhoedt. 2012. "Cloudlets: Bringing the cloud to the mobile user." *Proceedings of the third ACM workshop on Mobile cloud computing and services.*

Wang, Kaiqiang, Minwei Shen, Junguk Cho, Arijit Banerjee, Jacobus Van der Merwe and Kirk Webb. 2015. "Mobiscud: A fast moving personal cloud in the mobile network." *Proceedings of the 5ᵗʰ Workshop on All Things Cellular: Operations, Applications and Challenges.*

Wang, Shiqiang, Guan-Hua Tu, Raghu Ganti, Ting He, Kin Leung, Howard Tripp, Katy Wan and Murtaza Zafer. 2013. "Mobile micro-cloud: Application classification, mapping, and deployment." *Proc. Annual Fall Meeting of ITA (AMITA).*

Wang, Shiqiang, Rahul Urgaonkar, Ting He, Kevin Chan, Murtaza Zafer and Kin K Leung. 2017. "Dynamic service placement for mobile micro-clouds with predicted future costs." *IEEE Transactions on Parallel and Distributed Systems* 28 (4):1002-1016.

Wong, Vincent WS, Robert Schober, Derrick Wing Kwan Ng and Li-Chun Wang. 2017. *Key technologies for 5G wireless systems*: Cambridge University Press.

Xie, Yu, Ivan Wang-Hei Ho and Elmer R Magsino. 2018. "The Modeling and Cross-Layer Optimization of 802.11 p VANET Unicast." *IEEE Access* 6:171-186.

Yi, Shanhe, Zijiang Hao, Zhengrui Qin and Qun Li. 2015. "Fog computing: Platform and applications." 2015 *Third IEEE Workshop on Hot Topics in Web Systems and Technologies (HotWeb).*

You, Changsheng and Kaibin Huang. 2016. "Multiuser resource allocation for mobile-edge computation offloading." *Global Communications Conference (GLOBECOM), 2016 IEEE.*

You, Changsheng, Kaibin Huang, Hyukjin Chae and Byoung-Hoon Kim. 2017. "Energy-efficient resource allocation for mobile-edge computation offloading." *IEEE Transactions on Wireless Communications* 16 (3):1397-1411.

Yuen, Steve Chi-Yin, Gallayanee Yaoyuneyong and Erik Johnson. 2011. "Augmented reality: An overview and five directions for AR in education." *Journal of Educational Technology Development and Exchange (JETDE)* 4 (1):11.

Zhang, Ke, Yuming Mao, Supeng Leng, Alexey Vinel and Yan Zhang. 2016. "Delay constrained offloading for mobile edge computing in cloud-enabled vehicular networks." *2016 8ᵗʰ International Workshop on Resilient Networks Design and Modeling (RNDM),*

Zhang, Yuan, Hao Liu, Lei Jiao and Xiaoming Fu. 2012. "To offload or not to offload: an efficient code partition algorithm for mobile cloud computing." *2012 IEEE 1st International Conference on Cloud Networking (CLOUDNET).*

Zhao, Yun, Sheng Zhou, Tianchu Zhao and Zhisheng Niu. 2015. "Energy-efficient task offloading for multiuser mobile cloud computing." *ICCC.*

Zhu, Jiang, Douglas S Chan, Mythili Suryanarayana Prabhu, Preethi Natarajan, Hao Hu and Flavio Bonomi. 2013. "Improving web sites performance using edge servers in fog computing architecture." *2013 IEEE Seventh International Symposium on Service-Oriented System Engineering.*

. Vehicular Networks   ISBN: 978-1-53615-978-3
.ditors: P. H. J. Chong and I. W-H. Ho   © 2019 Nova Science Publishers, Inc.

Chapter 6

LOCATION PRIVACY FOR THE NEXT GENERATION NETWORKS: ACHIEVING LOCATION PRIVACY IN HIGHLY CONNECTED AND AUTONOMOUS VEHICLES

Philip Asuquo[1],* Yue Cao[2], Shihan Bao[1], Waleed Hathal[1], Ao Lei[1] and Haitham Cruickshank[1]
[1]Institute for Communication Systems, University of Surrey, Guildford, United Kingdom
[2]School of Computing and Communications, Lancaster University, Lancaster, United Kingdom

ABSTRACT

There is an unprecedented revolution in the transportation industry due to the growing interest in connected and autonomous vehicles (CAVs). This has led to the rapid development of cloud-based infrastructures and services with huge amount of traffic related information

---

*Corresponding Author's E-mail: p.asuquo@surrey.ac.uk

generated and utilized. In vehicular communications, each vehicle periodically broadcasts safety messages and these messages may be exploited to compromise the location privacy of the user. Although several pseudonym changing schemes have been proposed to provide location privacy protection, these schemes do not guarantee location privacy protection. This chapter proposes an Infrastructure-Assisted Pseudonym Changing Scheme (IPCS). IPCS aims to provide location privacy against trajectory attacks thereby reducing the linkability of the pseudonyms. We demonstrate through analytical evaluation and simulation results that IPCS is very effective and provides a stronger location privacy protection when compared to existing privacy enhancing schemes.

INTRODUCTION

In the last few years, there have been dedicated research efforts in vehicular communications ranging from challenges in networking and communication technologies to security and privacy protection. Recently, there has been a growing interest in smart cities, which has influenced transportation systems (Lim et al. 2017). In addition to Direct Short Range Communication for Vehicle-to-Vehicle (V2V), vehicles now have access to 4G LTE in-car Internet services. Again, spatio-temporal information are sent to vehicles based on their locations using GPS technology as described in the ETSI Standards for Cooperative Awareness Messages (CAM) and Decentralized Environmental Network Message (DENM) (Pingley et al. 2011). As discussed in (Niu et al. 2014), Connected and Autonomous Vehicles (CAVs) will broadcast different classes of messages from one-hop to certain geographic areas. This implies that safety, traffic efficiency management, infotainment, and network coordination applications will broadcast different types of messages that will include GPS information. In addition to the security requirements in vehicular communications which include; confidentiality, authentication and security, privacy is another requirement which must be addressed (Buttyan et al. 2009). Privacy in vehicular communications is achieved with changing of identifiers (pseudonyms) frequently. This approach was adopted by the current security standard IEEE 1609.2 (Standards Committee 2016).

Vehicular communication consists of vehicles and infrastructure (Road-Side-Units), where vehicles send periodic broadcast to neighbouring vehicles

(Vehicle-to-Vehicle V2V) or (Vehicle-to-Infrastructure V2I). This beacon messages sent by each vehicle contains its speed, location, direction of travel etc. for safety and the optimization of traffic routes (Youssef, Atluri, and Adam 2005). The availability of this information may lead to the leakage privacy from the disclosure of location information. Protecting the location privacy of users in vehicular communication is quite challenging, as changing pseudonyms (vehicle identities) may not be very effective with a global attacker (Chow, Mokbel and Liu 2006). Despite the significant research effort on pseudonym changing strategies (Youssef, Atluri, and Adam 2005), achieving an effective location privacy is still an open issue.

RELATED WORK

In this section, existing location privacy enhancing techniques are reviewed. These privacy enhancing approaches (Silent periods (Huang et al. 2014), (Sampigethaya et al. 2007), (Li et al. 2006), Mix-zones (Freudiger, Shokri, and Hubaux 2009), (Buttyan, Holczer, and Vajda 2007) and Location obfuscation) have been widely discussed in literature to address location privacy in vehicular communications. A user-centric scheme for mitigating location tracking is proposed in (Li et al. 2006). In the Swing technique, the pseudonyms are changed by the vehicles when their speed and directions are changed. This makes it difficult for an attacker to correlate the locations of the node before and after an update by utilizing the movement predictions of the nodes. In the Swap technique, location privacy is maximised by the exchange of the vehicle identifiers. The vehicles exchange their pseudonyms with a probability of 0.5 during an update and then enter a silent period. However, indistinguishability is only achieved by the cooperating vehicles from the vehicle that initiated the pseudonym change. In (Sampigethaya et al. 2007), authors pay attention to the mitigation of unauthorized location tracking and LBS profiling from service providers. They identify the vulnerabilities from accumulated location history of vehicles over time. They also consider the vulnerabilities associated with additional information from visited locations from places of interest using geographical maps thereby enabling profiling of personal interest. They propose a scheme (AMOEBA) based on the group navigation of vehicles for user and location privacy. AMOEBA uses a group concept to provide location privacy.

A random silent period is used to provide unlinkability between the locations of a vehicle. They consider a scenario where a target vehicle joins the network and broadcast safety messages. This target vehicle remains silent and updates its pseudonym from C to C' then broadcast with C' after a random silent period. In (Eichler 2007), the author discusses the general issues on pseudonym changing in VANET. They focus on the influence of the mobility of the vehicles on pseudonym changes by adjusting the silent period based on the mobility of the vehicle. They identify two parameters (node re-interaction and quiet time) which must be assessed to improve the efficiency of location privacy achieved by pseudonyms. These parameters are mainly influenced by the node mobility characteristics. In order to achieve a high degree of unlinkability between the pseudonyms, they claim that an optimal interval for pseudonym change must be adapted to the node interaction interval. Different from the approaches in (Eichler 2007), (Sampigethaya et al. 2007), a silent period technique SLOW (silent on low-speed) is proposed in (Buttyan et al. 2009). The SLOW protocol does not need an infrastructure or cooperation from neighbouring vehicles. When the speed of the vehicle drops below a pre-defined threshold, vehicles do not transmit messages. They define this period as the silent period where vehicles can change their pseudonyms. They describe a scenario in an urban area that is crowded whenever a group of vehicles stop at the traffic signal point. They also create mix-zones at the points where there are maximum uncertainties about a vehicle. The authors claim that SLOW ensures a smooth synchronization process when the pseudonym is changed in the silent period. SLOW also reduces the burden of large verification of digital signatures when the vehicle density is large. The authors in (Sampigethaya et al. 2012) look into the tracking of broadcast communication of vehicles by adversaries. They propose a location privacy scheme (CARAVAN) to unlink the locations of a vehicle. They describe two tracking methods (simple and correlation tracking) used by adversaries to link two possible locations of a vehicle and take into account the mobility and application features of VANETs. CARAVAN combines a silent period enhancement technique with group navigation to prevent the tracking of vehicles. The group navigation provides unlinkability between the vehicle's pseudonym and the LBS application that is accessing the service. When an application request is received from a vehicle, this request is forwarded by the group leader using its own address to the registration authority. through the RSU. A session key is provided by the registration authority to both the LBS provider and the vehicle after the validation of the application request. The entire communication between the vehicle and the LBS provider is encrypted by this key. Mix-zones enhance location privacy using anonymous communication zones. These zones are mostly road intersections where the speed and direction of a vehicle is likely to change. When a vehicle enters a mix-zone, it stops sending messages and updates its pseudonym. The effect of changing pseudonyms frequently in location privacy is examined by the authors in (Buttyan, Holczer, and Vajda 2007). In this approach, traffic is generated on non-trivial road maps with realistic parameters. The authors assume that the antennas are positioned by attackers in the network to overhear communication. In their analysis of the effectiveness of mix-zones, they conclude that the optimal frequency of pseudonym change depends on the attributes of the mix-zones such as the location, size and the number of entry points. In (Freudiger et al. 2007), mix-zones are created using cryptographic techniques CMIX at road intersections within the broadcast distance of the RSUs. The CMIX protocol distributes symmetric keys using traditional asymmetric cryptography for the establishment of the cryptographic mix-zones. In the Cmix-zone, all broadcast messages by vehicles are encrypted with the symmetric key distributed by the RSU. The authors claim that CMIX makes it difficult for an attacker to link the identity of a vehicle since the same key is used by all vehicles. In (Lu 2011), (Lu 2012), the authors propose changing of pseudonym at social spots (PCS) as a strategy to achieve high location privacy. Vehicles temporarily gather at social spots such as free parking lots that may be close to a shopping mall or at road intersections when the traffic light turns red. They state that a social spot becomes a mix-zone if pseudonyms are changed by all the vehicles before leaving that spot. An indistinguishable information is broadcast as safety message which shows the location of the vehicle as a social spot at a velocity of 0 with an unlinkable pseudonym. They show that when pseudonyms are changed by all the vehicles simultaneously, the high density makes it difficult for attackers to track the vehicles. However, pseudonym changing at social spots does not provide sufficient privacy protection when the vehicle density is low. Yu *et al.* (Yu 2016) propose a MixGroup scheme for location privacy. Based on sporadic observations, they exploit meeting opportunities to change pseudonyms and improve location privacy. Observations are made from real vehicle traces based on social spots and sporadic observations.

MixGroup is used to construct an extended pseudonym group region where vehicles can change their accumulated pseudonyms. Each group has a group leader and a group identifier. When a vehicle enters a group, the group leader will assign a group ID with a certificate and a private key to the new vehicle after authentication. The group ID, certificate and the private key are used for changing pseudonyms and broadcasting safety messages. An entropy-optimal negotiation procedure is used to facilitate the process of exchanging pseudonyms among vehicles. They quantitatively measure the risk and benefits associated with the pseudonym exchange using a pre-defined pseudonym entropy. In (Hoh et al. 2007), a delay is introduced into the anonymization process. The basic idea is using a path confusion algorithm to perform a posteriori analysis of the path of the users. Assuming two users pass through an intersection similar to (Beresford and Stajano 2003) at time t_0 and t_1 respectively where $t_0 < t_1 < t_0 + t_{delay}$. The posteriori analysis is performed at t_{delay}. The paths intersect in a way that anonymity is created. Although two users were not in the location at the same time, the user location is not known by the LBS until both have crossed the intersection point. In this scheme, the real time operation is compromised by the introduction of delay. If the anonymity accumulated after $t_0 + t_{delay}$ is insufficient, the path confusion algorithm may not release the location of the user to the LBS. A mutual obfuscating path (MOP) (Lim et al. 2017) is proposed for location privacy in connected vehicles. MOP is used to retrieve spatio-temporal information in real time. Different from other approaches, MOP does not make use of the intersections in the user's path. MOP takes advantage of the dedicated short range communication (DSRC) radios to obfuscate location tracking. They consider a communication range of $200 - 400m$ as the DSRC beacon when two vehicles communicate using the LBS server to determine whether the MOPs can be generated. MOP is performed when a vehicle receives a beacon. As explained in (Lim et al. 2017), assuming vehicle A wants to mutually obfuscate the path with vehicle B, the kinematic information such as the current location loc_{cur}^B, speed $speed_{cur}^B$ and the direction dir_{cur}^B are used to define a threshold for the convergence time T_{thld}. The MOP process requires cooperation from neighbouring vehicles. According to the authors, a selfish or non-cooperative vehicle threatens its own privacy by not cooperating since the LBS uses posteriori reasoning to guarantee the mutual obfuscation of all connected paths.

In this book chapter, we propose an infrastructure-assisted location privacy scheme using the system model in (Emara 2017). We use the context-aware broadcast classification to develop IPCS which guarantees location privacy.

PROBLEM STATEMENT

In this section, the system model is briefly introduced as well as the assumption and design objectives.

System Model

We assume that each vehicle has an on-board unit (OBU) which broadcasts application protocol messages as defined in (Meyerowitz and Choudhury 2009). Each broadcast message contains the current state of the vehicle, a pseudonym and time-stamp. For each vehicle, pseudonym changing occurs every 5 minutes. The proposed model consists of Intelligent Transportation Systems (ITS) Stations; the vehicles, road side units (RSUs) and the trusted authority (TA). It is assumed that each vehicle is equipped with a GPS receiver and maintains messages from neighbouring vehicles within its communication range with Multi-Target Tracking (MTT) algorithm described in (Emara 2016), (Emara, Woerndl, and Schlichter 2013). The MTT algorithm is useful in the predication of the state of a vehicle even when its radio is turned off. This also helps in improving the safety awareness of a broadcast message. We combine the MTT algorithm with a context-aware similarity protocol to determine the appropriate time for a vehicle to change its identity.

1. Vehicles: Each vehicle is equipped with an OBU that supports communication using IEEE 802.11p (DSRC). Each vehicle can communicate with other vehicles and the RSUs.

2. RSU: It is assumed that the RSU is a trusted entity that cannot be compromised. RSU can communicate with vehicles within its range and other RSUs. The validity of messages from vehicles can be checked by the RSUs.

3. TA: The TA is a trusted third-party that acts as a registration centre for

RSUs and OBUs. The TA uses a secure layer transmission protocol to communicate with the OBU and RSU.

We develop a context-based class broadcast for different application specific protocols as defined below.

- Category 1: This category consists of one-hop periodic broadcast messages such as Cooperative Awareness Message (CAM) defined in ETSI ITS-G5 or Basic Safety Message defined in IEEE 1609.

- Category 2: This group defines protocols that broadcast event messages such as emergency information. One of such protocols is the Decentralized Environmental Notification Message (DENM) Which is an event trigger message and can only be detected by a few vehicles. Some DENM messages have higher priority than CAMs and BSMs.

- Category 3: We consider application protocols that broadcast messages that are non-urgent in category 3 such as infotainment and geographic applications.

Security and Privacy Requirements

1. Authentication: Data authentication ensures that the receiving vehicle can verify that the message was sent by an appropriate entity. Most importantly, this message has not been tampered or modified.

2. Non-Repudiation: This property ensures that the message sender is accountable for message generated. If a broadcast message lacks the non-repudiation property, a compromised or malicious vehicle can claim that the message was generated by another vehicle.

3. Identity Privacy Preserving: The identity of the vehicle must be preserved from untrusted sources. Malicious users should not be able to analyze multiple messages sent by the same vehicle to compromise its identity.

4. Collision Resistance: Colluding vehicles should not be able to generate a signature that is valid.

5. Unlinkability: The unlinkability of a message to its originator is similar to traceability. It is important to provide tracking immunity by unlinking broadcast messages which have items of interest such as coordinates and points of interest.

INFRASTRUCTURE-ASSISTED PSEUDONYM CHANGING SCHEME (IPCS)

In the proposed scheme, it is assumed that traditional PKI is used for key management and key initialization is performed by the TA. After registration with the TA, a vehicle V_i loads its buffer with pseudo-locations. We use historical location from MTTA described in (Emara, Woerndl, and Schlichter 2013).

Pseudo-Location Swapping Algorithm

To achieve location privacy using k-anonymity, a location swapping algorithm is introduced. The identity of each vehicle is checked before swapping, the uncertainty of the relationship between the vehicle's identity and its location is improved. When a vehicle V_i sends a broadcast message which is received by a neighbouring vehicle V_j, after their handshake, V_j chooses a random pseudo-location in its buffer which is exchanged with V_i. To reduce computation and overhead cost, we assume that V_j gets certificate from the TA and only needs to communicate with V_i using encryption. The location swapping algorithm is described in Algorithm 1. V_j sends a verification request to the TA when it receives a broadcast message from V_i which contains the identity of the sender $(V_j||pubk_i||V_i)$. The TA encrypts the queried content using the public key in Eq. 1.

$$E_{pubk_{TA}}(V_j||pubk_j||V_i) \tag{1}$$

TA verifies the authenticity of V_j and checks for the corresponding public key $pubk_i$. Upon successful authentication, TA send V_i's public key to V_j. V_j decrypts the message and obtains V_i public key which is used to encrypt the information sent.

$$E_{pubk_i}(V_i||pubk_i||TA_i) \qquad (2)$$

$$Sig_i(V_i||pubk_i||TA_i) \qquad (3)$$

V_i receives and decrypts the message, then verifies the signature. After V_i and V_j are mutually authenticated, V_j and V_i randomly select pairwise pseudo location in their buffers and send it to each other. V_j sends queries to the RSU after swapping pseudo-locations and chooses a $k-1$ pseudo-location randomly. V_j uses its pseudonym to send its k locations to the RSU. This guarantees the uncertainty of the k locations from a GPA stationed at a traffic intersection. This ensures that the locations in V_j buffer is disordered when it encounters a neighbouring vehicle.

Algorithm 1 Location Swapping Algorithm

1: **Input:** pseudo-locations in buffer $V_j l_1^{t-1}$, $V_j l_2^{t-1}$....,$V_j l_S^{t-1}$
2: **Output:** $V_j l_1^t, V_j l_2^t,...., V_j l_S^t$
3: **Data:** Testing set x
4: send query to TA:$E_{pubk_{TA}}(V_j||pubk_j||V_i)$
5: V_j receives V_i certificate from TA
6: V_j mutually authenticates V_i
7: A_s=(random())mod(S)
8: swap l_A^{t-1} with V_i
9: update $V_j l_1^{t-1}$, $V_j l_2^{t-1}$, ..., $V_j l_S^{t-1}$ to $V_j l_1^t$, $V_j l_2^t,...., V_j l_S^t$

Similarity-Based Context-Aware Protocol

The proposed scheme relies on the RSUs for pseudonym changing to occur. As discussed in (Gerlach and Gutler 2007), location privacy of a vehicle highly depends on the traffic distribution. RSUs are used to develop context-aware information to trigger pseudonym change. Since RSUs are regarded as trusted authorities, we develop a multidimensional context-aware message based on broadcast messages described in (Jerbi et al. 2008). This is modelled similar to location dynamic map described in ETSI TR 102 863 (Dressler et al. 2018). We use a multidimensional context similarity approach to build a context-aware system for RSUs based on three subclasses:*context, node and services*. Context information contains spatial and temporal range, velocity, type of vehicle, length of vehicle, time, list of neighbouring vehicles in a predefined interval. Service information contains safety applications such as CAM and DENM messages, commercial applications that fall under geographic and infotainment applications.

The RSUs periodically broadcast event messages to neighbouring vehicles. These messages are similarity-based recommendations derived from multidimensional context awareness which can be also used to prioritize safety messages to be verified when using digital signatures. The pseudonym change is triggered when the event similarity is 1 as explained in the next section, this happens if there is no DENM message in the queue. Although this can be implemented in a V2V scenario, we reduce the computational burden on vehicles as they still need to perform cryptographic operations for safety messages received by neighbouring vehicles and RSUs.

Similarity-Based Context Awareness

We assume that there are three contextual dimensions *context, node and services* and real values are assigned to each contextual condition. The contextual values are normalized within the range [0,1]. We use context awareness to quantify the similarity in contextual conditions and corresponding task. Jaccard Index J is used to compute the similarity index events in broadcast messages.

$$J(T_1, T_2) = \frac{|M_1 \cap M_2|}{|M_1 \cup M_2|} \qquad (4)$$

where J represents the contextual conditions in the intersection of two events (broadcast messages). We extend Jacquard's Index to add relevance to event messages M and define this multidimensional context aware similarity as:

$$J_R(T_1, T_2) = \frac{\sum\limits_{X \in |M_1 \cap M_2|} Rel(x, M_1) + Rel(x, M_2)}{\sum_{x \in |M_1|} Rel(x, M_1) + \sum_{x \in |M_2|} Rel(x, M_2)} \qquad (5)$$

As shown in Eq.5, we consider all the events found in both context (broadcast messages) in the intersection sets and sum up their relevance value with each context. The more an even is relevant to contextual condition, the more the

contextual similarity is increased. To reduce the computational burden on the
OBUs, the RSU periodically broadcasts a context-aware message periodically
based on historical information gathered by neighbouring vehicles as described
in Algorithm 2.

Algorithm 2 Context-Aware Pseudonym Changing Scheme

1: Upon receiving broadcast from neighboring vehicles
2: Construct context awareness
3: Construct node awareness
4: Construct service awareness
5: Calculate $J_R(T_1, T_2)$ for $\{context, node, services\}$
6: **if** $J_R(T_1, T_2) \geq 7$ **then**
7:     Broadcast Pseudonym Change Alert
8:     **if** $Condition \leq 5$ **then**
9:         Query Updates
10:     **end if**
11: **end if**

Privacy Metrics

Location Entropy

The degree of privacy under a GPA is measured using entropy. Location
entropy is defined as $E_t = \sum_i p(i, t) \log p(i, t)$. Entropy E_t is the quantitative
measure of the uncertainty of the attacker. E_t measures the uncertainty of correctly tracking a vehicle over time t. Lower values of E_t indicate more certainty
or lower privacy (Lim et al. 2017).

Tracking Success Ratio

The ratio of successful tracking is the measure of the attacker's belief about
a tracked item over time. A_{S_T} is equivalent to $p(u, t)$ where u is the tracked
vehicle and t is the tracking time (Gedik and Liu 2005).

Adversary Model

We consider a global passive attacker (GPA) deployed with low-cost receivers with the ability to eavesdrop on all messages. The GPA is placed on road intersections where the traffic is dense and the RSUs are deployed. Different from the approach in (Hasan and Burns 2011), we assume that the RSUs are trusted entities but attackers can eavesdrop on broadcast messages sent to the RSU. The main aim of the attacker is to reconstruct beacon traces by correlating the traces when a vehicle changes its pseudonym. We use Global Nearest Neighbour (GNN) which evaluates each observation in a track gating region and chooses the best one to be incorporated. This provides more accuracy when compared to Nearest Neighbour Probabilistic Data Association (NNPDA) used in (Conti, Willemsen, and Crispo 2013).

PERFORMANCE EVALUATION

We implement our proposed scheme using Veins simulation environment (Sommer, Dietrich, and Dressler 2007). Veins is based on two simulation toolkits SUMO and OMNET++ which have been well described by the authors in (Sommer et al. 2008). A 7-km freeway scenario was configured which includes cross traffic . Veins was configured to perform network simulation within a region centred at the middle of the 7-km highway. We deployed 30 to 120 vehicles that send beacon updates every second while traveling inside the area of $6km \times 6km$ for 14 minutes. To give more intuitive results on users' privacy, we also provide a tracking success ratio A_{S_T}. It measures the chance that the attacker's belief, when tracking target u over time t, is indeed true. Thus, A_{S_T} is equivalent to $p(u, t)$ of actual target u, since $\sum_i p(i, t) = 1$ at any time t. Note that A_{S_T} is unknown to the attacker (except at the very beginning: $A_{S_0} = p(u, 0) = 1$. This is because the attacker becomes unsure which $l(i, t)$ belongs to target u over time as vehicle u performs the Mutual Obfuscating Path (MOP) (Lim et al. 2017) process while driving.

Simulation Results

Figure 1 (MOP) and Figure 2 (IPCS) show the the entropy of tracked vehicles over time which is measured as the location entropy. The attacker's uncertainty reduces as the number of vehicles reduce (n=number of vehicles). This means that tracking success of a targeted vehicle becomes high when traffic density is low. In Figures 1 and 2, we compare our work with MOP (Lim et al. 2017) and the result shows that our scheme increases the uncertainty of the attacker. IPCS achieves a higher location entropy when compared to MOP which distorts the GPS routes by the addition of random noise. The result clearly shows that the attacker's uncertainty about the targeted vehicle increases even when the number of vehicles is 30 for both MOP and IPCS. However, IPCS performs better than MOP in the lowest density conditions and when the number of vehicles have increased.

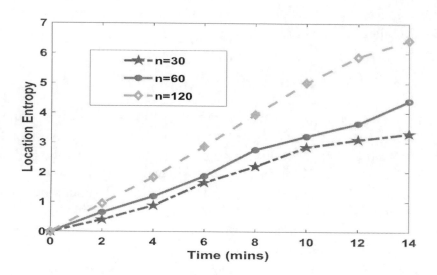

Figure 1. Location Entropy of MOP

In Figures 3 and 4, we show the success ratio of the attacker in reconstructing the vehicle's trajectory. In Figure 3, it can be seen that the tracking success ratio of MOP decreases from 1 to 0.4 after four minutes for 30, 60 and 120 vehicles. For IPCS, the tracking success ratio decreases to about 0.3 and further reduces to 0.05 which is slightly better than MOP after 14 mins as shown in Figure 4. It can be seen that in the sparse scenario where $n = 30$, with MOP, the success success ratio decreases to 0.65 after 4 mins and drops close to 0.4 after 10 mins as shown in Figure 3.

Compared to our proposed scheme in Figure 4, the success ratio of the at-

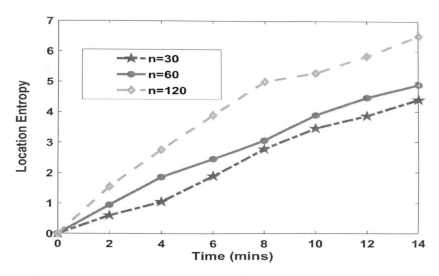

Figure 2. Location Entropy of IPCS

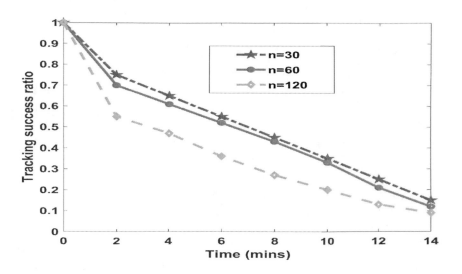

Figure 3. Tracking Success Ratio of MOP

tacker decreases to 0.57 after 4 mins and 0.2 after 10 mins. The result demonstrates that IPCS provides a stronger privacy protection in less dense scenarios when compared to MOP in Fig. 3. It can also be seen that when the number of

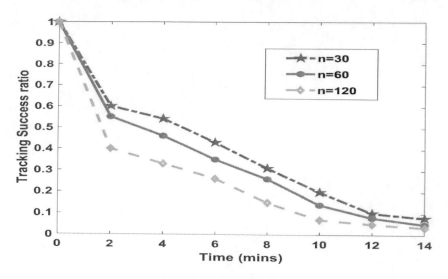

Figure 4. Tracking Success Ratio of IPCS

vehicles increase to 60 and 120. IPCS performs better than MOP significantly with lower attacker success ratio as shown in Figures 3 and 4. These results demonstrate the privacy protection that these techniques guarantee. Although both techniques have similar results, IPCS slightly responds faster than MOP.

CONCLUSION

Protecting the location privacy of connected and autonomous vehicles has been considered an open issue in ITS security and privacy due to the nature of vehicular broadcast and its frequency. In this chapter, we have proposed two infrastructure assisted solutions to support location privacy. The aim of these proposed strategies is to maximize the location privacy protection of connected and autonomous vehicles in vehicular communication. Our results show that the proposed scheme guarantees the location privacy when compared to other schemes.

REFERENCES

Beresford, Alastair R., and Frank Stajano. 2003. "Location privacy in pervasive computing." *IEEE Pervasive Computing* 1:46-55.

Buttyan, Levente, Tamas Holczer, and Istvan Vajda. 2007. "On the effectiveness of changing pseudonyms to provide location privacy in VANETs." In *European Workshop on Security in Ad-hoc and Sensor Networks*, pp. 129-141. Springer, Berlin, Heidelberg.

Buttyan, Levente, Tamas Holczer, Andre Weimerskirch, and William Whyte. 2009. "Slow: A practical pseudonym changing scheme for location privacy in vanets." In *2009 IEEE Vehicular Networking Conference (VNC)*, pp. 1-8. IEEE.

Chow, Chi-Yin, Mohamed F. Mokbel, and Xuan Liu. 2006. "A peer-to-peer spatial cloaking algorithm for anonymous location-based service." In *Proceedings of the 14th annual ACM international symposium on Advances in geographic information systems*, pp. 171-178. ACM.

Conti, Mauro, Jeroen Willemsen, and Bruno Crispo. 2013. "Providing source location privacy in wireless sensor networks: A survey." *IEEE Communications Surveys & Tutorials* 15, no. 3:1238-1280.

Dressler, Falko, Florian Klingler, Christoph Sommer, and Reuven Cohen. 2018. "Not all VANET broadcasts are the same: Context-aware class based broadcast." *IEEE/ACM Transactions on Networking* 26, no. 1:17-30.

Eichler, Stephan. 2007. "Strategies for pseudonym changes in vehicular ad hoc networks depending on node mobility." In 2007 *IEEE Intelligent Vehicles Symposium*, pp. 541-546. IEEE.

Emara, Karim. 2016. "Poster: PREXT: privacy extension for veins VANET simulator." In *2016 IEEE Vehicular Networking Conference (VNC)*, pp. 1-2. IEEE.

Emara, Karim. 2017. "Safety-aware location privacy in VANET: Evaluation and comparison." *IEEE Transactions on Vehicular Technology* 66, no. 12:10718-10731.

Emara, Karim, Wolfgang Woerndl, and Johann Schlichter. 2013. "Vehicle tracking using vehicular network beacons." In *2013 IEEE 14th International Symposium on "A World of Wireless, Mobile and Multimedia Networks" (WoWMoM)*, pp. 1-6. IEEE.

Freudiger, Julien, Maxim Raya, Félegyház, Panos Papadimitratos, and Jean-Pierre Hubaux. 2007. "Mix-zones for location privacy in vehicular networks." In *ACM Workshop on Wireless Networking for Intelligent Transportation Systems (WiN-ITS)*, no. CONF.

Freudiger, Julien, Reza Shokri, and Jean-Pierre Hubaux. 2009. "On the optimal placement of mix zones." In *International Symposium on Privacy Enhancing Technologies Symposium*, pp. 216-234. Springer, Berlin, Heidelberg.

Gedik, Bugra, and Ling Liu. 2005. "Location privacy in mobile systems: A personalized anonymization model." In *25th IEEE International Conference on Distributed Computing Systems (ICDCS'05)*, pp. 620-629. IEEE.

Gerlach, Matthias, and Felix Guttler. 2007. "Privacy in VANETs using changing pseudonyms-ideal and real." In *2007 IEEE 65th Vehicular Technology Conference-VTC2007-Spring*, pp. 2521-2525. IEEE.

Hasan, Ragib, and Randal Burns. 2011. *Where have you been? secure location provenance for mobile devices.* arXiv preprint arXiv:1107.1821.

Hoh, Baik, Marco Gruteser, Hui Xiong, and Ansaf Alrabady. 2007. "Preserving privacy in gps traces via uncertainty-aware path cloaking." In *Proceedings of the 14th ACM conference on Computer and communications security*, pp. 161-171. ACM.

Huang, Yan, Favyen Bastani, Ruoming Jin, and Xiaoyang Sean Wang. 2014. "Large scale real-time ridesharing with service guarantee on road networks." *Proceedings of the VLDB Endowment* 7, no. 14: 2017-2028.

Jerbi, Houssem, Franck Ravat, Olivier Teste, and Gilles Zurfluh. 2008. "Management of context-aware preferences in multidimensional databases." In *2008 Third International Conference on Digital Information Management*, pp. 669-675. IEEE.

Li, Mingyan, Krishna Sampigethaya, Leping Huang, and Radha Poovendran. 2006. "Swing & swap: user-centric approaches towards maximizing location privacy." In *Proceedings of the 5th ACM workshop on Privacy in electronic society*, pp. 19-28. ACM.

Lim, Jaemin, Hyunwoo Yu, Kiyeon Kim, Minho Kim, and Suk-Bok Lee. 2017. "Preserving location privacy of connected vehicles with highly accurate location updates." *IEEE Communications Letters* 21, no. 3: 540-543.

Lu, Rongxing, Xiaodong Lin, Tom H. Luan, Xiaohui Liang, and Xuemin Shen. 2011. "Anonymity analysis on social spot based pseudonym changing for location privacy in VANETs." In *2011 IEEE International Conference on Communications (ICC)*, pp. 1-5. IEEE.

Lu, Rongxing, Xiaodong Lin, Tom H. Luan, Xiaohui Liang, and Xuemin Shen. 2012. "Pseudonym changing at social spots: An effective strategy for location privacy in vanets." *IEEE transactions on vehicular technology* 61, no. 1: 86-96.

Meyerowitz, Joseph, and Romit Roy Choudhury. 2009. "Hiding stars with fireworks: location privacy through camouflage." In *Proceedings of the 15th annual international conference on Mobile computing and networking*, pp. 345-356. ACM.

Niu, Ben, Qinghua Li, Xiaoyan Zhu, Guohong Cao, and Hui Li. 2014. "Achieving k-anonymity in privacy-aware location-based services." In *IEEE INFOCOM 2014-IEEE Conference on Computer Communications*, pp. 754-762. IEEE.

Pingley, Aniket, Nan Zhang, Xinwen Fu, Hyeong-Ah Choi, Suresh Subramaniam, and Wei Zhao. 2011. "Protection of query privacy for continuous location based services." In *2011 Proceedings IEEE INFOCOM*, pp. 1710-1718. IEEE.

Sampigethaya, Krishna, Mingyan Li, Leping Huang, and Radha Poovendran. 2007. "AMOEBA: Robust location privacy scheme for VANET." *IEEE Journal on Selected Areas in communications* 25, no. 8: 1569-1589.

Sampigethaya, Krishna, Leping Huang, Mingyan Li, Radha Poovendran, Kanta Matsuura, and Kaoru Sezaki. 2005. *CARAVAN: Providing location privacy for VANET*. Washington Univ Seattle Dept of Electrical Engineering.

Sommer, Christoph, Armin Schmidt, Reinhard German, Wolfgang Koch, and Falko Dressler. 2008. "Simulative evaluation of a UMTS-based car-to-infrastructure traffic information system." In *IEEE GLOBECOM 2008, AutoNet Workshop*.

Sommer, Christoph, Isabel Dietrich, and Falko Dressler. 2007. "Realistic simulation of network protocols in VANET scenarios." In *2007 Mobile Networking for Vehicular Environments*, pp. 139-143. IEEE.

Standards Committee. 2016. IEEE Standard for Wireless Access in Vehicular Environments–Security Services for Applications and Management Messages. *IEEE Std* 1609.2-2016.

Youssef, Mahmoud, Vijayalakshmi Atluri, and Nabil R. Adam. 2005. "Preserving mobile customer privacy: an access control system for moving objects and customer profiles." In *Proceedings of the 6th international conference on Mobile data management*, pp. 67-76. ACM.

Yu, Rong, Jiawen Kang, Xumin Huang, Shengli Xie, Yan Zhang, and Stein Gjessing. 2016. "MixGroup: Accumulative pseudonym exchanging for location privacy enhancement in vehicular social networks." *IEEE Transactions on Dependable and Secure Computing* 13, no. 1: 93-105.

Chapter 7

SECURE AND TAMPER-RESILIENT DATA AGGREGATION FOR AUTONOMOUS VEHICLES AND SMART MOBILITY

Sananda Mitra*, Sumanta Bose, Sourav Sen Gupta,
Anupam Chattopadhyay and Kwok-Yan Lam
School of Computer Science and Engineering,
Nanyang Technological University, Singapore

Abstract

The future of transportation is going to change forever with the advent of Autonomous Vehicles and their integration within Smart Mobility framework. To achieve full autonomy, the vehicles need to be manufactured as complex Internet-of-Things (IoT) enabled cyber-physical systems. However, the security and safety vulnerabilities of self-driving cars are quite unlike that of the conventional cyber-physical systems. Data aggregation plays a crucial role in the safety of an autonomous vehicle embedded within the smart mobility architecture, which involves real-time information across the network. In this chapter, we primarily focus on the security and tamper-resilience of data aggregation in AVs as a part of the smart mobility infrastructure, based on the backbone of distributed ledgers. A distributed ledger structure is an ideal candidate due to its intrinsic features of consensus-driven synchronization and maintenance of

---

*Corresponding Author's E-mail: sananda.mitra@ntu.edu.sg.

transactional information without any single point-of-failure, like a central authority or storage. A consortium blockchain network is observed to be the most suited distributed ledger instantiation as it can be mapped to the internal network of an AV with consensus entrusted on the pre-decided AV internal units. The core data aggregation platform is therefore designed and instantiated as a consortium blockchain network, after thoroughly analysing the attack surfaces and appropriate countermeasures.

INTRODUCTION

The concept of a *Smart City* goes above and beyond its technological backbone, as it needs to integrate social and political aspects as well. The six key pillars of Smart City, as identified by Siemens (Seimens AG 2015), are Smart Living, Smart Mobility, Smart Society, Smart Economy, Smart Government and Smart Environment. Within these, Smart Mobility is a key component to achieve sustainable development of any city. In this connection, one may envision a Smart City as a complex system which employs a mesh of Internet-of-Things enabled sensors and cyber-physical devices to acquire, aggregate and utilise information for efficient management of the city's assets and resources.

Smart Mobility

One of the key pillars of smart city, *Smart Mobility Infrastructure*, focusses on information acquisition from fixed assets, portable devices, and autonomous vehicles (AVs) to monitor and manage smart traffic and smart transportation. The idea of smart mobility goes beyond alternative forms of transportation (Land Transport Authority, Government of Singapore 2014). Smart mobility is built on the core principles of flexibility, efficiency, integration, eco-friendliness, safety and accessibility (Frost and Sullivan 2014), as in Figure 1.

   Smart mobility infrastructure is being adopted in several leading cities that are paving the way for others to follow. Columbus, Ohio, for example, is collecting traffic data to identify and address safety issues such as collision hotspots and potential signal malfunction. It is soon to become the first smart city in the United States of America. Another example is Singapore, where growing number of residents (over 5.6 million) and vehicles (almost 1 million) in an island limited by land area has been the catalyst in the creation of an intelligent transport system to help the commuters enjoy a hassle-free travel. Strategic planning of Singapore's Smart Mobility 2030 goal revolves around the next generation

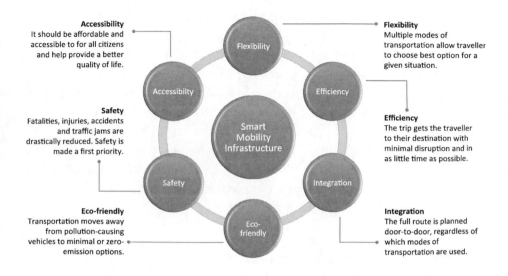

Figure 1. Key Principles of Smart Mobility Infrastructure.

of transportation with focus on information, interaction, assistance and green mobility. Key strategies to achieve these goals, as outlined in (Land Transport Authority, Government of Singapore 2014), are: (*i*) to implement innovative and sustainable smart mobility solutions; (*ii*) to develop and adopt intelligent transport system standards; and (*iii*) to establish close partnerships and co-creation.

Autonomous Vehicles

AVs are the most crucial elements in smart mobility. Introduction of driverless cars for private and public transport in smart cities shall require a secure, efficient, robust and scalable design for the transportation framework. Intelligent transportation system will necessitate AVs to interact and integrate information from a range of entities like intra-vehicular control units (vehicle-to-vehicle *aka* V2V), smart roadside units (vehicle-to-infrastructure *aka* V2I) and even smart devices with mobile roadside citizens (vehicle-to-pedestrian *aka* V2P).

Autonomy of vehicles within a smart city is not an isolated mechanism. With the advent of cloud, fog and mist computing (Corsaro 2016), it is appropriate to consider an AV as a Cyber-Physical System (CPS) embedded within an *intelligent* grid of infrastructured and infrastructureless information agents. The autonomy of the AV may be considered as a three-phase learning mechanism:

Perception — The first phase is perception, which denotes the interaction of the AV with information agents for data accumulation. The agents may be within the vehicular system or in the overall Smart Mobility environment.

Decision — The second phase is decision, which the the process of drawing inference from the accumulated data, through artificial intelligence algorithms, often executed in real-time for control and cognitive resolution.

Actuation — The third phase is actuation, whereby the implementation of cumulative cognitive decisions are undertaken, with adequate feedback and response, to ensure autonomous navigation and operation of the vehicle.

Security Concerns

In prevalent smart mobility platforms, real time data is integrated through the information and communication substructure as shown in Figure 2. Ensuring security and privacy of the data flow is pivotal for safe and reliable transport. In a recent work (Dominic, Chhawri, Eustice, Ma, and Weimerskirch 2016) at University of Michigan, researchers have proposed a threat identification model to analyze the likelihood and severity of potential threats by accounting for the attacker's skill level and motivation, the vulnerable vehicle system components, the ways in which an attack could be achieved, and the repercussions, including for privacy, safety and financial loss. In another relevant work (Petit and Shladover 2015), researchers have extensively studied the potential threats, the vulnerable components and eventual consequences. Similar studies (Wolf, Weimerskirch, and Paar 2004) reveal that the threats posed to an AV not only compromises road safety (Gerla, Lee, Pau, and Lee 2014), but may also be detrimental to the entire smart mobility infrastructure (Garip, Gursoy, Reiher, and Gerla 2015). Cybersecurity is still an overlooked area of research in AV technology, even though many threats and vulnerabilities exist, and more are likely to emerge as the technology progresses to higher levels of autonomy. It is therefore crucial to analyse the likelihood and severity of potential cyberthreats to intra-AV and inter-AV networks.

Realisation of the security issues arising from data flow network within an AV is critical to the eventual understanding of higher-level security concerns in the smart mobility ecosystem. We start by examining the data flow in autonomous vehicles as a part of the smart urban mobility architecture. In 2018 (Mitra, Bose, Sen Gupta, and Chattopadhyay 2018), we have explored a

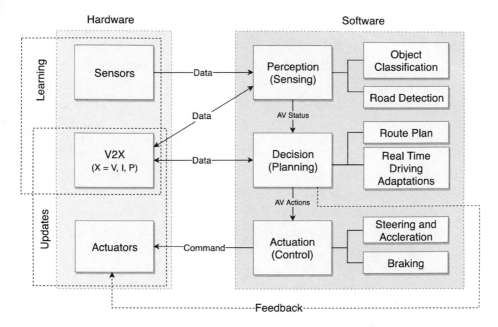

Figure 2. Data Flow Diagram of Autonomous Vehicles.

secure and tamper resilient framework based on Distributed Ledger Technology (DLT) for data aggregation in AVs for fixing the existing safety loopholes. In this chapter we show that a secure and tamper-resilient ledger can be a dependable source of information beyond the AV, for manufacturers, service providers and insurance companies. The smart mobility infrastructure can also monitor and harvest immutable and validated data from the ledger. Secure remote monitoring, over-the-air updates or diagnostics, dynamic evaluation of insurance value, etc., will be of major relevance to complete the overall picture of smart urban mobility.

AVS AND SMART MOBILITY

Over the past decade, the average commute time of urban citizens have increased considerably. Connected in-vehicle services like onboard infotainment and diagnostics are now major contributing factors for buying choices of vehicles, along with the ever-existing demand for seamless and hassle free commute. A promising solution for smart transportation are the AVs, as they provide improved efficiency in traffic flow and road safety. As discussed earlier, the full potential of AVs can only be realised through a complete understanding of its various components, comprehensive knowledge of the internal data management network, interpretation of its dependency on the smart mobility framework, and a thorough risk assessment of the entire cyber-physical architecture.

Information Units

The data flow and aggregation in an AV, depends on the harmony of several *information units*, such as vehicular perception sensors, intra-vehicular control units and communication modules as shown in Figure 3. The *Powertrain Unit* and the *Chassis Unit* are the two major control units overseeing engine and gears control, steering control, breaks, airbag opening etc. The *Body Unit* monitors central locking, lights, air conditioning, while the *Infotainment Unit* allows in-vehicle entertainment (radio, HDTV etc.) and information systems like GPS navigation. Communication via radio, and telecommunication services are supervised by telematics and V2X module (Sung, Juan, and Wang 2008).The analysis of the collective information by the Advanced Driver Assistance Systems (ADAS) help in charting a safe and optimal route for the AV. ADAS also issues intermittent diagnostic warnings.

Successful operation of AVs depends largely on the the ability to communicate and co-ordinate with the Vehicle-to-everything (V2X) framework. V2X data communication is a synergy of different IoT technologies like Vehicle to Vehicle (V2V), Vehicle to Infrastructure (V2I) and Vehicle to Pedestrian (V2P). V2V communication provides 360 degree awareness of speed change, range, direction of travel, braking, and potential hazards of other vehicles via wireless communication. Information generated from different vehicles can be aggregated before it is delivered to other vehicles. But V2V communication is not enough for taking adaptive cruise control decisions, as the range of V2V communication is up to 300 meters or about 10 seconds at highway speeds. To have information like road conditions and traffic flow outside the visual range of the car, the AVs are also expected to communicate with static roadside units. Reliable and low latency data communication is also required to ensure safety and issue security alerts to pedestrians or cyclists.

---

[1] © 2018 IEEE. Reprinted, with permission, from S Mitra, S Bose, S Sen Gupta, A Chattopadhyay, "Secure and Tamper-resilient Distributed Ledger for Data Aggregation in Autonomous Vehicles," 2018 IEEE Asia Pacific Conference on Circuits and Systems (APCCAS), pp. 548–551.

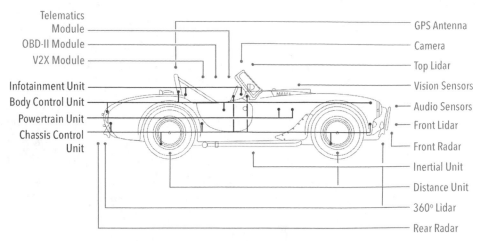

Figure 3. Information Units in typical AVs: •{ Intra-vehicular Control Units, •{ Perception Sensors, and •{ Peripheral Communication Modules.[1]

Stages of Data Flow

The complex data flow network in an AV is modelled in three functional stages, data generation (telematics and diagnostics), data acquisition (perception and communication), and data processing (decision and actuation), as follows.

Data Generation — Data generation in AVs is aided by a range of perception sensors such as LiDAR, RADAR, surround view front/rear cameras, inertial sensors etc. To enable complex driving assistance AVs requires multiple redundant information sources which is a combination of information from perception sensors supported by V2X communication. Sensors collect surrounding data and provide them to the on-board Electronic Control Units (ECUs). Navigation of an AV requires the connected ECUs inside the vehicle to generate a substantial amount of data, in the order of terabytes per hour (Accenture 2018). The variety of data generated inside the components of an AV include diagnostic data, behavioural data for autonomous driving, reports on failures and crashes, and data for in-vehicle entertainment. On-board flash storage is no longer a viable option for storing such volume of data generated inside and communicated to it. The industry is actively looking into sustainable hybrid models for data storage, with full-stack integration of in-vehicle storage units to the cloud.

Data Acquisition — Acquisition is the process of fusing the data collected by the sensors with the help of standard in vehicle communication protocols.

Communication between the control units is of paramount importance to navigation fidelity. Standard communication protocols for safety critical (powertrain and chassis) and non-critical operations are Controller Area Network (CAN), CAN Flexible Data-Rate (CAN FD), FlexRay, Local Interconnect Network (LIN), Media Oriented Systems Transport (MOST) and Ethernet (Wolf, Weimerskirch, and Paar 2004). CAN is a multi-master message broadcast bus system that supports serial communication between different ECUs. While CAN is mostly used for low speed in-vehicle communication (1 Mbps), CAN FD and FlexRay are suitable for real time safety critical operations as they are capable of high speed communication, robust error detection and fault tolerance. LIN is a low-cost sub-bus for CAN and is mostly used for non-mainstream body electronics, where speed, error handling and fault tolerance are not of utmost importance. MOST and Ethernet are high bandwidth protocols used for infotainment and telematics. In addition, there are five OBD-II signalling protocols, including classical CAN, in any AV. Data fusion in the conventional sense requires interconnection between the internal communication protocols as well as external V2X ecosystem like IEEE 802.11p, Wi-Fi, Bluetooth, 3G/LTE, etc. for data exchange (Rettore, Santos, Campolina, Villas, and Loureiro 2016).

Data Processing — The AI-driven computing module is responsible for processing the intra-AV data, and analysing the information accumulated from the smart mobility framework to model the environment around the vehicle. It takes informed decisions regarding navigation, maintenance, route determination, parking etc., and is the crux of automation that creates a safe and secure perception-decision-actuation loop based on data.

DATA AGGREGATION ARCHITECTURE

In order to design a robust data aggregation framework for smart mobility infrastructure, we need to consider the practical security challenges. The security and privacy concerns regarding the smart mobility data will eventually guide us to formulate the design principles for data aggregation and analysis.

Security Challenges

In a smart mobility infrastructure, V2X technology allows vehicles to communicate via wireless exchange to have a co-ordinated sense of the environment and to take preemptive actions for seamless navigation. Use of wireless channels for communication exposes the V2X system to various threats and attacks. To understand the security scenario, we must identify the actors involved in V2X communication. The main actors of such a network (Zhong, Zhong, Huang, Yang, Shi, Xie, and Wang 2019) are as depicted in Figures 4 and 5, the real-life V2V, V2I and V2P.

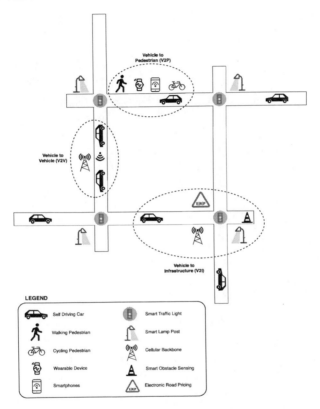

Figure 4. The V2X communication infrastructure — Vehicle-to-vehicle (V2V), Vehicle-to-infrastructure (V2I), and Vehicle-to-pedestrian (V2P) networks.

Traffic Centres (TC) — Responsible for identity verification, certificate management, remote monitoring and control of entities and conditions.

Road Side Units (RSU) — Placed within infrastructural components or standalone; responsible for managing V2X communication with vehicles.

On Board Units (OBU) — Sensors, cyber-physical devices, ECUs or on-board computing platforms present within an autonomous vehicle.

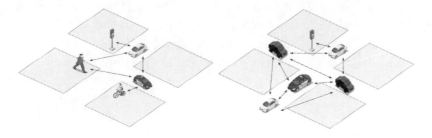

(a) Hybrid V2X communication. (b) High-speed V2X communication.

Figure 5. Real-time communication substructure for autonomous navigation.

Smart Devices — Devices with pedestrians or in other AVs, able to communicate with the vehicles to ensure pedestrian safety or for diagnostics.

The desired security principles for V2X communication between the actors are — (i) proper identification and authentication of the actors, (ii) verification of data integrity generally by redundancy, (iii) confidentiality of communicated and stored data, (iv) authorised provisioning of services, (v) availability of information or over-the-air updates, (vi) privacy preservation for user data, and (vii) accountability of information source. Even though the security requirements for V2X is of primary importance in smart mobility, we need to consider three reference domains in the smart mobility architecture — (a) V2X communication network, (b) AV in-vehicle data network, and (c) service information platform, like diagnostic services, insurance, certification authority, etc. These three domains should be considered separately as each one presents unique characteristics in terms of overall security of the smart mobility infrastructure (Woo, Jo, and Lee 2015).

Security threats based on the reference domains (V2X network, in-vehicle network, and service network) include, but are not always limited to — malicious use of a vehicle providing misleading information to other vehicles, malicious entity posing as a roadside unit providing fake information to passing vehicles, generating high volume of fake messages or replay messages for denial of service within the V2X domain, posting malicious information to the in-vehicle data aggregation system, attacking adjacent road side units and vehicles in a specific area so that they cannot communicate with the V2X framework, and privacy violation by analysis of network traffic to obtain vehicle specific data. Most research works in this area till date have focused on simply encrypting the data, on both the vehicular system and the wireless channels, without evaluating the complete space of solutions.

Attack Surfaces

Ironically, the capabilities provided to an AV by the V2X platform can make the system fall prey to more vulnerabilities. Increased complexity of ADAS systems exposes more attack surfaces in the smart mobility architecture. *Autonomous Cruise Control* presents quite a challenging scenario for security management with increasing levels of autonomy. To ensure performance efficiency and safety, secure communication between vehicle control units is extremely important. (Miller and Valasek 2015) showed the possibility of malicious attacks on AVs via mobile telephone network. They hacked a Chrysler Jeep by injecting messages into the CAN bus through the V850 controller designed to communicate with it and took control over its engine unit to disable its brakes. Similar attacks furthermore showed that even though an adversary can attack an AV remotely there is no remote means to fix the attacks (Schellekens 2016).

Security threats creep into the smart mobility framework more so because real time safety is the essence in these systems. Consider the Chassis Control Unit issuing a braking signal; there is no double guessing. In recent efforts made by automotive companies like Tesla and Chrysler, security updates were sent to manufacturers via remote patching or using USB sticks. Both these methods have severe cybersecurity flaws. If the manufacturers can communicate with the vehicle processor and post remote updates, so can a hacker, provided an entry point is compromised. Plugging USB keys for updates can have dire consequences as it would very hard to verify whether the device can be trusted or if it is malware free. Researchers have shown that spoofing of GPS systems and sensor manipulation are significant threats (Bagloee, Tavana, Asadi, and Oliver 2016). Table 1 lists potential attacks, security issues of targets, and possible countermeasures of the mobility domains.

Safety of an AV depends on security solutions conceived for the ubiquitous system, encompassing vehicles and the intra-vehicular network. There is not enough evidence in the literature to provide us with definitive prerequisites and guidelines for developing an appropriate data management framework for autonomous navigation that can rule out all cybersecurity threats. In certain scenarios, a distributed ledger based data aggregation seems to resolve a numbe of existing issues pertaining to security and privacy, and brings forth the inherent benefits of consensus-driven decentralisation (Mitra, Bose, Sen Gupta, and Chattopadhyay 2018).

Table 1. Security issues and countermeasures in Smart Mobility Platform

Attack	Access	Target	Issue	Countermeasure
Packet Injection (in CAN Bus)	Remote	AV ECUs, ADAS, OBD II	Integrity	Identification, Authentication, Blockchain
Eavesdropping	Remote, Proximity	AV Sensors, V2X Platform	Confidentiality, Privacy	In-vehicle Data Encryption
Firmware Tampering	Remote, Physical	OBD II Port, AV Processor	Integrity, Availability	Authentication, In-vehicle Data Encryption, Root-of-Trust, Blockchain
Side-Channel Attack	Remote	AV Processor, ADAS, OBD II	Confidentiality, Privacy	Authentication, Access Control
Identity Spoofing	Remote, Proximity	AV Sensors, GPS System	Integrity	Packet Filtering, Authentication
Packet Sniffing	Remote	AV Telematics, V2X Platform	Confidentiality, Privacy	Authentication, Intrusion Detection, Encrypted Comm.
Routing and Map Poisoning	Remote	AV Telematics, V2X Platform	Integrity, Availability	Authentication, Intrusion Detection
Distributed DoS and Blackhole	Remote, Proximity	AV Actuators, ADAS, Network	Availability	Identification, Authentication, Intrusion Detection
Data Remanence	Remote, Physical	Flash Storage in AV, OBD II	Confidentiality, Privacy	Deep Formatting, Access Control
Data Tampering	Remote, Proximity, Physical	Flash Storage, ECUs, OBD II, V2X Platform	Integrity	Authentication, Encrypted Data Storage, Blockchain
Fault Injection (in CAN bus and FlexRay)	Remote, Proximity, Physical	ADAS and Computing Devices	Integrity	Authentication, Access Control, Blockchain
BotNet	Proximity	V2X Platform	Integrity, Availability	Trust, Reputation, Segregated Computing

Design Considerations

In light of the security challenges faced by AVs, as discussed above, the current need of the hour is a secure and tamper-resilient data aggregation mechanism within a set of participating entities with a shared state. This is the forte of Distributed Ledger Technology (DLT), such as blockchain. There are manyfold advantages of DLT, particularly with respect to state-of-the-art data privacy and real-time automation through smart-contracts (Buterin 2015). DLT facilitates a networked database that is consensually shared and synchronised across multiple parties that may be hosted in diverse logical or physical geographies. It allows transactions to have publicly verifiable 'witnesses', thereby making the proof-of-data tamper-resilient. The participant hosting each node of the network can access and own identical copies of the shared records. Modifications or appends made to the ledger are reflected and copied to all participants through a consensus mechanism (Cachin and Vukolic 2017). Blockchain is a specific kind of distributed ledger that guarantees data provenance, data validity and immutability across the network.

Design Principle — We observe that the internal network of an AV can be envisioned as a consortium blockchain with consensus depending on pre-decided peers, as explored in our previous work (Mitra, Bose, Sen Gupta, and Chattopadhyay 2018). Distributed ledgers offer a shared state of transaction or contract records that have been approved through a consensus mechanism executed in a consortium of participating entities. It eliminates the need of a central authority to keep a check on manipulation, and the secure tamper-resilient ledger becomes a dependable source of information for manufacturers, service providers and insurance companies. The smart mobility infrastructure can also monitor and harvest immutable and validated data from the ledger. Remote monitoring of AVs for safety, over-the-air updates or diagnostics, and dynamic evaluation of insurance value, will be of major relevance to complete the overall picture of smart urban mobility. Parties monitoring and retrieving data from AVs can also be the peers in a consortium blockchain to share the data. Channel design of such consortium structures must ensure selective involvement of peers in the sharing of data and remote administration, as well as guarantee privacy of sensitive data. Safety-critical operations in an AV require real time decisions, while data aggregation through blockchain can be a robust but computationally heavy operation. If it is required to incorporate data aggregation in real time decision control loops in an AV, the solution must use extremely high throughput DLT design, supported by a low-latency consensus mechanism.

Smart Contracts — Computer programs executed in a blockchain network, containing a set of rules under which the participating entities agree to interact with each other, are called smart contracts. They enforce automated agreement triggered under certain circumstances. In the context of an AV, smart contracts can formalise the relationships between its core components, data modules and data flow channels. The transaction rules (agreement) of the smart contract define the conditions, rights and obligations, to which the multiple participating entities of the protocol consent. This can be predefined, and the agreement may be attained by simple opt-in actions. In case of autonomous navigation, the smart contract ruleset can be formalised with the rights and obligations pre-established. The contract may then be automatically executed by the network of the concerned data modules (infotainment, chassis control, telematics and V2X). The smart contracts executed in an AV can bring tremendous cost savings, as they are capable of tracking performance in real time. Controlling and compliance can happen on the fly. Smart contracts need information oracles, which feed the contract with external information for its functionality. Key virtues of a well deployed smart contract are being *self-verifying*, *self-executing* and *tamper-resilient*. Smart contracts can turn deterministic legal obligations into automated processes, guarantee a greater degree of data security and privacy, reduce reliance on trusted intermediaries, lower data aggregation costs, and automate real-time processes.

REFERENCE INSTANTIATION

In this section, we design and instantiate the internal network of an AV, and the smart mobility infrastructure, as a consortium blockchain with consensus amongst the major actors (peers and modules) of the cyber-physical network.

Design of Blockchain

Based on network structure, identity and trust among the peers blockchain network have been classified into three categories, namely public, private and consortium (Buterin 2015). While Ethereum (Vogelsteller, Buterin, et al. 2017) promoted blockchain from a ledger of records to a decentralized trusted operating system equipped with smart contracts, Hyperledger (The Linux Foundation 2016) and Corda (Hearn 2015) propelled it into the arena of consensus-driven enterprise networks. This is where an automated blockchain framework interfaces with the AV ecosystem in the context of data aggregation and automation.

The information on the blockchain is securely and accurately stored using cryptographic primitives and can be accessed using cryptographic keys and digital signatures. Once the information is logged in the network, it acts as an immutable database, governed by the network protocols. While centralised ledgers could be prone to cyber-attack, it is inherently harder to attack distributed ledgers owing to the presence of distributed copies among network participants that needs to be attacked individually and simultaneously for an attack to be successful. Further, these records are made resistant to malicious changes by a single party not meeting the consensus criteria. The distributed ledger contains a verifiable and tamper-resilient proof of every transaction in the network, and ensures three key properties for data.

Provenance of Data — Ensures a verifiable source of origin for all records and transactions in the network, thus eliminating any conflict by design.

Validity of Data — Facilitates a distributed verification mechanism of all records and transactions in the network, adhering to some pre-defined robust multi-party consensus mechanism across a decentralised network.

Immutability of Data — Guarantees the secure storage of all records or transactions in the network, with tamper-proof cryptographic primitives (hash functions) that are resistant to malicious changes by a single party.

We observe that data aggregation network in an AV resembles a consortium blockchain network, which operates under the federation of multiple groups of entities, with the consensus dependent on a pre-decided subset of participants, as in Figure 6, the IoT landscape of autonomous vehicles and smart mobility.

Data Aggregation Framework

In Figure 6, we present a conceptual model of the complex IoT interconnection and data flow network within and around an AV. The intra-AV data communication consists of the three step data aggregation, and communication to the smart mobility infrastructure. The smart mobility data from different V2X IoT platforms are aggregated using vehicle as a resource (Abdelhamid, Hassanein, and Takahara 2015). The information from each mobility substructure is communicated to the cloud for storage, analysis and remote monitoring. In this chapter, we design our smart mobility blockchain framework based on this reference architecture.

Autonomous Navigation — We first discuss the operational layout of the autonomous navigation data flow, based on consortium blockchain, as in Figure 7. The figure shows Components, Modules and Channels for the model, where *Autonomous Cruise Control* is divided into *Perception–Decision* unit and *Decision–Actuation* unit. This design was proposed in our previous work (Mitra, Bose, Sen Gupta, and Chattopadhyay 2018).

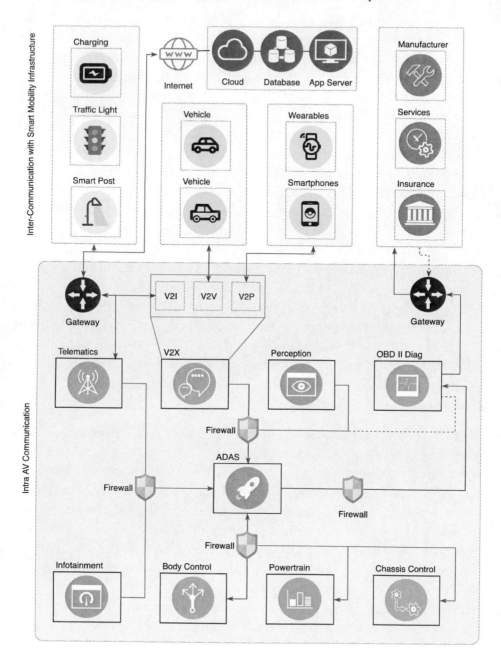

Figure 6. The IoT Landscape of Autonomous Vehicles and Smart Mobility.

The in-vehicle modules namely powertrain, chassis, telematics, infotainment, V2X form a consortium, and contribute peers to create the data-flow channels. Two data flow channels, *navigation sensor channel* and *navigation actuation channel*, control the navigation events and record them in a shared ledger. The navigation sensor channel comprises of sensors and peripheral communication ports of each module, and the actuation units and ECUs are contributed to the navigation actuation channel. Authenticated sensor data are recorded in the form of smart contracts through the central Decision (Control) module. The mutually authenticated data from the peers will be used by ADAS to take a consensus-backed decision. The actuation units and ECUs receive the decision via navigation actuation channel. Overall security and privacy of the system is ensured by source attestation and recipient attribution using smart contracts.

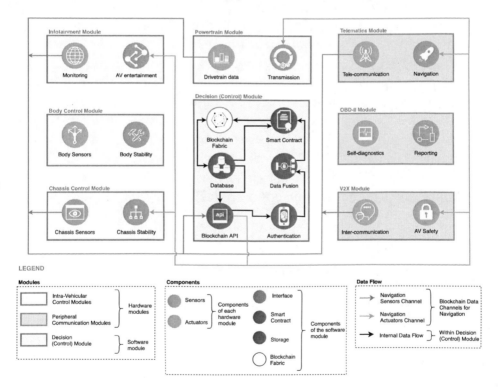

Figure 7. Components, Modules and Data Flow Channels for *Autonomous Navigation* with an underlying Blockchain framework for Data Aggregation.[2]

Smart Mobility

Beyond the scope of our previous work, we extend this framework to assimilate the complete smart mobility landscape, with peers and data channels pertinent to the smart mobility IoT landscape. Figure 8 refers to the consortium blockchain architecture for smart mobility. The consortium blockchain will allow participants to access the distributed ledger and smart contract services only as a part of segregated channels. Other than the parties participating in the consortium network authorized Government agencies may have access to the root hash and prerogative to probe and verify the blockchain status. Similar to our previous work, the consensus within the smart mobility blockchain will depend on the subgroup of entities forming the channels.

The mobility framework is at first logically sub-divided into two functional segments pertaining to real time navigation control and diagnostics or other services which may not be essentially real time. For real time navigation control V2V, V2I, V2P, remote monitoring agencies and geolocation satellite will contribute peers and will have private communications within the scope of co-ordinated cruise control channel. All transactions relating to cruise control will be performed within the cruise control channel. Manufacturers, service providers and insurance agencies will contribute peers to the diagnostics and secure update channel. Level 1 blockchain can incorporate copies of ledger updated and maintained by Level 2 chains. The hierarchical structure instead of a monolithic one is suggested to counter storage inefficiency and on chain latency.

Security and Scalability

In certain scenarios, a blockchain based data aggregation resolves a number of existing issues (Wolf, Weimerskirch, and Paar 2004) pertaining to security and privacy in an AV (Parkinson, Ward, Wilson, and Miller 2017). As additional security measure, a trusted execution environment based on modern technologies (Intel Corporation ; ARM Limited) may also be provided at the Decision (Control) Module for secure execution of the core data fusion. With the trusted execution environment, the authenticated data fusion will provide consistency and accountability guarantees during secure processing of data for training of the on-board AI core.

---

hyay, "Secure and Tamper-resilient Distributed Ledger for Data Aggregation in Autonomous Vehicles," 2018 IEEE Asia Pacific Conference on Circuits and Systems (APCCAS), pp. 548–551.

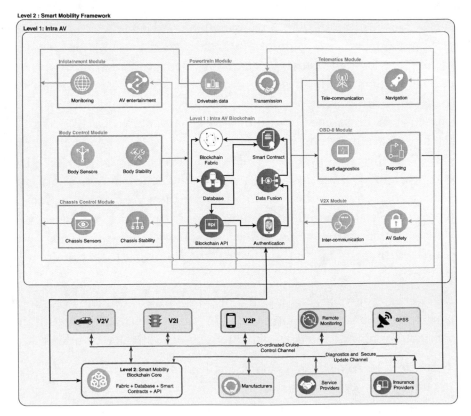

Figure 8. Consortium Blockchain Architecture for Smart Mobility.

Safety critical operations in an AV demands real-time response which makes the response time a crucial factor. Blockchain based data aggregation being inherently computationally heavy operation may increase the waiting time for responses. Using blockchain data aggregation within a real-time decision loop in an AV will require an extremely high throughput DLT, supported by a low-latency consensus mechanism like pBFT (Castro and Liskov 2002). One may also consider a modular design of the consortium network to allow for a highly efficient consensus based on sharding (Kokoris-Kogias, Jovanovic, Gasser, Gailly, Syta, and Ford 2018).

The solution to scalability in a traditional database system is to increase computational power (i.e., add more servers) to handle the added transactions. In our example of a decentralised AV blockchain network, however, every data aggregation instance needs to be processed and validated by every node. Thus to get faster, we need to add more computational power to every node in the network. In permission-less (public) blockchains, we have little or no control over the public nodes in the network. Therefore, there is a trade-off between low transaction throughput and high degree of centralisation in most permission-less blockchain with decentralised consensus protocols.

In case of permissioned (private) blockchain networks like our AV blockchain, we have more control over the network nodes, and hence over the scalability. With the growing size of a network, the computational power, storage and bandwidth requirements of the participating nodes increases. This may lead to the risk of centralisation. In order to scale the AV blockchain protocol, we must have a mechanism to limit the number of participating nodes necessary to validate each transaction, while still ensuring the AV network's trust on the validity of each transaction. In this context, the following three requirements are imperative.

(a) Since every node does not have the responsibility to validate every transaction, they must have a game-theoretic trust mechanism to ensure that transactions not validated by them are securely validated by others.

(b) There must be some way to guarantee the availability of transaction data. In other words, even for a transaction valid from the perspective of a node that has not directly validated it, unavailability of that transaction data (due to malicious attack, node power loss, etc.) would lead to a deadlock, and no other node can validate or create new transactions.

(c) In order to achieve scalability, different nodes must have the capability of processing transactions in parallel. As blockchain state transition also has several non-parallelizable components, there are certain restrictions on transitioning blockchain state, balancing scalability and parallelizability.

Some possible approaches of scaling the AV blockchain protocol are as follows:

State Channels — State channels allow interactions that were normally meant to occur within the blockchain to instead occur off the main chain. This is done in a cryptographically secure way without increasing the risk of any participant, while providing significant improvements in cost and speed. In future, state channels could be a critical part of scaling the AV blockchain to support higher levels of use, as recent reports have shown (Miller, Bentov, Kumaresan, and McCorry 2017). One option to create a state channel solution for AV data aggregation is as follows.

1. Part of the AV blockchain would be locked using multi-sig (or a smart-contract), which can only be updated if a specific set of participants agree.

2. Participants would make updates amongst themselves by constructing and signing transactions privately, without posting them on main chain.

3. Later, participants would submit the state back to the AV blockchain, which would close the state channel and unlock the state again.

Steps 1 and 3 (as above) involve blockchain operations which are published to the network and have to wait for peer validation However, Step 2 does not involve the main chain at all. It can contain an unlimited number of updates and can remain open indefinitely. In this sense, the AV blockchain can be used purely as a settlement layer to process the data aggregation instances, which help lift the burden from the underlying blockchain network. Not only can the transactional capacity be increased with state channels, but they can also provide two other crucial benefits — increased speed and lower overhead.

Plasma network — Plasma, a recently introduced technology, is a promising solution for scaling blockchain computation (Poon and Buterin 2017). It can be visualised as a series of contracts running on top of a root blockchain. The validity of the state is enforced by the root blockchain in the Plasma chains using 'fraud proofs', which is a mechanism by which nodes can determine if a block is invalid. To implement this, the AV blockchain must be structured in a tree hierarchy, where each branch must be treated as a blockchain that has its own blockchain history and computations that are map-reducable. The child chains can be called 'Plasma blockchains', each of which is a chain within the main AV blockchain. The Plasma blockchain does not disclose the contents of the blockchain on the root chain. Instead, only the block header hashes are submitted on the root chain, which is enough to determine validity of the block. If there is proof of fraud submitted on the root chain, then the block is rolled back and the block creator is penalised. As a result, the root blockchain would process only a tiny amount of commitments from child blockchains, which in turn decreases the amount of data passed onto the root blockchain and allows for a much larger number of computations. In addition, data is only propagated to those who wish to validate a particular state. This makes the validation process for data aggregation in AVs more scalable by eliminating the need for every node to watch every chain. Instead, they only watch the ones they are impacted by in order to enforce correct behaviour and penalise fraud. Fraud proofs allow any node to enforce invalid blocks and ensure that all state transitions are validated. Additionally, if there is an attack on a particular chain, participants can rapidly and cheaply do a mass-exit from the corrupt child chain.

Off-chain Compute — This can be an enabler in scaling transactions in blockchain networks, like TrueBit for smart contracts (Teutsch and Reitwießner 2017). Essentially, just like state channels, this approach would use a layer outside the blockchain to do the heavy lifting. It is a system that verifiably executes computations off-chain that would be otherwise computationally expensive to execute on-chain. It can be implemented for the AV blockchain as follows.

1. Instead of every node, specific participants in the network (*solvers*) perform the computations made by data aggregation smart contracts and submit the transaction log, along with a virtual deposit. If the log is correct, then the Solver is rewarded and its deposit is returned. If the Solver cheats, its deposit is forfeited and any dispute is resolved on the AV blockchain using the 'Verification Game'. The V2X, V2I, V2P entities in the smart mobility blockchain architecture may act as the Solvers.

2. Verification Game — A pre-defined set of participants in the network (Verifiers) check the Solvers' work off the chain. The solution is accepted by the system if no error is reported by any Verifier. If a Verifier does dispute the correctness of the Solver's solution, the game proceeds in a series of rounds to settle the dispute on the blockchain, where 'Judges' in the network with limited computational power adjudicate all disputes. The system is built to ensure that in a modest round of interactions the Judges can settle the dispute with a relatively small amount of work compared to that required for performing the actual task off the chain. infrastructural entities may act as Verifiers, while the Government may act as Judge.

3. At the end of this game, if the Solver was in fact cheating, it will be discovered and penalised. If not, then the challenging Verifier will pay for the resources consumed by the false alarm, thus balancing the system.

Overall, the protocol allows any information module (node) in the AV to initiate a data aggregation instance, and any other module (node) to receive a reward for completing it, while the system's incentive structure guarantees the correctness of the data aggregation transaction log. And by moving the computations and verification process off the blockchain into a separate protocol, it can scale to large numbers of transactions per unit time without significant constraints.

Sharding — This is similar to database sharding in traditional software systems, where each horizontal partition of the data in a database (called a shard) is stored on a separate server instance. This helps spread the load across different servers. Similarly, with blockchain sharding, the overall state of the blockchain is separated into different shards, and each part of the state would be stored by different nodes in the network (Luu, Narayanan, Zheng, Baweja, Gilbert, and Saxena 2016). Transactions that occur on the network are directed to different nodes depending on which shards they affect. Each shard only processes a small part of the state and does so in parallel. In order to communicate between shards, there needs to be some message-passing mechanism. To implement sharding in an AV, it would necessitate the creation of a network where every node only processes a small portion of all transactions (within its own module), while still maintaining high security.

To test the applicability of each of the aforesaid scalability solutions in case of smart mobility, is beyond the scope of this chapter. This, however, may prove to be an exciting future direction of research in smart mobility infrastructure.

CONCLUSION

In this chapter, we highlight how the emergence of autonomous vehicles and the smart mobility infrastructure will revolutionise the concept of Smart City, by promoting a more flexible, efficient, integrated, safe and accessible adoption of future transportation. For this to materialize, Level 4 AVs as of 2019, and level 5 AVs of the future, will have to be conceptualised and manufactured as complex Internet-of-Things enabled Cyber-physical Systems embedded within an intelligent grid of static and dynamic information agents.

We reason that the security and safety risks for the autonomy of such self-driving cars outweigh those of conventional cyber-physical systems. We have discussed in detail about several potential attacks, targeted assets security issues and possible countermeasures of the mobility domains. The most crucial undertaking in ensuring autonomous navigation safety is fortifying the 'data aggregation' mechanism both within and outside an AV integrated into a smart mobility framework. We ensure the security and tamper-resilience during data aggregation as a two level distributed ledger structure instantiated as consortium blockchains. The Level 1 blockchain corresponds to the within-AV data aggregation, instantiated within each vehicle, responsible for the secure and tamper-resilient data aggregation initiated from the local information units such as infotainment, body control, chassis control, powertrain, telematics, OBD-II, and V2X modules. And the Level 2 blockchain is necessary to support the smart mobility infrastructure connecting multiple AVs, pedestrians using wearable devices and smart infrastructural elements such as traffic light, lamp post, charging units, etc. This second level global blockchain network can also be a facilitator for secure and tamper-resilient data aggregation encompassing on-road vehicles, roadside infrastructure, electronic road pricing system, parking facilities, electric charging stations, diagnostic networks, AV manufacturers, insurance agencies, service centers etc. As an extension to this work, we plan the practical implementation of our model on an actual AV platform.

Acknowledgments

The authors would like to acknowledge the support from SPIRIT, the centre for Smart Platform Infrastructure Research on Integrative Technology, Nanyang Technological University, Singapore, and ERI@N, the Energy Research Institute, Nanyang Technological University, Singapore.

REFERENCES

Abdelhamid, S., H. Hassanein, and G. Takahara (2015). Vehicle as a resource (vaar). *IEEE Network 29*(1), 12–17.

Accenture (2018, March). *Autonomous Vehicles: The   Race   is   On.* https://www.accenture.com/us-en/insights/communications-media/autonomous-vehicles-data-challenges.

ARM   Limited.   *ARM   Security   Technology   –   TrustZone.* https://www.arm.com/products/security-on-arm/trustzone.

Bagloee, S. A., M. Tavana, M. Asadi, and T. Oliver (2016). Autonomous vehicles: challenges, opportunities, and future implications for transportation policies. *Journal of Modern Transportation 24*(4), 284–303.

Buterin, V. (2015). *On Public and Private Blockchains.* Ethereum Blog.

Cachin, C. and M. Vukolic (2017). *Blockchain Consensus Protocols in the Wild.*

Castro, M. and B. Liskov (2002). Practical byzantine fault tolerance and proactive recovery. *ACM Trans. Comput. Syst. 20*(4), 398–461.

Corsaro, A. (2016). Cloudy, Foggy and Misty Internet of Things. In *7th ACM/SPEC on Intl. Conf. on Performance Engg.*, pp. 261–261.

Dominic, D., S. Chhawri, R. M. Eustice, D. Ma, and A. Weimerskirch (2016). Risk Assessment for Cooperative Automated Driving. In *Proceedings of the 2nd ACM Workshop on Cyber-Physical Systems Security and Privacy, Austria*, pp. 47–58.

Frost and Sullivan (2014). *Future of Mobility.* https://ww2.frost.com/research/visionary-innovation/future-mobility.

Garip, M. T., M. E. Gursoy, P. Reiher, and M. Gerla (2015). Congestion attacks to autonomous cars using vehicular botnets. In *NDSS Workshop on Security of Emerging Networking Technologies (SENT)*, San Diego, CA.

Gerla, M., E.-K. Lee, G. Pau, and U. Lee (2014). Internet of vehicles: From intelligent grid to autonomous cars and vehicular clouds. In *Internet of Things (WF-IoT), 2014 IEEE World Forum on*, pp. 241–246. IEEE.

Hearn, M. (2015). *Corda: A distributed ledger.* https://docs.corda.net/head/_static/corda-technical-whitepaper.pdf.

Intel Corporation. *Intel Trusted Execution Technology.* https://www.intel.com/content/www/us/en/architecture-and-technology/trusted-infrastructure-overview.html.

Kokoris-Kogias, E., P. Jovanovic, L. Gasser, N. Gailly, E. Syta, and B. Ford (2018). Omniledger: A secure, scale-out, decentralized ledger via sharding. In *2018 IEEE Symposium on Security and Privacy, SP 2018, Proceedings, 21-23 May 2018, San Francisco, California, USA*, pp. 583–598.

Land Transport Authority, Government of Singapore (2014). *Smart Mobility 2030.* https://www.lta.gov.sg/content/ltaweb/en/roads-and-motoring/managing-traffic-and-congestion/intelligent-transport-systems/SmartMobility2030.html.

Luu, L., V. Narayanan, C. Zheng, K. Baweja, S. Gilbert, and P. Saxena (2016). A secure sharding protocol for open blockchains. In *Proceedings of the 2016 ACM SIGSAC Conference on Computer and Communications Security*, Vienna, Austria, October 24-28, 2016, pp. 17–30.

Miller, A., I. Bentov, R. Kumaresan, and P. McCorry (2017). Sprites and State Channels: Payment Networks that Go Faster than Lightning. *CoRR abs/1702.05812*, 1–24.

Miller, C. and C. Valasek (2015). Remote exploitation of an unaltered passenger vehicle. *Black Hat USA 2015*, 91.

Mitra, S., S. Bose, S. Sen Gupta, and A. Chattopadhyay (2018). Secure and tamper-resilient distributed ledger for data aggregation in autonomous vehicles. In *2018 IEEE Asia Pacific Conference on Circuits and Systems (APCCAS)*, pp. 548–551. IEEE.

Parkinson, S., P. Ward, K. Wilson, and J. Miller (2017). Cyber threats facing autonomous and connected vehicles: Future challenges. *IEEE Trans. on Intelligent Transportation Systems 18*(11), 2898.

Petit, J. and S. E. Shladover (2015). Potential Cyberattacks on Automated Vehicles. *IEEE Trans. Intelligent Transportation Systems 16*(2), 546–556.

Poon, J. and V. Buterin (2017). Plasma: Scalable Autonomous Smart Contracts. http://plasma.io/plasma.pdf.

Rettore, P. H. L., B. P. Santos, A. B. Campolina, L. A. Villas, and A. A. F. Loureiro (2016). Towards intra-vehicular sensor data fusion. In *19th IEEE Intl. Conf. on Intelligent Transportation Systems*, Brazil, pp. 126.

Schellekens, M. (2016). Car hacking: Navigating the regulatory landscape. *Computer Law & Security Review 32*(2), 307–315.

Seimens AG (2015). *Smart Mobility - A tool to achieve sustainable cities*. http://www.vt.bgu.tum.de/fileadmin/w00bnf/www/VKA/2014_15/150212_Smart_Mobility_v5_TUM.pdf.

Sung, G.-N., C.-Y. Juan, and C.-C. Wang (2008). Bus Guardian Design for automobile networking ECU nodes compliant with FlexRay standards. In *IEEE Intl. Symposium on Consumer Electronics*, pp. 1–4.

Teutsch, J. and C. Reitwießner (2017). *A scalable verification solution for blockchains*. https://people.cs.uchicago.edu/ teutsch/papers/truebit.pdf.

The Linux Foundation (2016). *Hyperledger.* https://www.hyperledger.org/projects/fabric.

Vogelsteller, F., V. Buterin, et al. (2017). *Ethereum Whitepaper.* https://github.com/ethereum/wiki/wiki/White-Paper.

Wolf, M., A. Weimerskirch, and C. Paar (2004). Security in automotive bus systems. In *Workshop on Embedded Security in Cars.*

Woo, S., H. J. Jo, and D. H. Lee (2015). A practical wireless attack on the connected car and security protocol for in-vehicle can. *IEEE Transactions on Intelligent Transportation Systems 16*(2), 993–1006.

Zhong, S., H. Zhong, X. Huang, P. Yang, J. Shi, L. Xie, and K. Wang (2019). *Connecting Things to Things in Physical-World: Security and Privacy Issues in Vehicular Ad-hoc Networks*, pp. 101–134. Springer International Publishing.

ABOUT THE EDITORS

Peter Han Joo Chong, PhD
Professor and Head of Department
Auckland University of Technology, Auckland. New Zealand
E-mail: peter.chong@aut.ac.nz

Dr. Peter Han Joo Chong is currently a Professor and Head of Department of Electrical and Electronic Engineering at Auckland University of Technology, Auckland, New Zealand. He received the PhD degree from the University of British Columbia, Canada, in 2000. He is an Adjunct Professor at the Department of Information Engineering, Chinese University of Hong Kong, Hong Kong. He was previously an Associate Professor (tenured) in the School of Electrical and Electronic Engineering at Nanyang Technological University (NTU), Singapore. Between 2011 and 2013, he was an Assistant Head of Division of Communication Engineering. Between 2013 and 2016, he was a Director of Infinitus, Centre for Infocomm Technology. From February 2001 to May 2002, he was a Research Engineer at Nokia Research Center, Helsinki, Finland. Between July 2000 and January 2001, he worked in the Advanced Networks Division at Agilent Technologies Canada Inc., Vancouver, Canada. His research interests are in the areas of mobile communications systems including MANETs/VANETs, V2X and Internet of Things/Vehicles.

Ivan Wang-Hei Ho, PhD

Assistant Professor

The Hong Kong Polytechnic University, Kowloon, Hong Kong

E-mail: ivanwh.ho@polyu.edu.hk

Dr. Ivan Wang-Hei Ho is currently an Assistant Professor at the Department of Electronic and Information Engineering, The Hong Kong Polytechnic University. He received the B.Eng. and M.Phil. degrees in Information Engineering from The Chinese University of Hong Kong, and the PhD degree in Electrical and Electronic Engineering from Imperial College London. In 2007, Ivan spent a summer working at the IBM T. J. Watson Research Center, Hawthorne, NY. After his PhD graduation, he was with the System Engineering Initiative at Imperial College London as a Postdoctoral Research Associate. In 2010, he co-founded P2 Mobile Technologies Limited at Hong Kong Science Park and served as the Chief R&D Engineer. He primarily invented the MeshRanger series wireless mesh embedded system, which won the Silver Award in Best Ubiquitous Networking at the Hong Kong ICT Awards 2012. He is an Associate Editor for IEEE Access and IEEE Transactions on Circuits and Systems II, the TPC Co-chair for CoWPER and PERSIST-IoT Workshops in conjunction with IEEE SECON 2018 and ACM MobiHoc 2019 respectively. His research interests are in wireless communications and networking, specifically in vehicular networks, intelligent transportation systems (ITS), Internet of things (IoT), and network coding.

INDEX

Related Nova Publications

DATA SHARING: RECENT PROGRESS AND REMAINING CHALLENGES

EDITORS: Yousef Ibrahim Daradkeh and Korolev Petr Mikhailovich

SERIES: Computer Science, Technology and Applications

BOOK DESCRIPTION: Coherence of the information world is needed to approve technology concerning data sharing. This book gives to a wide range of readers the possibility to know what problems exist in the field.

SOFTCOVER ISBN: 978-1-53614-677-6
RETAIL PRICE: $82

INDEPENDENT COMPONENT ANALYSIS (ICA): ALGORITHMS, APPLICATIONS AND AMBIGUITIES

EDITORS: Addisson Salazar and Luis Vergara

SERIES: Computer Science, Technology and Applications

BOOK DESCRIPTION: Considering adequate data preprocessing, ICA can be implemented for any kind of data including imaging; biomedical signals; telecommunication data; and web data. In this framework, this book embraces a significant vision of ICA that presents innovative theoretical and practical approaches.

HARDCOVER ISBN: 978-1-53613-994-5
RETAIL PRICE: $230

To see a complete list of Nova publications, please visit our website at www.novapublishers.com

COMPUTATIONAL MECHANICS (CM): APPLICATIONS AND DEVELOPMENTS

EDITOR: Jacob Yuen

SERIES: Computer Science, Technology and Applications

BOOK DESCRIPTION: In this collection, the authors examine how modeling impact of solid particles contributes to an understanding of the fundamental mechanisms of erosive wear.

SOFTCOVER ISBN: 978-1-53613-672-2
RETAIL PRICE: $95

IoT: PLATFORMS, CONNECTIVITY, APPLICATIONS AND SERVICES

AUTHOR: Abdulrahman Yarali

SERIES: Computer Science, Technology and Applications

BOOK DESCRIPTION: The confluence of standards/technologies and ability to connect massive smaller devices, objects, and sensors, inexpensively and easily have created a hyper-connected world bridging the virtual and physical to generate, process, exchange and consume data for the Internet of Things (IoT).

HARDCOVER ISBN: 978-1-53613-400-1
RETAIL PRICE: $230